HF
5827.85
.D38
2000

HWBI

D1169909

9

DISCARD

Living up to the Ads

New Americanists   A Series Edited by Donald E. Pease

Living Up

to the Ads

Gender Fictions of the 1920s

Simone Weil Davis

Duke University Press   *Durham & London*   2000

In slightly different versions, sections of chapter 4 of the present
work appeared in French (translated by Maggy Chambon) as "La
Mise en Scène des Femmes dans la Publicité," in *Mimesis: Imiter,
représenter, circuler, Hermes* 22 (fall 1998): 167–77; and sections of
chapter 5 of the present work appeared as " 'The Burden of
Reflecting': Effort and Desire in Zelda Fitzgerald's *Save Me the
Waltz,*"in *Modern Language Quarterly* 56, no. 3 (September 1995):
327–61.

Printed in the United States of America on acid-free paper ∞

Typeset in Adobe Garamond by Keystone Typesetting, Inc.

Library of Congress Cataloging-in-Publication Data appear on
the last printed page of this book.

Contents

Illustrations

For my parents

Acknowledgments

A huge thank you to my inspired and inspiring daughter, Sofia Szamosi, whose no-nonsense and often hilarious commentary on advertising lit my path.

I am grateful for the backing of the Department of English at the University of California at Berkeley and the Mellon Foundation, which made my research possible, as did a 1993 travel grant provided by Duke University. And thanks to Ellen Gartrell and the staff at the Duke University Library, without whom the J. Walter Thompson Archives would have remained a swirling sea of cardboard boxes and mysterious files. I also appreciate the assistance provided by the staff at Radcliffe's Schlesinger Library. Moreover, this book would not have been completed without the postdoctoral fellowship I have so enjoyed as a professor of gender politics at New York University's John W. Draper Interdisciplinary Master's Program in Humanities and Social Thought.

Many along the way helped me to continue, and allowed the work to grow with their support and careful reading of earlier versions. The merits of the project, in large part, are due to those acknowledged below; all errors of interpretation or fact are mine and mine alone.

My adviser at Berkeley, Mitchell Breitwieser, offered the perfect mix of ready confidence, challenging intellectual prodding, and wry wit; I am profoundly indebted. Also at Berkeley, crucial assistance, commentary, and citations from Donald McQuade and Lawrence Levine allowed the project to develop. At New York University, let me heartily note the inspiration, friendship, and support extended by the Draper program: from Director Robin Nagle and my colleagues, to the staff and students.

Thanks to Susan Schweik, Paula Fass, and James Young for their encouragement and perception. I am indebted to friend, colleague, copanelist, and reader Jen Scanlon for expert advice and pivotal support. Kathy Peiss gave me a fruitful citation early on, and Christine Stansell extended both friendship and invaluable commentary at several key junctures in my writing. The following friends and colleagues were sufficiently savage, and absolutely generous, as critical readers of parts of the manuscript at various stages: unending gratitude to Kristina Brooks, Kimberly Drake, Nico Israel, David Potash, Arthur Riss, Cindy Schrager, and Steven Rubio.

I am indebted to both the research and theorizations of Jackson Lears. Few cultural critics have paid more attention to the history of advertising in the United States. His work has been pivotal to the scholarly understanding of commodity culture, as its many citations here will exemplify. I hope to build on and deepen that theoretical contribution by bringing the gendering of advertising relations center stage in a way that Lears does not.

Several sections of this book either appeared in print or were presented at conferences. Let me express my appreciation to editors, commentators, and panelists at the following venues. The valuable insights of colleagues— including Ulrich Baer and Nikhil Singh—were brought to bear on chapter 1 at an NYU colloquium, in the spring of 1997. I presented chapter 2 in 1996 at the Berkshire Conference on the History of Women: thanks very much to Jen Scanlon and Ellen Garvey, as well as the audience there. Parts of chapter 4 were aided first by audience commentary at an American Studies Association panel in 1995, and later by inclusion in a special issue of *Hermes* (fall 1998), edited by Susan Ossman, which grew out of an international conference on mimesis held at the Sorbonne Université's Laboratoire Communication et Politique in May 1997. My discussion of Nella Larsen's *Quicksand* in chapter 4 was deepened by critiques received at a 1996 NYU colloquium (Avital Ronnell, Jennifer Wicke, and Faye Ginsburg deserve particular mention), and a Princeton University conference the following year, Women: Center Stage. *Modern Language Quarterly* published an earlier version of chapter 5 in its September 1995 issue (special thanks to Paula Dragosh), and this material continued to grow due to audience response at a New York University (NYU) public lecture in 1997.

Hannah Davis Taïeb, Erika Reynolds, Rachel Stocking, and Sue Grayzel, four heavy hitters in my heart, provided me with uncommonly constructive feedback. Encouragement from three dear friends—Victoria Randlett, Elizabeth Young, and Laura Camozzi Berry—convinced me that the task of writing was worth the ardor, and Elizabeth's last-minute read increased the chances of that bearing fruit. More gratitude than I can convey goes to Heath Putnam for his white-hot analysis and multitiered sustenance. And thanks to New York buddies Sarah Bassett, Barbara Browning, Jayati Lal, Peggy Phelan, Aaron Retica, Peter Secor, and John Wojda for an array of intangible, indisputable benefits. For help with the illustrations, I am much obliged to Natalie Friedman and Cyndie Burckhardt. Thanks to Aaron Davis and Candy Girling, Max and Gabriel Davis, and André Taïeb and Hannah Davis Taïeb for opening their homes and hearts to Sofia while her mother lurched about in archival stacks.

I'm tremendously appreciative of the editorial support of Ken Wissoker and Richard Morrison at Duke University Press, and the three readers to whom they sent the manuscript (two have emerged from anonymity—Jen Scanlon and Rachel Bowlby—so I get to thank them by name). Guidance from Ken and Richard, along with suggestions from all three manuscript readers, made the revision of the book possible; fond gratitude for their expert assistance and commentary.

The project is dedicated to my parents, Natalie Zemon Davis and Chandler Davis, whose unswerving, multifaceted faith and support over the years have meant so much to me, as has their commitment to creative thought and inventive, ethical living.

Introduction

Does advertising "work"? Do ads actually determine consumer decisions and choices? Maybe advertisers and their critics both overstate the powers of suggestion. How preposterous to think that we would be fooled, agog over an ad that wears its agenda on its screaming neon sleeve. As consumers, we all feel like well-versed readers, sophisticates—while we may guffaw or sigh over a well-crafted ad (or an especially bad one), we readily discern the manipulative ploys of advertisements, and when we decide what to buy, we would like to think that we rely more on word of mouth and personal experience than hypnotic commercial command. This point has certainly been made.[1] Perhaps the thing is this, though: Ads *do* "work," but their primary function is not to lead a consumer to choose between brands. Rather, through inundation, ads serve to produce an all-around ambiance that encourages consumerism in toto, making it seem as desirable and natural as air.[2] Advertiser Christine Frederick noted in a 1929 manual: "I always think of advertising as a tremendous moving-picture device to keep ever and constantly changing before us, in film after film, reel after reel, all the good things that manufacturers make everywhere, set in a dramatic scenario which compels attention through the touch of advertising genius."[3] In the seventy years of technological innovation and marketing consolidation since Frederick's comment, advertising has become an ever more influential part of a hegemonic matrix of social and economic institutions. We do indeed attend its panorama and, whether slack-jawed or skeptical, are gripped by all these "good things . . . set in a dramatic scenario."

At first it was just a byproduct; then, it became a stated goal of the commercial endeavor. To practitioners, it was implicit that the advertising industry should help shape popular notions of identity—and by extension, gender, race, and class. Jackson Lears remarks that "national advertisers . . . participated in the construction of the modern subject—a normative self that suited the emerging corporate structure of power relations in the early-twentieth-century United States."[4] *Living Up to the Ads* examines both fictional and commercial representations of identity from the 1920s, the decade that secured a place for advertising at the heart of American business. Considering fiction by Sinclair

I

Lewis, Bruce Barton, Zelda and F. Scott Fitzgerald, and Nella Larsen, along with advertisements and other data emerging from the advertising industry (such as memoirs, manuals, meeting minutes, and newsletters), this book determines what sort of gendered subjectivities were, in fact, under construction.

Advertising Selves

By the twenties, the prizing of sincerity and self-reliance characteristic of nineteenth-century advice literature had given way, in writing pitched toward the urban and suburban classes of the United States, to the endorsement of a more theatrical, even salesmanlike selfhood. From *The Great Gatsby* to adman Bruce Barton's portrait of Jesus, *The Man Nobody Knows,* popular books of the period lauded and lamented the effects of this "selling self." This shift, so linked to the emergence of a commodity culture, was part of a complex of changes. As advertising became an increasingly established component of business as usual, not one but three new *metaphors for personhood* were introduced into the popular arena, means of structuring one's thoughts about identity that were compelling, gendered, and suggested by the commercial transaction. These subject positions—the adman, the consumer, and the "vehicle" or advertising model who transmits the message between them—were both evocative and omnipresent enough that they began to circulate culturally as gendered and raced tropes for identity itself.

As the corporate world became the United States's designated new epic sphere, popular and commercial narratives increasingly located masculine selfhood in the persuasive impact one had on others, rather than in the monadic integrity of self-reliance. The *adman* (so denominated despite the presence of some women in the field) borrows "influence" from the domain of the feminine to create a new machismo of persuasion. Racial exclusions that kept nonwhites almost entirely out of this sphere and often stigmatized Jewish advertisers by characterizing them as the definitive hucksters meant that the persuading salesman with the winning personality was envisioned in his WASP whiteness—regardless of the race or ethnicity of the readership of these narratives.[6]

The *consumer,* then and still conceived primarily as female, is supposed to manifest her "rainbow moods" most entirely via the selection and purchase of commodities, the expressive lexicon from which she is to assemble and display her identity.[7] Cast by the industry as the ultimate object of scrutiny, the consumer must be read, interpreted, "mimicked" (even by female copywriters), and seduced. But she, too, advertises, as she performs the spectacle of her gender. Here, the portrayed generic consumer modeled a certain kind of classed whiteness, which was ultimately depicted as inherent to American feminine consumption—in part, because national advertisers did not yet have faith in the buying power of nonwhite niche markets, and consequently, often left them unaddressed in commercial narratives.[8]

The *vehicle,* or the female advertising model pitching and posing with the product, works to convey the message between the adman and consumer. She functions as a metaphor, her own commodified but canny presence representing and augmenting the appeal of the commodity with which she poses. The representational work performed by an advertising model, who uses her charm to bolster the allure of something *else,* seems a telling distillation of the work of the objectified female, generally, in American commodity culture.

All three of these gendered identities were picked up, remodeled, exploited, and explored as figures for selfhood by fiction writers and other American consumer-participants. Whether for the "selling self," the consuming female, or the posing vehicle, the task of self-presentation seems to come hand in glove with a shame and anxiety about the self that is being hauled on stage. Despite the supposedly diametric opposition between the knowing salesman and the "sucker" who succumbs to his address, despite the hierarchical and classed distinction between entrepreneurial magnate P. T. Barnum and the comely hired "attraction" featured on his poster, all these marketized subject positions are shaped by the pressure to make an impact on others and, thereby, turn a "profit."

One 1920 ad for nail polish, designed to invoke the urgent physical anxiety so often incited by advertising, gave readers the choice between "Embarrassed Fingers That Shrink from Scrutiny or Charming Fingers That Seek the Light!"[9] Animated with the melodramatic emotional agency of little people, the digits in this copy must negotiate between the antipodes of shame and self-display. This same axis determines the orbit of the models for subjectivity discussed in this work. The need to self-present, or "seek the light," is paradoxically bound to the equally pressing need to "shrink from scrutiny," to hide those flaws, hungers, doubts, and ambivalences that might bring into question one's commitment to self-spectacle and the profit motive. Invested with the heightened attention given to that which must be hidden, these "shameful" qualities, partly because they are regretted, often become the secret locus of personal identification.

Emerging from the architecture of the commercial transaction, these subject positions became, for the American public(s), not only available but almost unavoidable. As Judith Butler writes, "the *conditions of intelligibility* are themselves formulated in and by power, and this normative exercise of power is rarely acknowledged as an operation of power at all."[10] Self-promotion, consumption, assemblage, and display—these became the means whereby many people organized their thinking about selfhood, gender, and the fashioning and expression of an identity. The deep gendering of these positions in the commercial mise-en-scène worked to underscore and retain the power imbalance between them, by making it seem to be a "natural" story of the difference between men and women.

The models for subjectivity generated by the nationalized commercial endeavor also performed racial work, helping to universalize and even celebritize an implicit middle-class whiteness in the presumed audience, what Michael Uebel calls "'autonomy effects'—the ways in which [whiteness] appears as a generality."[11] The ascendancy of commercial culture made these effects more pronounced through the content of the ads themselves—where every "you" addressed was assumed to be white, and nonwhite figures were almost invariably servants. Additionally, national brands and nationwide advertising meant the curtailment or partial suppression of an array of localized commercial practices that were far more expressive of diverse ethnic, class, and racial positions—from the mom-and-pop market to the truck-bed performances of the patent medicine salesman and the hand-painted sign hoisted outside the neighborhood beauty salon. To an extent, then, this commercial project is blanketed by an artificially universal, imposed whiteness, experienced by many Americans of color, as we will see, as either displacement or insult. Yet in order to explore the workings of power in the commercial arena, I emphasize the realm of gender relations (also inherently racialized), in part because gender was so explicitly, indeed obsessively addressed.

Because of advertising's sheer ubiquity and invocation of extremely personal concerns, the provision of models for self-fashioning is probably the most important aspect of its influential power—far more significant in terms of the cultural changes wrought than are the explicit directives of individual advertisements. In 1929, historian and industry advocate Frank Presbrey enthused that advertising had encouraged the "growth of a national homogeneity in our people, a uniformity of ideas which, despite the mixture of races, is found to be greater here than in European countries [which would] . . . seem to be easier to nationalize."[12] He saw this capacity to consolidate and mold public desires, especially in light of American diversities, as key to advertising's success as a nationalizing social force, what he called a "civilizer" (613).

The means whereby this "homogeneity" was (incompletely) fostered were multiple. First, as the complex of institutions that make up market capitalism gained more social and economic power, advertising really became a presence, indeed a condition, of American culture, media, business, and even the landscape. The sheer amount of time that people spent selling, advertising, and buying—especially living as they were within a landscape awash with "consuming images"[13]—had a massive impact on the American identity, as a verb will invariably shape its subject.

At least in theory, those new tools for self-fashioning, promulgated in part by the advertising industry, were more porous and geared less toward autonomy and self-regulation than the models for identity construction circulating in the United States of the nineteenth century. With immigration and internal migration at an all-time high, with the rapid-fire insurgence of new economic forms, urban centers, technologies, and relations to work fostered by factory labor and corporatization, a vacuum was created that could not be filled by the last century's models for subjectivity and gender. Or so the story goes. Perhaps this vacuum, this "clean break" disjuncture between nineteenth- and twentieth-century "ways of being," was mainly a construction generated and cherished by a modernity born out of self-mythologization, and fired in the kiln of the First World War. At any rate, new ways of thinking about and enacting selfhood were simultaneously being forged and snatched up by people who often were negotiating environments for which they felt unprepared, people engaged in increasingly industrialized or corporatized work relations as well as ever more commercialized contexts for interaction.[14]

As has been theorized by Jackson Lears and others, during the early twentieth century, people living in the United States became more likely to think of their identity as rooted in their consumer and leisure practices than in their role as producers. Though the advertising industry has always proffered images of work and the workplace, it increasingly positioned selfhood as resident among an individual's leisure pursuits. To some extent, this shift forestalled the unsettling conclusions that an alienated workforce might otherwise have been likely to reach. Efficiency experts like Frederick Winslow Taylor and of course Henry Ford, by discouraging worker solidarity and encouraging a mechanistic approach to labor, "pushed" identity cathexis out of the workplace; the "pull" was

provided by commodities, which with the help of energetic and creative advertisers and improved avenues of distribution promised an easily accessorized
leisure self outside the forty (or sixty) hours. Although consumerism obfus-
cated the role of work, it also transformed it, since "work," too, is a fluid
category only discernible as one element in the complex of relations that
determines its nature.[15] One goal of the present study is to locate and articulate
some of the psychological work performed on and off the job, often covertly
and under some duress, by subjects seeking social intelligibility in the context
of commodity culture.

Advertisers contributed consciously to popular discourse about selfhood in
several ways. They generated many of the period's success manuals, thereby
helping to weave together a modern portrait of masculine achievement and
authority, and they also delved energetically into the study of commercial
psychology, making the female consumer the predominant subject of their
interpretation. In their manuals and memoirs, advertisers zealously theorized
the secrets of salesmanship and the psychological workings of the female
shopper—although these "secrets" were never particularly shrouded by the veil
of professional discretion. In fact, advertising's celebration of its own capacity
to persuade and its purchase on the audience psyche is less a buried subtext of
the commercial enterprise than an omnipresent metanarrative. Industry analysis of its craft and target blurred into industry promotion. As a result of this
very public investigation, advertising's interpretation of psychology and its
contribution to it were absolutely central in shaping popular notions, about
both the burgeoning field of psychology and the human psyche itself.

To understand the social impact of this industry on gendered subjectivity,
one must also consider the ads themselves, and more specifically, their role in
determining the nature of modern objectification of women. As Karl Marx
famously depicted it, with the emergence of commodification, the object itself
took on a new fetishized power, exalted and animated by its nimbus of exchange value.[16] The crucial, enabling links between this "vivification" of the
commodity object and the objectification of the woman whose image is used to
sell is a special focus of this book. The centuries-old symbolic function played
by women in both religious allegory and secular national imagery surely predetermined that this function would continue to manifest itself in the face of a
commodity culture. The female in an ad lends all her desirability and anima-
tion to the product; at the same time, the totemic grandeur of the commodity
icon, and its fixity, are projected on the "thingified" woman. The woman thus

objectified is engaged in representational labor, a set of performative tasks that proves both pleasurable and burdensome.

The figure of the confidence man, close cousin to the adman, has been well theorized, as has that of the female consumer.[17] By discussing the advertiser and consumer together, alongside the "vehicle" who transmits the message between them, this book questions the causative—and often destabilizing—set of relations out of which these figures spring. Gendered distinctions between the advertiser and the shopper that "he" addresses, between the manipulator of human drives and the female vehicle who works to provoke them, seem to fade away in the face of the tension between zealous self-promotion and mortified self-disguise with which all these figures must cope.

Some of the similarities between consumption and production are inherent to marketplace relations, and yet they have often gone untheorized: to maintain the hierarchy between producer and consumer, it is necessary that these parallels be obscured. The gendering of that divide—in which producers are envisioned as male, consumers as female—has been central to maintaining this hierarchy. Both critics and proponents of commodity culture have emphasized the differences between a male-coded production ethos supposedly based in rationality and industry, and a feminized consumerism ostensibly driven by desire. By contrast, *Living Up to the Ads* considers the phenomenological links between them.

Look in any library index under the key words *consumer behavior,* and after scanning twenty titles or more, you will gather that consumers must "behave" far more than producers appear to. Why does behaving—such a vulnerable, unwilled verb—seem the special provenance of the consumer? What makes the drives that lead producers to "behave" fall out of view? Like Michel Foucault's eagle-eyed disciplinarians snugly shielded in their Benthamite panopticon, or the Wizard of Oz working his levers behind a drawn curtain, the generators of our commercial economy have created a system that will allow them to supersede surveillance, at least in their capacity as producers. Let me write my way into the heart of that taboo. Roots that predate, and consequently inform, both industrial and finance capitalism, reveal the connections between consumer and producer "behavior."

Systemic Shame

In *The Protestant Ethic and the Spirit of Capitalism,* Max Weber posits a causal link between Protestant worldly asceticism and economic rationalism.[18] This rationalism, Weber argues, sanctifies and organizes the profit motive by defining it as devolving from a Puritan valuation of industry. This logic creates a "psychological incentive," even a "categorical imperative," for capitalist production as a proof of one's salvation, he asserts (146 n. 1, 160 n.5). Weber's groundbreaking text does not address the relationship between Protestant psychology and capitalist consumption, however, except contrarily: he depicts Puritan "anti-Mammonism" as a force that militated against the development of a consumerist psychology.

As an aside, paralleling Weber's project in the *Protestant Ethic*, Werner Sombart attempted in 1911 to consider capitalism's philosophical linkage to Judaism. *The Jews and Modern Capitalism* is a complex, flawed work[19]—like Weber's, very much addressing the conceptualizations of its day, whereby the "spirit" of a people could be codified. Though Sombart later aligned himself with Nazism, his work was initially lauded *and* reviled by Jewish and gentile readers, including anti-Semites. Sombart somewhat tentatively cites Jews as the earliest advertisers, remarking, "The 'deafening invitation' . . . which came from the small [eighteenth-century Jewish clothes dealer] is now made by the million-voiced advertisements of our business life. If the Jews are to be considered the originators of the system of 'getting hold of the customers,' their claim to be the fathers of modern advertising is equally well established" (139). Like Weber, Sombart's emphasis is on the rationalism (and male sexual sublimation) that he sees fueling capitalist production. Desire only factors into the economy he describes as innately Jewish when it is channeled via suppression into rational capitalism, and both consumption and women drop almost entirely from his analysis.[20]

To return to Weber (whose work was much more widely known in the United States of the twenties than was Sombart's): although one must acknowledge that the Puritan lauding of thrift and the corollary distrust of luxurious display were profound components in the Protestant culture of the eighteenth and nineteenth centuries, another feature of the Protestant model for subjectivity is nonetheless much aligned with the advertising industry's later formulations about the consumer's identity. One should, indeed, consider the former a significant forebear to the latter. This alignment is not surprising. The split that Weber claims is so crucial to the Protestant sensibility—between the virtue of acquiring wealth and the vice associated with spending it—seems a strained, collapsible distinction: production and consumption are clearly interdependent, mutually constitutive parts of the same economic system.

Weber is not alone in arguing for this split, however—the psychologies of production and consumption are popularly conceived and presented as entirely distinct, almost mutually exclusive, requiring textual frames so segregated that their commixture seems almost forbidden.[21] What is it about the Protestant ethic that prepares for and fuels the spirit of consumption?

Advertising's double-valenced address of the consumer-subject reflects a two-tiered model of individuality constituted largely by a Protestant sensibility. In both the Protestant and commercial arenas, the individual is hailed simultaneously with two contradictory addresses.[22] The first runs as follows: "You, the individual, have direct access to the truth." Since its inception in the Reformation, Protestantism defined itself as a liberation of the individual from the supervisory mediation of the church. Ostensibly, Protestant selfhood is to be understood as constituted most supremely by this capacity for direct communion with God's truth. Advertising also takes as its founding premise the secular but significantly resonant myth that the individual's democratic liberty is most fully realized in his or her right to make selections as a consumer. For example, Paul Cherington, director of research at the J. Walter Thompson Company, said in 1922 that "consumption is no longer a thing of needs but a matter of choices freely exercised."[23]

Or see Christine Frederick, who describes the newfound freedom of the modern American woman primarily as the freedom to shop: "She is less sentimental, and more aggressive and sure of her tastes. She is not afraid to be an individual, and this reflects itself in desiring specialties and novelties and new patterns and new colors. She knows precisely what she wants, even in color and line" (23). This new woman's assertiveness, individuality, desire, and will are all structured around—and limited to—the task of consumption. She can garner the information she needs from the advertisements she scans and then make up her own mind about what to buy; brand diversification affords her the consummate opportunity to exert her personal agency in the world. Since John Milton's day, Protestant tenets have influenced the development of democratic principles, including those concerning individual rights, so the link between civic and spiritual "choice" here is not accidental. Though the context for advertising's claim about consumption is more political than religious, its depiction of an individuality defined above all else by its direct access to a larger truth mimics the Protestant model for selfhood. In other words, Protestantism and advertising allegedly exalt individual Christian and consumer subjects as unaided recipients of information, freed of any reliance on an intermediary.

Yet both the Protestant and commercial arenas, concurrent with the apparent exaltation of one's status as an individual, offer an unending subcurrent of incited anxiety about one's inherent odiousness (whether physical, spiritual, social, or all of the above), and insecurity about one's status as an elect or nonelect. The second address extended to Christian and consumer subjects alike is almost all subtext then, and runs like this: "You, the individual, are probably in a state of wretchedness, and what you must do is to act 'as if' and hope that you are, in fact, among the elect." Your actions will not transform you, nor will they become you. The tortured logic of simulation requires a signal disjuncture between you, the compelled strategist, and your works, the proffered evidence, because you generate works for show, for proof: they will be "the technical means, not of purchasing salvation, but of getting rid of the fear of damnation" (Weber 1976, 115). Thus, a presumed, incited, and aggravated sense of shame is the force behind the need to emulate, which Thorstein Veblen places at the heart of most consumer practices.[24]

The much touted power of consumer choice is undercut by this shifting of judgment away from the to-be-selected product and onto the consumer him or herself. If it doesn't do for you what it does for the character in the ad, it is due not to the product's deficiencies but your own inhering vileness. In her 1923 article, "The Snob Appeal," J. Walter Thompson's Frances Maule assumes as given that people feel horrible about themselves, and that this "inferiority complex" is our deepest motivator and the most important lesson made available by psychology.

> According to these new explorers into human motives [psychoanalysts], we all suffer from an eating sense of our own unimportance. . . . When we wear the garments of the cosmopolitan great lady who "assembles, tries and admits to a place in her life only the choicest" . . . we are made to feel that [she has] "nothing on us." And this is what we all want, really, more than anything else in the world. This is the "grand and glorious feeling" which we are seeking all the time.[25]

As conjured by the advertising industry, the consumer's individuality is constituted by isolation—an isolation caused by his or her shying away from the scrutinizing gaze of others.[26] The only viable alternative to sheer retreat or public humiliation is to step behind a battery of shielding commodities that will disguise and, especially, protect one from detection. In *Captains of Con-*

sciousness, a study of advertising in the 1920s, Stuart Ewen remarks that "the negative condition was portrayed as social failure derived from continual public scrutiny. The positive goal emanated from one's *modern* decision to arm himself [*sic*] against such scrutiny with the accumulated 'benefits' of industrial production."[27]

Behind the individual agency that the invited act of consumption will supposedly manifest, then, lurks a sadder selfhood, created by the need to withdraw. As one deodorant ad from the twenties put it, the consumer requires "complete protection against even the most fleeting possibility of reproach."[28] Advertisements routinely invoked an astonishing degree of personal, physical shame: "How to Keep Free from a Wretched Glisten"; "How to Prevent the Homeliness that Creeps upon You Unawares"; "He was his own worst enemy . . . oh why had he neglected the bath that morning, the shave, the change of linen?"[29] Roland Marchand has cataloged other examples of such ads, in which job opportunities are lost and marriage proposals rejected because of indiscretions like body odor and the "slovenliness" of ungartered socks (212–15). Whether these ads instill, aggravate, or merely reflect widespread anxieties about untamable physicality, their cumulative effect bespeaks a profound shame in the posited reader. For the audience, the sharp jolt of self-recognition, the identification, is with the blemishes or flaws that the ads heave into the limelight for exposure.

The mortifications and compensatory drives of the consumer have been suggested, teased into being, ranked, and tabulated by zip code, chakra, race, and every other distinguishing denomination. Consumer shame of all sorts, from physical embarrassment to class anxiety to the dread of alienating loved ones, is analyzed and incited by advertisers and marketeers—the supposed prevalence of this individual-as-flaw model, and the resultant vulnerability of the potential consumer, are almost truisms. By contrast, the shame associated with production is heavily vaulted and disavowed. Both the fear of vulnerability and exposure, and the consumeristic model for desire and purchase as an unending loop, can be understood as indicating the phenomenology of capitalist production as well as consumption, again implying the artificiality of the hierarchical distinction drawn between the two spheres. The cyclic, infinite process whereby consumer shame leads to consumer desire, which leads to purchase followed by a resumption of doubt and shame, uncannily parallels the unending circuits through which capital races as it changes from currency to commodity and back again. As Marx discusses the "law which gives capital no rest and continually whispers in its ear 'Go on! Go on!' " his language evokes a remarkable compulsion and vulnerability.[30] In *The Nature and Logic of Capitalism*, Robert Heilbroner writes:

> Capital, unlike the use values that embody prestige and power in tributary societies, exists in a constant state of vulnerability as it passes through its never-ending circuits. . . . Continuous dissolution and recapture is the essence of the process of competition. . . . Capital is powerful only insofar as it continuously runs the gauntlet of circulation. . . .
>
> Competition . . . [means] the inescapable exposure of each capitalist to the efforts of others to gain as much as possible of the public's purchasing power.[31]

"Running the gauntlet of circulation" and enduring "inescapable exposure," the advertiser, on the frontlines of capitalist production, would seem particularly desirous of the "complete protection against even the most fleeting possibility of reproach" that she or he promises to the consumer. Weber calls up just this mobilizing force of agitation when he remarks on the producer's need for the "complete protection" of proof: "The religious valuation of restless, continuous, systematic work . . . as the surest and most evident proof of rebirth and genuine faith, must have been the most powerful conceivable lever for the expansion of . . . the spirit of capitalism" (1976, 172). Advertisers and commentators on commercial culture typically ascribe both fear of exposure and repetitive, bottomless desire to the consumer. Extending Heilbroner and Weber's notions implies that the phenomenology of consumerism needs to be correlated far more closely than is common practice to that of capitalist production.[32]

Once the consumer was determined by academic researchers to be worthy of study, "she" was found to have already been smeared on a specimen tray by market researchers, each of "her" impulses and desires defined, cataloged, and ready for scholarly dissection. By contrast, what fuels the impulse to produce and keep on producing in a capitalist economy is often either overlooked as self-evident or exalted as an almost metaphysical exemplar of the life force. Despite the proliferation of selling and business "how-tos," the "why-dos"—the motivations behind production—remain the wagging fingers on an invisible hand.

Reading Stories and Ads

Not only are production and consumption symbiotically inextricable, but producers of commercial narratives are consumers of them as well, influenced by the discursive pool to which they contribute. Yet how can one reasonably extrapolate from representations of gendered subjectivity to lived experience? This book is precisely about this interplay, about the relationship between people and representations. Depictions of gendered selfhood in ads and fiction both mirror and shape the popular psyche, but the processes of reflection and influence bring with them all sorts of experiences that are not embedded in the narratives themselves. For instance, to the extent that members of the audience of commercial culture attempt to simulate the stances they see adopted in advertisements, the work of simulation or approximation becomes itself the site of identification, more profoundly so than does the specific nature of that which we strive to imitate and become. By calling this practice of approximation "work" and arguing that people identify (even if only secretly and partially) with the labor of staging such simulations, I mean to highlight both the performative, productive nature of simulation and the sense of compulsion that drives such performances. Ad "work," however, is not unmixed drudgery. Most typically, the pleasure of performance and the erotics of the commodity braid together inextricably with the anxiety incited by that same culture to motivate and fuel such stagings. But the relationship between a representation and its audience is not the only significant interplay between text and life. Given the ambivalences and agendas of cultural producers, and the impact of both on their work, it is necessary to examine the relationship between the representations of subjectivity put forth by both advertisers and novelists, and the lives of those writers themselves.

The substance, form, and site of these two distinct genres—the literary and commercial—have interpenetrated at least since the rise of modern advertising.[33] In the twenties, much of a writer's income was derived from magazine stories: these literally shared the page with advertisements. Research like Ellen Gruber Garvey's on the promotion of the bicycle illustrates that "theme" stories were sometimes commissioned to work in tandem with ads, while many ads from the twenties follow the narrative form of little stories, drawing in readers by mimicking the fiction that adjoins them on the magazine page.[34]

The authors discussed in this book deal consciously with selfhood in the context of a commercial culture, and they are just as likely to borrow the discursive style of the copywriter or to reference particular advertisements and brand names as they are to depict their protagonists in the act of shopping or sales. The realism they all typically employ, whether sardonic or frank, is an engagement with the mode of the advertisement, and as we will see in chapter 5, the American surrealism experimented with by Zelda Fitzgerald in *Save Me the Waltz* also owes much to the commercial address and bourgeois cult of the commodity. Most important, they all use the metaphoric figures of advertisement, display, and consumption to develop the personae and plots they are creating.

These authors were not only "treating" the phenomenon of subjectivity and commodity culture, they were living in it, constructed by it, illustrative of it— as is the modern-day critic hoping to comment on them. Essentially, they were marketing themselves and their work to a predominantly middle-class consumer culture, addressing and simultaneously participating in it. At the same time, all the novels read at length here perform some kind of critique of this culture. Perhaps Sinclair Lewis's satire is the most openly critical of the texts examined, but in its time, it was also a best-seller and was itself "commodified," the term *Babbitry* fast taking on the cachet of a brand name or trademark. Certainly, none of these writers positioned themselves at an emphatic remove from mainstream cultural practices. At least in terms of class standing, these authors interrogated mainstream commercial culture "from within," and this very embeddedness links them directly to the advertisers considered in this book. The hegemony of the "center" was, of course, dubious: the Fitzgeralds were expatriates, Lewis was a radical, and Larsen addressed a specifically Black middle class. Still, none of these qualities marked them as practitioners of "fringe" or alternative cultural forms. And advertisers, in a similar irony, so often seen as producers or at least disseminators of hegemonic culture, generally understood themselves to be detached or removed from the society they addressed, and even the work in which they themselves engaged, suggesting that the core/periphery model for dominant and subcultural identification is fruitfully complicated.

Fiction itself was and is heavily advertised and promoted, and authors like the Fitzgeralds and Lewis both gained from and contended with the boons and exigencies of celebrity. Conversely, the advertising profession has always attracted artists and writers (something that the industry has often struggled to downplay), and at least two of the authors examined here were directly engaged: Lewis worked as advertising manager for George Doran for a year, and F. Scott Fitzgerald was hired by the J. Walter Thompson Company to judge a staged beauty contest for a Woodbury Soap campaign.[35] The distinctions, then, between the world, the endeavor, and the generic space of the advertiser and author were not deeply delineated.

The discussion of advertising is too often limited to an analysis of ads themselves.[36] This "New Critical" approach leaves out the dynamics, contradictions, and drama inherent to their production. The advertisers explored here, who were helping to create the same cultural landscape as the authors cited in this book (arguably, with more impact), were themselves theorizing vigorously about the significance of their endeavor and its impact on psychology. Since this is an intrinsically self-conscious industry, committed as it is to the task of presentation, the professional dialogue generated by its practitioners is illuminating. Rachel Bowlby's *Shopping with Freud*, which shares some of this work's operative tenets despite its more British focus, also reads sales texts and contemporaneous fiction in tandem, in order to depict and analyze some of the models for identity suggested by "consumer relations."[37] *Living Up to the Ads* differs in one central way, however: it challenges the preeminence of these models of subjectivity by examining the various strains and pressures on them. Bowlby, instead, works to *establish* that preeminence in the face of a class/mass dichotomy that she wisely wants to prove bogus.[38] Once that dichotomy is undone—and Bowlby does an excellent job of it—do we have to agree that "there is nothing outside the shop" (119)?[39] With her allusion to a Derridean void outside the text, Bowlby points us not to relativistic paralysis but to a methodology of historical and discursive analysis.[40]

Bowlby, Walter Benn Michaels, and Jennifer Wicke are among those scholars who have advised against imagining that art provides a sacrosanct sphere, a safety zone from which authors can produce "objective" commentary on commodity culture and its effects (Bowlby 27). Surely they are right: whether producing "art" or "scholarship," we want our books to sell. As Lewis remarked about scathing social satirist H. L. Mencken, "Hasn't Menck in his salad days written punk hack stories, and didn't he in *Smart Set* [a journal he coedited] days stand for those lousy ads?"[41] We cannot and should not speculate much about some "uncontaminated" selfhood in an alternate universe undefiled by capitalist relations. The fruitlessness of that endeavor, though, should not lead us to universalize or dehistoricize the effects of capitalist relations on our experience of identity and gender. Bowlby suggests that, for starters, we " 'pay' some attention to our surroundings and notice them for what they are" (119). Through an inventive renegotiation of the discursive logic with which we approach identity, we can denaturalize the life that we're leading "inside the shop." We greet ads as detritus, to be muted, ignored, dismissed, perhaps peeked at, recycled—certainly too banal to "work" on our senses of self. Similarly, beneath the radar of everyday life, the gendered simulations we engage in daily, and the interplay between the productive power of ads and our own production of these performances, typically go unremarked. Hauling the term *work* into the sphere of private stagings does not mean borrowing the romance of the proletariat as an unearned form of cultural leverage. Instead, this book seeks to render strange and thereby illuminate the day-to-day experiences of subjectivity in the commercial culture of 1920s' America.

Happily, analyses that deepen the conceptual linkages between the consumer and worker's experiences of gender are becoming more common. Though the class differences between a woman on an assembly line and a rich American expat like the characters in the Fitzgeralds' fiction are obviously of the utmost importance, and are elided only quite falsely, analyses of consumption and production across the twentieth century do need to be integrated with more and more subtlety as global capital continues to enjoy unprecedented hegemony.[42] Ultimately, when we pass an ad for, say, Guess jeans, perhaps with a thirteen-year-old model in thick makeup straddling a tub of popcorn and sucking on her finger, we should be able to make profound connections (not equations) between the "work" that the ad makes us feel we must perform (such as trying to make ourselves look sixteen while convincing our daughters not to look twenty), the work performed by the model, and the work engaged in by the women in the sweatshops where the jeans are constructed, even while we also apprehend the conditions that divide the women occupying these different sites. This book attempts to add to the just-forming conceptual framework for such linkages.

The Chapters

Warren I. Susman, Karen Halttunen, and others have described a shift in the modern period's conceptualizations of subjectivity: though the exact timing of this is open to debate, it is clear that at the start of the twentieth century, theatrical effect began to be emphasized in popular American discourse about selfhood, above the integrity of the autonomous self.[43] This "cult of personality" meant a popular reevaluation of "influence," a form of personal agency identified in the nineteenth century with the feminine. By and throughout the twenties, influence was masculinized and reinvented as persuasion. In order to convince others, one has to be "sold" oneself, or at least convinced of one's own right to wield mesmeric power. Therefore, persuasion must begin with self-justification, and self-justification is a process that seems to leave its mark as contradiction in the text.

Particularly striking in materials emerging from the advertising industry is a dramatic vacillation between equally constructed, often contradictory positions. Manuals and memoirs by advertisers like Carl Naether, Claude Hopkins, and others careen between critical confession (or exposé) and self-eulogy. But as we will see in chapter 1, even when we zero in on the eulogies themselves, we discover that they are uttered in two contradictory registers: advertising's civilizing project, envisioned as feminine, provides the "treble line" while the hypermasculinized "bottom line" sounds the bass. The naturalization of the profit motive as a universal driving force is one of the fundamental moves made in advertising texts—the bottom line is treated as a self-evidence beyond analysis, and one of the few remaining sites in the modernist period for the notion of an inhering, essential truth. For the advertising man who succeeds through persuasion, the "truth" of the drive for profit supersedes in importance the relative truth value of any advertising claims he makes. His self-image and construction of a masculinity specific to his profession depend on a contrast between himself, distinct and supposedly in control of the messages he generates, and the undifferentiated "masses" who believe those messages. This masculine selfhood, then, is most rooted in the disjuncture between oneself and one's commercial utterance, the chasm or gap that marks one's capacity to profit through effective persuasion.

The heroics of profit require that there be buyers motivated to part with their cash. To foster this, the industry sought to address and aggravate certain anxieties in the consumer, anxieties that she or he might seek to soothe through consumption. In chapter 2, capitalist machismo and the pressure to perform are examined using Lewis's *Babbitt*[44] and Barton's *The Man Nobody Knows*. These two books treat the same vision of masculinity in the arenas of both consumption and salesmanship, though from strikingly different vantage points. Each book depicts a model of masculinity based on contemporaneous principles of self-advertisement and success in the business world, and largely dependent on an almost mystical devotion to enthusiastic, progressive energy that it codes masculine. In the formulation of a modern masculine subjectivity, the sacralization of "pep" seems another version of the unquestioning imperative of the search for profit, the same driving force in its psychological rather than economic valence. Whether celebrating or critiquing "the pep paradigm," each book suggests that, paradoxically, the quest for a zesty image, and thus efficacious mastery over others, *generates* the shame that motivates self-disguise, a shame that actually builds up an enormous, covert, imploding energy.

Speculations about feminine rather than masculine shame propel chapter 3. The advertiser's task of interpreting, addressing, and then swaying the female consumer—palpable in products, and responsible for endless manuals and treatises—has colored (and gendered) the entire popular approach to the field of psychology. The manuals and memoirs of several trailblazing female copywriters are read here to delineate their theories of the female consumer, as well as to consider the disruption of the showman-and-sucker paradigm brought about by women's entry into a largely male advertising workforce. These adwomen exemplified what much of advertising psychology downplays: women's increasing consumption was often far more directly linked to their working outside the home than to their Veblenian drive toward home adornment. In fact, females were entering the workforce in general during this period in unprecedented numbers—and entering new professions. Middle-class women were attending college and seeking careers, frequently delaying or even eschewing marriage and procreation, and working-class women were moving from domestic employment to more public jobs in factories, offices, and shops. John D'Emilio and Estelle B. Freedman report that "in 1870, domestic service accounted for sixty percent of female employment . . . by 1920 it had dropped to eighteen percent."[45] The women who entered the advertising profession, then, symbolize the failure of the "masses" to remain in their (feminine) place, the fissures that shoot through the gendered divide between advertiser and consumer, and the unsettling of the sexual politics that informed that divide. From the archival record, it appears that the work of these adwomen—with its creative and yet compulsory "mock-ups" of gendered subjectivity—led to an intermingling of shame and pleasure, irony and conviction.

The last two chapters explore the fiction of the Fitzgeralds and Larsen alongside contemporaneous advertising materials; the literary and commercial texts use language instantly recognizable as emerging from the same discursive pool. Although occupying different racial and class positions, the female protagonists created by Larsen and the Fitzgeralds all approach the task of self-presentation in ways that parallel the work of the advertising "vehicle." Committed and confined to this model of subjectivity, the fictional characters understand that they must negotiate the task of representing and augmenting the perceived value of something or someone else. In chapter 5, I use both advertising copy and a surrealist text by Leonora Carrington to open up Zelda Fitzgerald's *Save Me the Waltz*, asking whether the vehicle's labor of representation, her "burden of reflecting," can be, not transcended, but transmuted to point toward some form of escape.

To make the case for the prevalence in the 1920s of three subject positions defined by the commercial enterprise requires a firm belief in the molding powers of commodity culture. But I also read signs of the hungers, choices, and allegiances that such models for subjectivity precluded. Of particular interest are the destabilizations of the adman/consumer/vehicle triad: those prompted by the human desires that both fuel and exceed the system; those linked to expressions of class, racial, ethnic, and other subcultural affiliations dishonored by the dominant culture; and those brought about by experiences of community that undercut the heralding and constitution of the individual as essentially alone with his or her purchase or sale.[46]

Certainly, the gendering of the divide between producer and consumer has failed to secure a perfect hegemony. Michel Foucault's model for shifting, dispersed, and mutable power relations elucidates this failure. In fact, the difference between producer and consumer is by no means stable, nor can the gender delineation between salesman and shopper ever remain discrete. For all of us, movement through a day involves sifting through an array of differing roles and relationships. Since producers are consumers, the power dynamics between them are inherently unstable as they also shoot through them. Foucault argues that "one is dealing with mobile and transitory points of resistance, producing cleavages in a society that shift about, fracturing unities and effecting regroupings, furrowing across individuals themselves" (1978, 96). Despite inequities, furthermore, people of both genders play both roles.[47] Finally, precisely because advertising was so successful at disseminating models and tropes for thinking about and performing subjectivity, the sheer applicability and ubiquity of this discourse meant that it was open to perpetual mutation when people reused it in their own lives. All "[d]iscourse transmits and produces power; it reinforces it, but also undermines and exposes it, renders it fragile and makes it possible to thwart it" (Foucault 1978, 101). When dedicated to the mounting of persuasive spectacle, as in the commercial address, this discourse's emphasis on artifice weakens significantly its reliance on a posited essential difference between men and women.

I am among those whose critical analysis betrays a hunger for signs of resistance against a cultural and economic hegemony rife with inequities. Yet I hope that this zest for a utopian moment will not lead me to equate resistance with transcendence, or to imagine that the critical or "detached" stance (whether commercial, literary, or scholarly) can be objective or unimplicated. To invoke the late twentieth century's permutation of the free will versus determinism debate, it seems an increasingly tiresome inevitability that scholars of culture today must position themselves along a narrow spectrum, providing their answers to questions that have become, in the end, pat: Just how successful are the containing powers of cultural hegemony? Just how much space remains for "extrahegemonic" expression, and how much of that can qualify as "resistance"? This book suggests close reading as one way out of this confining, almost Manichaean paradigm, allowing us instead to discern the irresolvable interplay between forces of containment or appropriation and resistance on a case-by-case basis.

Reading closely, one can hear cage rattling, imperfect fits, absences, creative reception, ironies, and glimpses of epiphany, perhaps shrouded by capitulation, but illuminating nonetheless. This throws into relief the agency residing—often latent—not within a transcendent subject envisioned as discrete from its cultural context, but within societal subject positions themselves. The revolutionary impetus in marxist thought was the revelation of the agency inhering in industrial labor, despite the obfuscations of that agency perpetuated by capitalist culture. Though there is no tidy parallel between psychological and industrial travail, other apparently disempowered social roles seem to be possessed of a strangely accreted, unacknowledged but still profound agency, as feminist scholarship and reception theory have shown. This agency hides in the same way as that of the Marxian laborer, like Poe's "purloined letter," vanishing in front of our eyes. Whether in Lewis's George Babbitt, the eager businesswomen in success manuals by advertiser Maule, or Larsen's protagonist Helga Crane, the productive effort, or the work required in self-performativity—the hiding and display—resonates with individual agency. Identity, then, refracts and shifts between persona and representation on the one hand, and vulnerability, effort, and "work" on the other. The disavowed shame and malaise that the white-collar employee secretly fears are central to his self, the complex negotiations with power and sheer industry of the woman engaged in consumption and gender spectacle—these are the unspoken cathexes and hidden labors that it is my task here to interconnect, acknowledge, and articulate.

Chapter 1

Doubled Truth

Uplift and the Bottom Line

The Industry

Advertising emerged as an identifiable profession in the mid-nineteenth century, functioning in its earliest forms as a kind of "space brokerage" whereby
agents sold ad space in newspapers. Whether the adman-in-the-middle should
represent the company with something to tout or the newspaper with a circulation to sell was something that it took a generation or two of entrepreneurially
minded advertisers to iron out. Meanwhile, this unregulated indeterminacy
meant that advertising was perceived as a somewhat dubious enterprise among
the businesspeople who used it; it likewise suffered from a bad reputation
among audiences in that it was linked with the "quackery" and deceptions of
patent medicines, the first products to be heavily advertised across the United
States.[1] P. T. Barnum, an early and voluble figurehead for the profession,
generated much excitement and a certain umbrage during the 1860s and 1870s
with his energetic humbuggery, which proved a sizable contribution to the
development of advertising and public relations principles.[2]

At the century's turn, wage earners, often immigrants and/or recently ur-
banized, were heterogeneous in their affiliations, predilections, and cultural
values, and frequently politicized in their dissatisfactions. One significant reaction was an increasingly aggressive call from business and government circles
for what department store magnate Edward Filene called consumer "education": "Mass production demands mass education. . . . [T]he masses must
learn to behave like human beings in a mass production world" (quoted in
Ewen 1976, 54). For Filene and others, the masses acceptably "humanized"
would commit their wallets, leisure time, and value systems to the logic of
the marketplace and commodity. Since many American salaries did not provide adequate disposable income for such wholesale dedication to consumerism, credit options emerged, and "by the end of the 1920s, Americans were
buying over 60% of their cars, radios, and furniture on the installment plan"
(Marchand 4).

That so much of this consumer "education" should be conducted by advertising professionals was partially a result of the industry's engagement with the First World War effort. Advertiser George Creel's Committee on Public Information proved as much a publicity campaign for the respectability and indispensability of advertising as for American involvement in the war, and advertisers' National War Advisory Board ushered the profession into the managerial elite even as it counciled the government.[3] The collaboration was recompensed: a "wartime excess profits tax which defined advertising expenditures as exempt business costs" helped motivate a widespread enlargening of advertising budgets (Marchand 6).

By the 1920s, advertising, already a significant presence in national and local commerce since the 1870s, took its place at center stage: American commerce would not be conducted without it. Organizations like the American Association of Advertising Agencies, which touted its oversight of professional standards and truth in advertising, had already laid the groundwork for the industry's legitimization and self-regulation. Statistics of growth in advertising volume, agency's incomes, and the percentage of distribution costs allotted to advertising all reflect huge gains made by the profession during this period. Between 1914 and 1929, U.S. advertising revenues increased from $682 to $2,987 million (Pope 22–29), and between 1916 and 1926, national magazine advertising grew by 600% (Marchand 7). As we will see, the newly emergent radio and cinema, both valuable forums for product placement and commercial address, also contributed to the industry's accelerated growth during the twenties. Additionally, systems of transportation and communication had been gradually improving since before the Civil War (and because of the infrastructure created by that war), allowing nationalized chain stores, product distribution, and commercial campaigns to burgeon simultaneously.[4]

The Incorporated Snicker

The early ad industry's first job was to sell itself as an indispensable component of American commerce.[5] Practitioners in this self-conscious industry worked to develop narratives of justification that explained and promoted the profession's role in the economy. One can trace acts of projection in advertisers' texts, where traits that actually appear to be endemic to the advertising project itself are ascribed to the observed consumer-object. The often contradictory means whereby advertisers rationalized their profession, then, wound up shaping the models for individual subjectivity that advertisers envisioned and promulgated.

From its inception among the patent medicine salesmen through today, advertising has evoked associations with the charlatanesque, the theatrical, the charming, the carnivalesque. In the face of these somewhat disreputable connotations, the industry has strived for many decades (and especially so in the 1910s and 1920s) to take its place among the new "expert" professions, which were using the guise of the specialist and the "plain speech" discourse of empiricism to invest themselves with the right to exert managerial authority over other people's lives (Lears 1990). To climb, the adman needed to negotiate the tension between these two models of narrative authority: the carnivalesque and normative. And this industry-specific tension between two visions of power can be understood as more widely significant, providing a key component of advertising's metaphoric impact on a culture it both shaped and reflected. Throughout *Fables of Abundance,* Jackson Lears emphasizes and revalues the disruptive, creative qualities of the carnivalesque element running through commercial culture's history, a fundamentally Bakhtinian formulation. Yet the difference between the "carnivalesque" and "normative" modes in commercial culture is ultimately less profound than is their collaboration in hegemonic formation.

Historian Marjorie Beale describes how French advertisers of the 1920s, struggling to overcome the reputation of charlatanry, worked to "pool" these modes of authority: they often cited the work, for instance, of Dr. Hippolyte Bernheim, who brought the "rigor" of scientific discourse to the terrain of the mesmeric, focusing on hypnosis and the use of visual images in his study of the powers of suggestion.[6] "Charlatanry" and "scientism" may be more aligned than would seem likely. American advertisers certainly hoped to employ both means. Whether you are persuaded by the sheer pleasure of the seduction, or because you have been daunted into submitting to the injunctions of an expert, you are letting an address from without change your behavior. Hence, the subjectivity of a seduction and the cool rationality of a logical presentation of the "facts" wind up as collaborating planes of influence in the advertisement. Advertising discourse often strikes a "realist" tone, whether via "hard facts" or "folksy" affability, but at the same time, ads engage in a disruption of normative narrative cohesion that is ultimately postmodern. The career of the typical, and indeed prototypical advertising personality P. T. Barnum exemplifies just this strange partnership. Barnum claims in his autobiography, *Struggles and*

Triumphs, that he offers his readers the potentially profitable realism of exposé—talking them through the "backstage" mechanics of a lifetime of practical jokes and staged humbuggery—yet instead, he performs the postmodernist
gesture of an exposure that reveals only more spectacle and the impossibility of
a real core to be unmasked.[7] "Now and then someone would cry 'humbug' or
'charlatan,' but so much the better for me. It helped to advertise," Barnum
brags (142).

Neil Harris and Jennifer Wicke have both remarked on the way that
Barnum addressed and incorporated his audience's interpretive savviness by
inviting its members to chuckle knowingly at the spectacle of their own hood-
winking. As Lears notes, this phenomenon is essential to advertising as a
whole.[8] On the face of it, many ads attempt to neutralize the critical faculties of
their audience by presuming the absence of such, giving rise to the ubiquitous
cry that advertisers talk down to consumers and view them as gullible to the
extreme. This states the case too simply, though. Despite the fact that some
advertisers did express great contempt for their audience, they did not fail to
prepare for a complex response to the advertising message on the part of the
"incoherent masses" they addressed. The target of an ad is not expected to take
in the main address of the ad purely, simply, ingenuously. Rather, the consumer's "leftover" interpretive sophistication, although apparently belied, does
not go untended to. This more perspicacious level of reception is simultaneously engaged through a sort of incorporated snicker, which works in tandem with the broad face of the "show" itself to create a two-pronged strategy
for audience absorption. In addition to the surface thrust of the ad's main
"story," the competitive drive of the advertiser who tells this story to manipulate the audience successfully becomes, itself, a metaspectacle, and this covert
valuation of the manipulative illusion seeks a spot at the heart of the American
identity.

The reflexivity of the advertiser asks not for scrutiny but applause, a reflexivity that supports the status quo, not subverting but partnering the normative
realism of the advertiser's pitch. The incorporated snicker is subtextual, sub-
liminal; it attempts to incite a sort of pleasure in the epiphenomenology of
persuasion and therefore can be seen as aligning with the carnivalesque mode
of achieving narrative power. Running concurrent with the overt narrative of
the ad, then, is the picaresque subtext of the advertiser's endeavor to charm and
persuade; the audience is supposed to be "sold" by the ad's surface story and
simultaneously soothed about their own susceptibility in the pleasure of ob-

serving the mechanics of persuasion as it unfolds.[9] Today, this endeavor is often more than implicit, as articles tracking successful ad campaigns proliferate in the popular media and contextualize the ads themselves with a scorekeeping metanarrative akin to sports coverage.[10]

The incorporation of the audience's skeptical faculties via the tongue-in-cheek stance is a common ingredient in modern narrative. Its linkage to the commercial process throws into question any formula that would too quickly read all irony and fractured narrative as indicators of resistance or subversion. Advertisers are consummate experts at experimenting with semiotic fractures, at creating impact by attending to and incorporating the different levels of reception set into motion by a narrative address. So this kind of fracturing of narrative is not implicitly subversive, even though it apparently does not rely on the myth of a unified whole that has been posited by deconstructionists as the main tool of a liberal bourgeois cultural hegemony. Anne McClintock asks "whether it is sufficient to locate agency in the internal fissures of discourse. Locating agency in ambivalence runs the risk of what might be called a fetishism of form." She cites Homi Bhabha: "Caught in the Imaginary as they are, these shifting positionalities will never seriously threaten the dominant power relations, for they exist to exercise them pleasurably and productively."[11] The advertising agenda is not to subvert or oppose, but to sell; audience pleasure in an advertisement's ironic, winking address will hopefully lead to the productivity of a sale. Advertisers, however, are not mustachio-twirling villains, driven to distort narratives by their lust for lucre. Rather, they are an ambivalent lot, by and large savvy, highly creative, and often of two minds about their work. The multileveled, sardonic quality of so many ads bespeaks the subtle, wry, even analytic, self-consciousness of the advertiser. Still, this acute, ambivalent consciousness does not change the fact that advertising typically gains in efficacy via just such multilevel approaches to commercial address.[12]

The advertising narrative's remarkable ability to appropriate and reincorporate subtexts and fissures is inherent to the Barnumesque mounting of commercial spectacle. In fact, the fracturing seems to strengthen rather than deconstruct that narrative. This may be possible because, spectacular appearances to the contrary, the notion of an inhering truth is not repudiated by the injection of the reflexive subtext in an ad. The concept of "essence" does live on in the commercial address—in a specific form: the supposed self-evidence of the profit motive, its introduction into the "plot" as a first cause beyond questioning or examination, often becomes the ground, in a modern capitalist culture, for the enduring notion of inhering, nonconstructed, fundamental essence or truth. For it is profit above all that is spectacularized both in the advertisement's picaresque subtext about persuasion and in industry manuals—profit, no matter what, Barnum explained; profit, the getting of which is a pleasure to behold even at one's own expense; profit, because any catastrophe can be transformed into good publicity; profit, the ultimate proof of commodification's limitless appropriative powers.

The Opposing Imperatives of Transcendence and M-C-M Prime

The self-evidence of the bottom line is a key principle at work in many advertising texts from the twenties. This profit-based textual structure, though, intersects with another structuring thematic element: the repeated insistence not on the need to make money, but on advertising's transcendent capacity to civilize. The "treble line truth" of the profession, coded feminine, is advertising's "uplift" function, allowing society to ascend to new heights of civilization; the "bass line truth," coded masculine and ultimately celebrated even more, is the "fundamental bottom line" or the profit motive.

Both the moral and profit-based stances play a part in mobilizing advertisers; in the 1920s, despite their uneasy relation to one another, both postures needed to be assumed, it seems, in order to enable and explain the commercial endeavor to its own practitioners. Often, the search for profit is treated as the advertiser's "real" motivation; both critics and proponents of the advertising industry are quite likely to treat the utopic, transcendent "justifications" for advertising as just that—justifications—far more flimsy, superstructural, and veil-like than the hard, solid, bottom line quest for profit. Yet most advertisers who painted their profession as an agent of civilization were driven by genuinely powerful concerns about and hopes for the twentieth century and the modern industrial project.

One avenue by which such ideals were brought to the commercial endeavor was the social gospel movement: a review of Susan Curtis's work in this area suggests that the utopic, even philanthropic stances of some advertisers were shaped by cultural cross-pollination.[13] As Curtis limns it, Protestant hunger for a revamped Christianity committed to social reform began to express itself as a bona fide social movement in the 1880s and 1890s; eventually, this led to social gospel's significant engagement with and influence on an emergent commodity culture. The influence, though, clearly flowed in both directions: this period of interchange had an impact on both American Protestantism and American commercialism. This push for an accessible, efficacious social reform movement, one that would ameliorate the lot of the common person while invigorating and modernizing the Christian experience, was ultimately incorporated and subsumed by the corporate commercial sphere, Curtis argues. It also set a tenor for the ad industry: if social gospelers began to figure Christian faith using the tropes of consumption, so too did advertisers (regardless of their religious or ethnic identifications), often describing their task as one of uplift and societal transformation.[14] Industry memoirs indicate that the vision of advertising as an instigator of social progress held authentic allure; at the least, the amount of time spent returning to the site of the transcendent claims in these texts implies that the advertising authors hungered after the utopic.[15]

So, the "transcendent" mode in advertisers' writing is apparently more than a hypocritical veneer, an artifice glazed for effect over some sort of naked greed for profit. Perhaps the most lively, least saccharin exemplar comes from Christine Frederick, whose 1929 manual *Selling Mrs. Consumer* became an industry classic. Here, she responds to a critique of consumer culture from an unnamed source.

As a writer recently facetiously put it:

> "The Anglo-Saxon male tradition is slipping! Our civilization is lush
> soil for the feminine, but barren soil for the masculine characteristics of
> history and legend. We make much ado over our so-called modern indus-
> trial age, but what is it except kindly taking in women's washing and
> calling it a laundry—doing women's scullery work and calling it a food
> factory—taking in women's sewing and calling it a textile industry? So we
> busily mix dough, ply the needle and bustle about with soap and laundry
> machinery and call ourselves he-men!"

> To this Mrs. Consumer can only reply that both men and women seem
> to be agreed upon what constitutes real civilization, especially since the
> World War so apparently finally warped and destroyed the last vestige of
> the male's romantic notion about war. Man has decided to glorify the
> fireside rather than the God Mars, and to graft upon himself some of the
> more humanitarian principles with which women have always been con-
> cerned. He will fight nature, not himself, make war upon disease, discom-
> fort, ugliness, hunger, ignorance, poverty and misery rather than upon
> other men. He will live gorgeously and luxuriously, not upon goods taken

from others in conquest, but upon goods which he himself manufactures and distributes. If this be feminine, then make the most of it! is woman's reply to the iconoclast. . . . A new concept of glory which is neither male nor female but *human* is being substituted by the American man, in which the prize is the lifting of living standards in this country, as well as in the backwards countries of all the world. . . . That it makes Mrs. Consumer the pivotal center of modern life is simply the logic of nature. (15–17)

Frederick modernizes a rather nineteenth-century version of woman's moral superiority linked to her role as homemaker, making the wheels of commerce seem merely accomplices to her realization of home-and-hearth desires— desires that are now revealed to be the standard-bearing heralds of a society on its way to Edenic fulfillment. Business falls quietly in step "behind" the posited woman, gaining moral prestige from her nineteenth-century status (a status predicated, at least in theory, on her circumscription to the home). For Frederick, modernity is not a triumph of the revitalized man of business over the claustrophobic conventionalism of the nineteenth-century angel of the house (as Bruce Barton would have it); rather, the angel in this "feminist" tale has succeeded in transcending the house that defined her, and commerce, its testosterone humbled and quieted by the recent horrors of the First World War, is ready to do her bidding.

This is just as Catherine Beecher seemed to wish it, when she ended her 1869 domestic manual, *The American Woman's Home,* with an explicit call for the amplification of the domestic sphere to include society at large.[16] Whereas earlier chapters in Beecher's book provide layout plans for efficient homes, in her penultimate chapter, the blueprint is of a church and school: "Thus the 'Christian family' and 'Christian neighborhood' would become the grand ministry" (459).[17] Fifty years later, for Frederick, the "grand ministry" is more Herbert Hooverian than Christian (business having taken over the reins), and it is worldwide. She links advertising's transcendent function to a global transition away from militarily enforced imperialism (no more "the God Mars") and toward the economically "suggested" imperialism implied by the "lifting" of living standards around the world. Advertising, contends Frederick, "is performing the task that churches have long given up—it is strengthening our characters. I am really serious. Advertising is truly forcing us to develop strength of will to resist its alluring temptations to buy articles which we do not need" (337). In protesting that she is "really serious," Frederick seems to suggest that as an argument in favor of the advertising industry, this "character-strengthening" line stretches the bounds of credibility. To thank advertisers for exercising the consumers' developing powers of resistance in the same discussion that has tabulated the benefits of introduction to "all the good things that manufacturers make everywhere" seems an act of rhetorical desperation, but it is typical of the contradictory nature of advertisers' texts, and perhaps, reflective of the strain between service and profit that results from these dual narrative presences.

The compatibility between these two goals, service and profit, was frequently theorized by business proponents, and even insisted on as the groundwork of professionalism.[18] For the influential Bruce Barton, for instance, the congruence of personal gain and altruistic service seems a cheerful coincidence, good luck being conflated with virtue much as it is for Horatio Alger. A key component in the effort to align uplift and the bottom line was the naturalization of the urge for profit. But the masculinized bottom line, as invoked by advertisers, is in the end no more universal, self-evident, or "natural" than is the feminized focus on uplift, just as the "bullet-like, raucous, over-emphatic" copy that 1920s' advertisers produced for a male audience was fully as constructed and bound by discursive conventions as the more verbose and indirect prose they generated when emulating "feminine" stylistics.[19]

There is a reason, though, that the profit motive functions as an unquestionable "motor" in many of these texts. The quest for profit does a wonderful imitation of a self-evident essence or truth, because it *is* essential within this economic context. Capital itself, Karl Marx suggests, is the "repetitive, expansive" process, the "never-ending cycle" of "Money-Capital-Money Prime" (M-C-M prime), whereby money must ever be transformed into commodities and then turned back into money, and so on.[20] This ongoing metamorphosis, which characterizes capitalism, is figured (and experienced) as a universal, a given, parallel to and shaping our ideas about the life force itself, beyond which we can hardly be expected to peer. Max Weber comments on this naturalization of an economic mode, or perhaps we should term it a *cosmification:* "The capitalistic economy of the present day is an immense cosmos into which the individual is born and which presents itself to him . . . as an unalterable order of things in which he must live."[21] In a 1926 J. Walter Thompson *Newsletter* article, the profit motive is universalized through the pathologization of its absence. The piece critiques scientist Joseph Henry, who discovered the electromagnetic telegraph four years before Samuel Morse did, but who shied away "perversely" from the marketplace.

> The notion of seeking a profit from his laboratory discoveries was quite foreign to his nature. . . . This inventor lived in a sort of fantastic world apart from his fellow men. . . . [T]he early association of telegraph interests with those of the telephone . . . were responsible for the rise of the great AT & T company. . . . It is really fortunate that in the present day scientists are freer from Professor Henry's viewpoint, and realize that the man who invents or discovers a valuable thing is no criminal because he profits by his invention.[22]

Here, the failure to make profit-based decisions is painted as aberrant and inherently antisocial, and enthusiasm for the consolidated powers of corporate entities like AT&T is linked to participation in the family of man and presumed to be axiomatic. Heilbroner explains that a central distinction between the capitalist profit motive and the desire for accumulation observable in other economies is capitalism's development of an effective ideological "answer" to the widespread precapitalist condemnation of avarice.[23] On the same distinction, Weber remarks that for "whole epochs . . . the feeling was never quite overcome that activity directed to acquisition for its own sake was at bottom a *pudendum*" (73). (Note the highly gendered term for shame that Weber employs here, evoking in passing the supposed feminine alignment with and hunger for goods.) Acquisitiveness is reenvisioned in capitalist culture "not as a disruptive 'passion' but as a steadying 'interest' . . . in the guise of commerce, [and is] thus seen to exert a civilizing effect" (Heilbroner 111). In the passage about the resistant scientist quoted above, the "fantastic," uncivilized passion depicted is not greed, but exactly that force that drove Henry away from the marketplace, and it is countered with the calmer, more socially grounded "interests" of the telegraph and telephone industries.

An April 1926 *Associated Advertising* editorial lauded the commercial facilitation of such "interests" as worthy of scholarly ratification. Arguing for college degrees in advertising, the author writes that "surely it is as worthwhile to bring comfort and happiness, through cheaper and better advertised commodities, into human lives as it is to remove an appendix or to plead a case before the bar."[24] Clearly, the impetus for this comparison is more a concern for the industry's "professional pedigree," as the author puts it, than for social reform: significantly, though, he must invoke the "civilizing" project to ratify that pedigree.

In *Women in Advertising in New York Agencies,* by contrast, Merle Higley quotes one male ad executive who would naturalize the profit motive by deflating the claims of "higher" interests, and higher learning, as naive and counterproductive.[25] According to Higley, this exec energetically voices—and genders—the "bottom line" approach, critiquing "college girls" for assessing copy without enough respect for its selling ability: "Some copy may be ugly and sound crude, yet the increase of the volume of sales is conclusive proof that the advertising for that product is good. This selling angle on copy, he says, is lacking to a great degree in the experience and viewpoint of female copy writers" (16). The executive's scorn for (feminized) aesthetic criteria instantiates Heilbroner's contention that "the expansion of capital is aided and abetted by the declaration that moral and aesthetic criteria—the only dikes that might hold back the flood tide of capital's expansion—are *without relevance* within the realm of economic activity" (118). Heilbroner's insight suggests a strain between the moral high ground that advertisers claim for their professional endeavor and the bottom line, which they toe with equal vigor.

Despite that tension, both the moral and profit-based stances were attractive motivators to advertisers of the 1920s, who seem to have had fairly complex attitudes about their work. Many who wrote about their craft simply moved between the two positions, allowing the contradictions to stand, apparently depending on the rhetorical exigencies of the moment, but probably also reflecting deep ambivalences of their own. For example, in *My Life in Advertising,* Claude Hopkins reminds his readers that "we are in business to get results. . . . We can pose as artists and geniuses only so long. Business men find us out. . . . Not literary work, not work which leads your lady friends to say, 'That's wonderful.' But practical selling. No man save a dilettante will ever try for anything else" (107–8). Hopkins chooses terminology that genders both the keepers and betrayers of the bottom line: it will take "men" to see through the artsy "dilettantes" (note the swishy word) who threaten the flow of corporate gain merely to impress their "lady friends." Twenty pages later, however, Hopkins takes a contradictory stance, striving to ascend to "higher levels." "No man . . . can afford to offend his own principles. The moment he compromises for money's sake he is lost. Not as a success, perhaps, but as an artist. As a man who contributes to his profession or calling and brings it to higher levels"

(127).[26] In this more laudatory invocation, the artistic realm (depicted as sanctified and unbesmirched by commerce) is not feminized; rather, it is a sphere for men, for those few manly enough to risk censure and rise above the greed of the marketplace. The contradictions between these two passages go unremarked.

Beyond Uplift: The "Vast, Shapeless Force"

Advertisers went on to forge a resolution of sorts between the industry's drive for corporate gain and its sense of social calling. This involved shifts in the way advertisers referred to their aim, their own authority, and their audience. Perhaps one of the most zealous proponents of advertising's transcendent function can help us see what this resolution entailed. Frank Presbrey's eulogizing *The History and Development of Advertising* provides a comprehensive, though biased, narrative and pictorial history of his profession to date. By 1929, as illustrated in Presbrey's text, the push for social reform seemed to be dissolving into a belief in a business-driven model of expansion and progress (that is, M-C-M prime), and the philanthropist's conviction that he somehow has the right to oversee social uplift segued into a secular (and sometimes almost Nietzschean) belief in the right of an elite managerial class to influence and lead the "incoherent, voiceless mass," as one advertiser put it. In other words, the service ethos mutated into a reverence for economic expansion. In order for this commitment to M-C-M prime to feel like a form of social service, the target of advertising needed to be envisioned differently—the masses had to be "massified," in essence, so that the manipulation of desire could be seen not as an ethical dilemma, but as one component of a great social program. Presbrey invokes advertising's civilizing function in the boldest terms imaginable, as when he heads a discussion of one successful ad campaign, "Bathtub begins its great social work" (425).[27]

Presbrey's final chapter is the book's most extended rehearsal of his broad claims about the industry: Advertising, a "civilizing influence" and "social force," has "helped bring about an all-round easing of toil and a consequent greater interest in the finer things of life" (608). "Advertising is probably our greatest agency for spreading an understanding and love of beauty in all things" (611). But perhaps Presbrey's most explicitly political project for the advertising industry is put forth here: "Modern advertising has made the life of the masses so much more pleasant by painting attractive pictures of the things that make it so, and has so completely demonstrated its ability to influence the thought of the people of all classes, that when it comes to the big, all-comprehensive job of achieving an ideal social state, the potent force of advertising will at least be one of the agencies through which it will be accomplished" (618).

What Presbrey calls for is hardly synchronous with the uplift and reforms envisioned by "social gospel" activists of an earlier era, especially in the degree to which Presbrey denies autonomy to the "classes" in need of influence. "The masses" here are seen neither as active agents nor infantilized recipients of philanthropy, but instead, as an undifferentiated, malleable material that can be shaped from the inside via advertising's transformational powers. This vast society-building enterprise is to be undertaken by a class of leaders, so implicitly worthy of the power that they wield that they go unnamed in Presbrey's passively constructed sentence, though advertisers apparently hope to be numbered among them.

Presbrey finishes his *History* with an appended speech delivered by President Calvin Coolidge in 1926 at the Annual Convention of the American Association of Advertising Agencies. In a fine instance of preaching to the converted, Coolidge impressed on his audience the merit of building on and expanding the desires of the American people; he evidently addresses the same quest for "an ideal social state" that Presbrey detailed above. In one key moment, the president describes a community of immigrant workers living around the industrial concern that employs them.

> Their wants were not large, so that under the American rate of wages they found it possible to supply themselves and their families without working anywhere near full time. As a result, production was low compared with the number employed and was out of proportion to the overhead expense of management and capital costs. Some fertile mind conceived of locating a good milliner in that community. The wares of this shop were generously advertised. (quoted in Presbrey, 621)

Shortly thereafter, of course, urgent new yearnings for bonnets sprang up throughout the community, and ultimately, those burgeoning consumer desires led to a remarkably positive chain of events. The men worked more, the plant produced more, "its cost units were reduced, its profits were enlarged, it could sell its product to its customers at a lower figure [but did it?], and the whole industry was improved. More wealth was produced" (621). Unquestioningly, in the name of capital accumulation, Coolidge advocates the interruption of what sounds a fairly pleasant scenario: initially, in his account, the immigrant workers were satisfied. Their needs (not yet American needs) were being met. This hypothetical fulfillment he depicts as untenable and appropriately aborted: the social work performed by the milliner's advertising agency in Coolidge's anecdote seems to be at the service not of some vision of a common good, then, but of the bottom line as a nationalizing imperative, its merit self-evident and its force the compelling motor that drives on the United States. The Americanization of these immigrants—that is, the aggravation of their material desires—as Coolidge depicts it, is not a metamorphosis undergone by active agents, but a transformation wrought on them so they can play their part in the generation of further profit.

His narrative, of a stagnant satisfaction giving way to a productive appetite for consumables, drowns out another construction of immigrant experience, whereby foreign-born workers like anarchist Emma Goldman, highly dissatisfied, fought for improved wages and working conditions rather than haberdashery, and were often forcibly suppressed, not only via advertisement, but with guns, clubs, dogs, fire hoses, and arrest. Coolidge rewrites the story of the immigrant worker, and energetic realization of the expansive M-C-M prime process stands in for the social gospel. "More wealth was produced." By whom was this wealth produced and for whose coffers was it destined? The passive phrase suppresses this information, and the desires and motivations of the individual consumer-workers that Coolidge describes are relevant only as they impact on capital accumulation. This is the resolution alluded to above, between service and gain, because Coolidge offers us the bottom line as transcendence, the angel of the house replaced by the invisible hand in the twentieth century's "grand ministry."

Demarcating a shift in the commercial approach to the audience of mass media, however, does not mean that advertisers prior to 1929 expressed only respect for their audiences. To the contrary, early examples of disdain abound, just as deferential appreciation for the popular perspective can also be evidenced in the industry after the year of the crash. For instance, Stephen Fox quotes one prominent advertiser of the 1890s, Charles Austin Bates, who remarked that "advertisers should never forget that they are addressing stupid people. It's really astonishing how little a man may know, and yet keep out of the way of the trolley cars" (73). The shifts that do occur among advertisers around the beginning of the depression are in the notion of service itself and the envisioning of the target of advertising as part of a large, undifferentiated mass, appropriately directed by a small, powerful elite. This no doubt reflects the advances in communications brought about by the rise of Hollywood, the birth of radio, and the continued emergence of nationalized brand name products, advances that made audience population pools ever more unindividuated in the advertisers' minds. Additionally, that class inflections and contempt should manifest with particular vigor at this point in American economic history is not especially surprising, considering both the stark relief into which class distinctions were thrown by the depression, and the labor unrest and radicalism that it helped to accelerate. For these and other reasons, over the course of many decades, the industry's mode of self-justification and means whereby its practitioners legitimated their profession shifted—slowly, and in fits and starts—further from the task of "uplift." Already by 1927, one J. Walter Thompson advertiser asserted at a staff meeting: "This is not an age of crusades. . . . [I]t is an age of vogues, and we could not sell the moral responsibility of the age very easily, but we might sell the vogue very easily."[28] And so they did.

The struggle apparent at J. Walter Thompson around 1930 was not between a service ethos and an open avowal of profit priorities. Rather, discussion was more likely to revolve around whether to address the "mob" on what advertisers imagined to be its "own" terms or to avoid the "emotional appeal" of the "lowbrow" approach. The larger issue behind this debate was about how to articulate the distinction between the "mob" and the adman who addressed it; the distinction itself was a given. Jackson Lears argues that invocation of this distinction allowed advertisers to resolve a long-standing conflict in regard to their own profession: "By reaffirming their sense of superiority to their audience . . . and developing a rhetoric of 'mass man,' advertising spokesmen could relax the tension between managerial and carnivalesque discourses: rationality for the few, irrationality for the many" (Lears 1994, 218).

The industry consensus at this time seems to be that advertisers themselves are naturally at a great remove from their audience, separated by merit, refinement, and class. Demographics would suggest that advertisers were easily alienated from "the common man." As detailed by Roland Marchand, advertisers were significantly richer, more highly educated, more concentrated in urban areas, and far more likely to have servants than were Americans in general (36–38). (That they were also significantly whiter, Marchand may have assumed to be axiomatic.) Advertisers, apparently married to this sense of a hierarchical divide between themselves and their audience, came up with different ways of asserting their perceived superiority, espousing either a highbrow disregard for popular opinion or the cynical detachment of a salesman catering for his own reasons to the uncultivated hoi polloi.

In a number of speeches made before his colleagues, longtime J. Walter Thompson adman William L. Day argues for dismissal of the "masses" as too lacking in direction to matter, preferring to seek out and address an intellectual elite whom he saw as inevitably leading the rest. His version of the social gospeler's call for uplift is a very different, nonphilanthropic model for leadership, based on an almost fascistic zest for the principle of a few great men (in fact, he reserves high praise for the efficacy of Mussolini and Stalin).[29] In a 1931 talk, Day invoked the "critical one percent," an "intellectual minority," he claims, that directs the minds and actions of the great mass of unnoteworthies that make up the bulk of the human race.[30]

> The Soviet Russian Revolution is not a revolution of the Russian masses. . . . The masses had nothing to do with the grasping of power by a small group of Jewish anarchists. . . . There is no case in history . . . where there has ever been a real rising of a people in in which the idea which caused the rising sprang from the incoherent, voiceless mass. The great mass has never had an idea. . . . [I]t is purely and simply a vast, shapeless force which is led in one direction or another by leaders. (Day 1931, 3–4) [I believe that] the theory that advertising must cater to the actual mass reader [is] of very doubtful worth. . . . This mass theory . . . controverts, if it is true, all the theories by which people have been forced into other kinds of action prior to the establishment of the fact [that the average consumer is "mentally fourteen years old"]. (4) [We should be concerned with captivating the "critical one percent" instead.] Are we really bettering advertising and bettering our results in removing the principle of authority and in substituting the principle of talking down to people? Aren't we too much concerned with reaching people, about reaching large numbers of them? Aren't we too worried about talking to them in the words that they are supposed to use? (11)

The highbrow refusal to "sink" to the level of the average consumer is the means whereby Day underscores his own right to a spot high above the fray he attempts to direct. Day's rather Ayn Randian, overblown vision of leadership was not the most prevalent stance taken in the profession—which is unsurprising if you consider that he dismisses the need to reach people. Others were outspoken proponents of the "lowest common denominator" approach. These advertisers develop a different strategy to distinguish themselves from the masses they addressed. Based on the principles of mastery and cynical detachment, this approach was probably more resilient than Day's elitism because less melodramatic. The spokespeople for this approach at the J. Walter Thompson Company were the young, more cutting-edge players like William Esty and guest speakers from Hollywood, who addressed staff meetings with ever greater frequency as the agency developed its ties with the movie business.

The alliance between these two professions on parallel paths was happy, and as time wore on, inextricably symbiotic. Lary May describes the rise of movies:

> Despite former barriers of class and ethnicity, film innovators turned the once-crude peep shows into a complex art form and a multi-million dollar business. From nearly a hundred small firms in 1912, eight major companies emerged in the twenties to centralize production, distribution and exhibition. With this transition from an entrepreneurial to a corporate industry, the motion picture establishment generated the star system, lavish theater palaces, and Hollywood—a national symbol for the modern consumer lifestyle.[31]

In the corporate consolidation of an industry originally typified by heterogeneity and the maverick entrepreneur, as well as in the increasing commitment to the marketing of images of affluence, the movie and advertising businesses were both parallel and mutually supportive.

The growing impact of this shared project made itself felt in the business philosophy of both industries. At J. Walter Thompson, the most of-the-moment advertisers and visiting Hollywood representatives seemed to argue that advertisers should cease any pretense of either leadership or service, acknowledge the bottom line as the profession's clear priority, and get on with the job of catering to the mob's lowbrow tastes.[32] In a speech to his fellow ad representatives, William Esty declared:

> We say the Hollywood people are stupid, the pictures are stupid: What we are really saying is the great bulk of people is stupid and personally I believe, if you are going out to trade with the natives you take along coral

beads, or calico or whatever they like and not fight with bookshelves or anything unless you are trying to improve them. I think that the improvement of the human race is for scientists, educators, etc.; I don't look upon it as a function of advertising where clients don't spend money trying to raise the level of intelligence of the country, even if it could be done.[33]

Note here that Esty does not contradict the claim that people are generally stupid. Instead, he goes to "trade" with his American "natives," not to convert or "civilize" them. The "coral beads, or calico" that advertisers and Hollywood professionals deployed to wow their audiences were often enough images of wealth, of sumptuous commodities lovingly arrayed around performers deemed beautiful enough to deserve them.

These members of the J. Walter Thompson community, when they do wax sentimental about advertising (or cinema) performing a service, tend to talk about breathing a little romance and glamour into humdrum lives, rather than any wide-scale amelioration of social conditions. Copywriter Mildred Holmes takes this view in a 1928 contribution to the agency's *Newsletter.*

"Be more commonplace, dear,"
Says the client to us
With a bit of a sneer
"Don't be so high hat—
Be more commonplace dear.
"Our market's the masses—
They live in a flat—
"They don't have a butler
nor kitchens like that."
But we turn to folk-lore
which has influenced man
And we find that in these tales

no kings get the ban.
They are full of the doings
of heroes and gods.
Princesses and nabobs
with riches in wads.
We all dream beyond us
The Lord made us so—
It was done to inspire us
with some place to go.
So it's not being snooty
to work down from above,
It's only presenting
what dreams are made of.[34]

Assumed about the "masses" that Holmes and her colleagues address is that no one suffers from the insufficiently developed wants that Coolidge's immigrants harbored prior to the milliner's arrival. Rather, they are all presumed to yearn for luxury. This yearning is depicted as innate not instilled ("The Lord made us so"), even though the topic that the advertisers discuss is precisely the inculcation and channeling of consumer desire.

James Quirk, editor of *Photoplay Magazine,* took up the cultivation of commodity lust in his 1930 presentation to J. Walter Thompson staff.[35] Quirk
sketched out some of the shared priorities that bound advertising and motion
picture professionals in a common project. "The motion picture industry is
engaged in selling a very intangible commodity or series of commodities—it is
engaged in selling romance, beauty, luxury, adventure and last but not least,
laughter" (3). Quoting Sam Katz , head of the cinema chain Publix Theaters,
Quirk continued:

> You nor I have any idea of the millions of men and women who live not
> only in sordid surroundings but in pretty plain environments and what I
> am selling them is escape. Those people come into my theatre, they pay
> fifty cents, they are saluted—do you know that in this town there are
> people who are saluted by no one, no one says "Yes sir" to them; they can't
> boss anybody (even married people) but they come in here and they are
> surrounded by luxury—or what they think is luxury—somebody bows
> down and salutes them and they are made very happy. (3–4)

In his catalog of values offered to Hollywood's public ("romance, beauty,
luxury, adventure . . . laughter"), Quirk leaves out mention of the pseudo-
prestige that ticket holders pay to enjoy, when as they settle into plushly
upholstered chairs and the lights dim in a Katz-run movie palace, they are
saluted by uniformed ushers. Quirk goes on to recount Cecil B. DeMille's
related conviction that people want to ogle luxurious sets in the movies themselves, suggesting that once the heavy velvet curtain rises, images of handsomely appointed homes, well-dressed women, and elegant state-of-the-art
automobiles will likely flicker across the screen. So, those who attend the
movies are regaled with cinematic images of wealth, and given a taste of faux
status as they do so, attended by ushers. To be explicit, Katz depicts a venue for
a sanctioned pornography of class: the "exotic dancers" onstage are the sala-
ciously displayed commodities on-screen, and the uniformed ushers who rove
through the audience, saluting and waiting to be "bossed," heighten the appeal
of the cinematic wealth with their fetishized presence and immediacy, imper-
sonating subservience just as a lap dancer mimics sexual intimacy. Absolutely
presumed is that the average American moviegoer longs not only for luxury,
but the chance to domineer.[36]

Nodding in the direction of the service ethos, Quirk tries briefly to suggest
that advertisers are "selling the desire to be better," and that "the motion

picture has done something unconsciously to the American people: the girl of today is an entirely different girl; her ideals have been raised, her ideas of men have been raised" (4). Quickly, though, he undercuts the rhetoric of uplift, segueing into a sad little story about an office girl going out on a date with a boy who is "not handsome probably" and makes only $18 a week. This girl, he explains, will yearn for Jack Gilbert and imitate Greta Garbo, though he makes this mimicry seem more pathetic than beneficial. In her poem quoted above, Mildred Holmes niftily conflates *all* dreams and ambitions with the yearning for commodities when she claims that the commercial display of luxury triggers in its lowbrow audience a God-given—and stereotypically American—impulse toward financial aspiration ("We all dream beyond us / The Lord made us so—/ It was done to inspire us / with some place to go"). Quirk seems harder pressed to ascribe social benefits to Hollywood's portrayals of the glamorous life. Stumbling off the virtuous high ground, Quirk loses track of his point about the office girl's ideals having been raised, returning instead to the fundamental arena of M-C-M prime: "It seems a pretty crude form of business to be in—doesn't it?—to trade on human emotions and love and the desire of men and women for romance: Yes it does, but you are doing it in this office every day. *If advertising is going to sell things* it must appeal first of all to the emotions" (5, emphasis added).

The remarks of William Esty in the same year were entirely consonant with Quirk's, Esty insisting in the previously quoted speech that "it is futile to try to appeal to masses of people on an intellectual or logical basis. The only way to do it is on an emotional basis" (5). With the commentary of Esty, Quirk, and Day, we are in different territory indeed than when a leading adman of the 1910s, Theodore MacManus, declared that, "I look upon the public as myself multiplied, and I've not yet reached the stage of diffidence and humility which permits me to write myself down as an Ass" (quoted in Fox 73). Esty imagines the hordes as "natives" rather than as himself multiplied. He will remain untainted by those he bedazzles, even though he "caters" to their lowbrow tastes for "calico," because the profit thereby secured will attest to his actual superiority to and elite differentiation from the masses. There is no desire to lead, just to sell. Compared to the chilly *Übermenschsprache* of Day, it sounds almost like populism when Esty insists that,

> today [an advertiser has] to read what the mob reads, understand what the mob likes; certainly go to the movies very frequently, and by that . . .

I mean the run of the mill movies. Because of this there is no doubt that
the people in Hollywood have found the greatest common denominator
of all humanity. . . . [I]t is just as important, for an advertising man, to
know all about the miniature golf courses as to understand the Rocke-
feller Foundation: Al Capone is just as much a part of American life as
Lindbergh; Jimmy Walker as Coolidge; Rudy Vallée as Hoover and Texas
Guinan as Aimee MacPherson. (5)

This isn't, however, a truly empathic alignment with this "greatest common
denominator," any more than was the attitude of "Fraud Hopkins," a spoof of
adman Claude Hopkins by J. Walter Thompson staff member Jim Young: "I
attribute all my success to my love of the common people. I love them because
they are so easy to fool. My millions have been extracted from their pockets."[37]
Esty's stance, in contrast to the strangely inconsequential snobbery of Day,
borrows some "folksy" ammunition from its finger-on-the-pulse pseudopopu-
lism, but ultimately (and paradoxically) derives its main punch from its asser-
tion of mastery over the masses that the advertiser understands well enough to
manipulate. "When minds are unsettled it is a good era for politicians and for
advertising people" (Esty 5). Smart enough to know how to speak to and
convince the "lowest common denominator," Esty assumes that his act of
mastery ensures that he himself will not be "reduced" as he participates in this
"pretty crude form of business."

Esty was not alone in this approach to the generation of popular culture. In
1932, the creative staff at J. Walter Thompson listened to a long report from
copywriter Mr. Crampton about his impressions of Hollywood. Much like
Esty, he defends Hollywood's supposed appeal to the "lowest common denominator," while reinforcing the notion that cultural producers are entirely
distinct from this "common" "public":

> The movie people do their job supremely well, and are not all such
> ignoramuses as we give them credit for being. There is in Hollywood a
> nucleus of the most sophisticated, cynical and clever people I have ever
> met in one city. They cut their cloth according to the customer, and it
> takes a clever tailor to do that. When you deal with an audience of nine
> billion, you have got to find the least common denominator, and if it is
> low, you take it and like it. These Hollywood people are making what the
> public wants. It may not be what you and I want. . . . But let's not make
> the mistake of patronizing Hollywood.[38]

Esty and Crampton offer a vision of the adman's identity that is predicated both on the snookering of a posited mass of suckers and the capacity to remain free from the manipulations in which one engages. This is an almost Kierkegaardian model of an internal sphere for freedom—a freedom whose terrain is within the individual psyche rather than the sociopolitical arena. It differs, though, from an existentialist concern with individual subjective experience in its dependence on the suprasubjective notion of a herd of sheep out there who do *not* remain free, whose very "massification" provides the context and proof for the internal liberation of the "sophisticated, cynical and clever" people who generate the cultural "feed."

In his examination of celebrity in late-nineteenth-century American culture, Philip Fisher describes a contrast that can be seen as roughly paralleling the relationship imagined here between adman and consumer. Discussing Thomas Eakins's 1889 "The Agnew Clinic," a painting that depicts a surgery performed before students, Fisher notes the profound distinction between the "massified" crowd of spectators (rendered uniform by shadow and resembling "wallpaper") and the "singular humanity" of the celebrity surgeon (the latter can only be envisioned in the context of its opposite). In Fisher's interpretation, the "full humanity" of the "star performer" in Eakins's painting is proved by the surgeon's differentiation not only from the spectating crowd, but also from "the thing-like existence of the anesthetized, faceless, uncovered body" of the patient. This third presence is analogous to the advertising model—the "vehicle"—whose image transmits the message between advertiser and consumer.[39]

The surgeon in Eakins's work is dubbed "homo erectus" by Fisher; his authority stems from both his superior knowledge as an instructor and his literal ascendance over the inert, naked body of the patient. Likewise, the adman gains his authority from his capacity to remain unswayed by the commercial address in which he engages, an authority that is clinched by its contrast from the supposed gullibility of those he addresses. The adman's alleged imperviousness to the seductions of his own rhetoric is connected to a cynical detachment from what he says, to an identity, in fact, that revolves around its disjuncture from utterance. Hence, Barnum's incorporated snicker, so palpable in ads as well as the great showman's approach to his audience, may serve a purpose for the advertiser him/herself, not to mention the audience. The need for an ironic fissure somewhere in the advertising address, a gap into which the cynical selfhood of the adman can be inserted, is an exigency at least as urgent as the need to occupy and deflect the audience's critical faculties (perhaps not so gullible after all). The notion of honesty does remain important within this worldview: the truly "modern" adman is honest in his stalwart refusal to laud his work as having social value—this pride in nonhypocrisy becomes the locus for concerns about honesty, thereby deflecting attention away from the relative truth value of the advertising endeavor itself.

But Robert J. Heilbroner's definition of "ideology" implies that Esty's confidence about his own immunity to its sway may be unfounded:

> The purpose of an ideology is not to mystify but to clarify; not to mislead the lower classes but to enlighten all classes. . . . Economics [an ideological structure] does not "legitimate" activities that in fact the ruling class knows in its heart of hearts to be wrong. It succeeds, rather, in offering definitions of right and wrong that exonerate the activities and results of market activity. . . . These powerful prescriptions, ground into the lenses through which the ruling class observes its own actions, provide the moral self-assurance without which it could not carry on its historic mission with such dedicated conviction. (117)

So the advertiser has no island on which to stand. Like Mickey Mouse as the Sorcerer's Apprentice picking up the magic wand in *Fantasia,* advertisers "conduct" forces that are in actuality beyond their control, and without aid, will be submerged beneath the waters they have sent spinning as surely as will the others who supposedly jump and quiver so obediently to the magic of the illicit wand. Yet the metaphor breaks down; there is no sorcerer anywhere, napping or otherwise, who wields the magic wand of ideology without also dancing under its spell. The beliefs held by advertisers about their own leadership and distance from the masses for whom they write are themselves "powerful prescriptions," ideological constructs that make this "pretty crude form of business" seem beyond examination or critique.

The same large-scale social messages that influence the "mob" operate on Esty, too. He may have liked to think that he frequented "run of the mill" movies just to manipulate the masses more effectively, but that did not, in fact, make him impervious to the cultural seductions and force of those pop hits. But also, the model he deployed to justify his own work indicates immersion in a certain cultural milieu, one that informed the sensibilities of many of the men in business—that is, the great man mythos (as depicted in his use of the tropes of colonization, such as "going out to trade with the natives") and the unquestioning infatuation with M-C-M prime as a "first cause."

And that is what fills the cynical gap between the address of the advertisement and the advertiser who has generated it, the "disjuncture from utterance" that is *the* marker of the advertiser's subject-stance. Inflating and extending that fissure between speaker and spoken is M-C-M prime, characterized above all by expansiveness: for the process of realizing profit is supposed to provide material "proof" that the advertiser's subjectivity is beyond question, that an advertiser is not in danger of being lumped with the "vast, shapeless mass."

Chapter 2

The Pep Paradigm

Masculinity, Influence, and Shame in *Babbitt*
and *The Man Nobody Knows*

Sinclair Lewis's 1922 white-collar satire, *Babbitt,* and adman Bruce Barton's
1925 portrait of a virile Christ, *The Man Nobody Knows,* were both tremendously popular in their day; the name Babbitt captured a type clearly enough
that it earned a place in the English dictionary, while Barton's book sold its first
250,000 copies in only eighteen months and has been read by new audiences
ever since.[1] Manhood and the commercial enterprise are the principal topics of
each book. Barton's text, ostensibly a presentation of the life and spirit of Jesus
Christ, is deeply engaged with the modern commercial sphere, which it seeks
to ballyhoo in the name of a revitalized Christianity. Although Babbitt is not
an adman, his work as a realtor revolves around salesmanship and includes the
periodic generation of advertising copy for his firm, and his subjectivity is
(famously) shaped by his life as a consumer. For "the large national advertisers . . . fix what he believe[s] to be his individuality. These standard advertised wares [are] . . . at first the signs, and then the substitutes, for joy and
passion and wisdom."[2] The extensive research Lewis conducted for his novel,
amassing notebooks crammed with idioms and "locutions" during his months
out in the "field," was perhaps even more like the work of the itinerant market
researchers of his day than the ethnographers with whom he has often been
compared.[3] With *Babbitt,* Lewis levels a broad, essentially progressive critique
of commodity culture's management of individual experience, whereas Barton's book energetically perpetuates the notion that male subjectivity is about
effective salesmanship.

Barton depicts the genesis of his book in an introduction that pits a well-
meaning but enervating Sunday school teacher against a restless young boy—
the author as a child, one assumes. In this opening passage, the Christian faith
is being presented to the young Barton by a woman, although in fact he must
surely have received his most important religious training from his father, who
was a prominent pastor. The gendering is important, as the problem with this

lady's Jesus is his failure to respect the gender divide: he's too much "like Mary's little lamb, something for girls—sissified."[4] The boy's discontent with this effeminate Christ (a "weakling," "kill-joy," and "failure") is shown as motivating the eventual writing of the book (12–13). The chapters that follow do not trace the chronology of the life of Jesus, but instead work more as a manual, providing lessons in manhood and sales methodology (synonymous here). Chapters entitled "The Leader," "The Outdoor Man," and "The Sociable Man" use highlights from the New Testament to depict Jesus as a vital, hearty "executive" of the spirit and leader of his disciples, and to lay out the principles for success; these are followed by analyses of Christ's rhetoric and strategies of persuasion in chapters entitled "His Method," "His Work and Words," and "His Way in Our World." The book concludes with a portrayal of Christ as he moves toward the crucifixion, his power of persuasion still center stage: even in these moments of complete degradation, he remains able to "call forth enthusiasm" sufficient to dazzle the "crucified felon" at his side (133).

George Babbitt is a real estate agent in the mythical, midsized, Midwestern city of Zenith. He is exactly as corrupt as all "average" businessmen; a conformist and materialist; "respectable;" fed his personality and opinions by magazines. Babbitt concentrates all his unexpressed and underdeveloped humanity into periodic bursts of warmth for his youngest child, Tinka, and a tender admiration of his best friend, Paul, whose maniacal, self-pitying hatred of his wife George reads as a sign of martyred artistic greatness. Vague, rebellious feelings really bloom in Babbitt after Paul shoots his wife and goes to jail. Babbitt tries to channel these feelings in different directions—booze, camping, an affair, a slight lean to the Left after getting a compliment from the town radical when he's feeling alienated anyway. He is in real danger of threatening his social security with all this dabbling—facing exile from his conformist peers—but "fortunately" his wife gets appendicitis, and retreating gratefully from his own revolt, Babbitt is welcomed back into the fold. His son *does* rebel, and in the novel's last pages, George supports his son's secret marriage and decision to leave college for mechanic work: downwardly mobile, at least he is living for himself.

Though written from almost diametrically opposed vantages, *Babbitt* and *The Man Nobody Knows* deal with strikingly similar cultural concerns; historian Stephen Fox is among those scholars who have noted that Barton's book "offered a Christianity all too appropriate to the day, Jesus Christ as George F.

Babbitt" (108). And indeed, George Babbitt and Barton's Jesus Christ are the same sort of happy, peppy, sociable, manly, profit-turning, growth-loving good fellows. Their masculinity inheres in an enthusiastic, forward-looking energy that also enables and structures their success as influential social agents: "personal magnetism" or "Zeal, Zest and Zowie" (Barton 24; Lewis 135).[5]

What is this energy? Michel Foucault would perhaps instruct us to call this mythologized magnetism "sex": in *The History of Sexuality*, he describes the bourgeoisie "as being occupied, from the eighteenth century on, with creating its own sexuality and forming a specific body based on it, a 'class' body with its health, hygiene, descent, and race: the autosexualization of its body, the incarnation of sex in its body, the endogamy of sex and the body."[6] Commercial popularizations of Sigmund Freud in the early decades of the century emphasized the urgency of the sexual instinct, and this sense of a voracious drive for gratification linked itself naturally to the allures and promises of consumer culture. As John D'Emilio and Estelle B. Freedman write, "an ethic that encouraged the purchase of consumer products also fostered an acceptance of pleasure, self-gratification, and personal satisfaction, a perspective that easily translated to the province of sex."[7] Certainly, this linkage of sex and consumerism is omnipresent enough that it barely needs to be stated—it works more like a founding principle of consumer society than a revelation to be unearthed. What is less obvious is a link between the "pep" of the commercial *producer* and the newly circulating model of a ravenous hunger for sexual satisfaction. D'Emilio and Freedman cite a *Good Housekeeping* article from the 1910s: "the sex instinct sought 'every kind of sensory gratification. . . . If it gets its yearning, it is as contented as a nursing infant. If it does not, beware! It will never be stopped except with satisfactions'" (223–24). Perhaps the confluence between the drive for sexual satisfaction and the drive for profit characterized by M-C-M prime—both celebrated as urgent, vital motors of commodity culture—was the means whereby sexuality continued in the twentieth century to be tied to a "specific 'class' body."

If we read the "pep" manifesto as an attempt to conflate masculine heterosexuality with the economic robustness of the bourgeoisie, we need also to understand it as doing racial work. The "good fellas" here, like the Son of God, exhibit a vigor and dominance that are explicitly coded white, and that forcefully eradicate differently racialized sexualities. Of course, nonwhite sexualities were by no means simply overlooked by the dominant culture during this period, even if they were unaddressed in national advertisements. Although African American and immigrant working-class leisure culture made a permanent impact on dominant ideas about women, recreation, and sexuality, the value of this impact was always charged and contested, and negative portraits of nonwhite sexualities were available everywhere. The twenties were one nadir of postslavery race relations in the United States, with lynching and Ku Klux Klan activity resurgent and still dependent on the charge of rape. In the popular discourse, Jewish sexuality was largely connected, still, to fears about white slavery, and Asian immigrants were often cordoned off from engagement in the popular cultural arena, especially in the realm of the erotic.[8] Zip, zest, and zowie are the outcroppings of the turn-of-the-century process that Gail Bederman tracks in *Manliness and Civilization,* whereby the white middle class remade its conception of manhood in light of modernity's changes, "discovering an extraordinary variety of ways to link male power to race."[9] Overtly sexualized narratives about manhood and racial identity—whether vilifying, glorifying, or exoticizing—functioned as a charged backdrop that forcibly located social power and pep in the court of the white male.

Richard Dyer reminds us that while "it is methodologically important to insist on the particularity of white masculinities, . . . it is the ability to pass themselves off as not particular that allows them to go on being, within the regime of representation that they produce, 'invisible.'"[10] The privilege and presumed omnipresence that is concomitant with this "invisible" whiteness in fact requires energetic interaction with and "domination" of others. As an attribute of a "class" and "race" body, pep must evidence itself through hierarchy: in *The Man Nobody Knows* and, with irony, *Babbitt,* zest is described as emanating from within, but its *proof* is the point, and that resides in the exterior world, in the power of pep to influence and persuade (or simply dominate) others. Bluster and aggression notwithstanding, in its dependence on this externally provided proof lies the vulnerability of a pep-based, businessman's white machismo.

In *Babbitt,* a tension develops between the exterior efficacy of self-staged "zowie," and an interior plane full of secrets, shame, and anxiety. Lewis suggests, possibly counterintuitively, that the shame and exterior staging fuel one another, induce one another. The quest for a zesty image, and thus for social power, generates the sense that much must be hidden, and this perceived need in turn motivates further self-disguisings. Of course, Barton's Jesus Christ is not bound by mortal ties to this dialectic, so he can embody the myth of limitless pep: his masculinized magnetic charm seems to pour from an endless fount and does not mask a secret shame. It is only by dint of a deified central character that Barton can construct a charismatic white-collar performance unchecked by and unlinked to secret shame. Christ's struggles, as when he retreats to the desert to search his soul, are not embarrassing, but the sort of deep-seated conflicts that only exemplify his virile spirit. Unlike the Son of God, however, Lewis's Babbitt loses the vim requisite for leadership and falls short of the mark, stirred by his own humanity into a restless, questioning malaise. While apparently belying the self-confident pep of the exterior performance and figured as a drawing off of vigor, this internal anxiety actually proves a storehouse of surreptitious, compressed energy.

In Babbitt's world, all doubts and desires not successfully incorporated under the rubric of sales or consumer practices are seen as liabilities, inherent flaws, dangerous drains on personal force. In fact, this force is not lessened by such secret doubts, but rather redistributed, lifted away from the zesty pursuit of the bottom line, and toward questions, perceptions, and allegiances not sanctioned by commodity culture's "pep paradigm." What secrets might lurk in the breast of Babbitt, a man ostensibly committed to self-salesmanship and the large-scale social system that contextualizes it? Of what might he be ashamed? Lewis seems to suggest that shame and discomfort about the ruthlessness of the capitalist endeavor coexist with an anxious need to hide those very doubts and differences lest they betray the presence of marginal tendencies. This can lead to vigorous, recurrent restatements of conformist sentiment, as the characters in *Babbitt* bond with one another against themselves, distancing themselves from their own potential marginality.

Among the widespread causes of suppressed male discomfiture during this period are significant changes in gender identity wrought by shifts in the workplace. The business world's recasting of an ideal manhood involved the reinvention as masculine of traits that had typically been ascribed in the nineteenth century to the feminine arena: both the power of influence and capacity to tolerate tedium without complaint were now part of the manly sphere. The bluster associated with the masculinization of these previously feminized traits indicates an unease with the transition. This is due not only to a prejudice against anything deemed female, but more profoundly to the fact that both these traits (toleration of tedium and reliance on the circuitous agency of influence) are linked with the delimited personal power afforded to most male participants in a newly corporatized United States. Indeed, the reason these particular qualities had been associated with the feminine was that women held positions lacking direct social power.

In both *Babbitt* and *The Man Nobody Knows*, proponents of the national business enterprise invoke tropes of masculinity to resolve the disjuncture between the cog-in-a-wheel corporatism increasingly integral to the nation's business climate and the rugged individualism so long prized as an American virtue. In this strategy of resolution through gendering, traits and behaviors deemed masculine, and therefore desirable, include traditional male arenas like hunting and militarism, but also all sorts of social practices, business endeavors, and organizational bonding rituals requisite to the functioning of the nation's managerial class. Popular authors and advertisers, many of them representatives of the corporate realm just being fashioned, reinvented business as the masculine epic sphere of the modern age as a strategy to help business workers celebrate their endeavor, as well as cope with and suppress discontent.[11] As Elizabeth Lunbeck has outlined, "industrial psychiatry" emerged in the late teens and was often referenced by advertising authors, adding the clout of science to this positing of a masculinity geared toward unflagging acceptance of the marketplace and work front.[12] *Babbitt,* a work of cultural critique, demarcates the gendered stress and limits of this strategy in the face of the doubts and hungers it leaves unaddressed.

Both Barton's laudatory and Lewis's critical texts can seem hopelessly dated now, in these postpep days of late-twentieth-century capitalism. After all, we live in an era when midlevel managers, terrified that they belong to a disappearing class, attend Tom Peters and Peter Drucker workshops, and self-medicate with Prozac, hoping to radiate positive energy—by any means necessary.[13] (Indeed, one recent book by Bob Briner seems a nineties' "copy cat" of Barton's best-seller, offering insight into "the management methods of Jesus" to contemporary readers in the corporate world.[14]) They may, however, be peculiarly timely.

The Prophet with a Punch

It is hardly surprising that Barton's Christianity serves business: the son of a popular Congregationalist pastor, Barton cofounded Batten, Barton, Durstine, and Osborn. BBD&O, still a phenomenally successful advertising agency, ranked fourth largest in the United States during the 1920s.[15] Throughout *The Man Nobody Knows,* Barton is explicit in his central motif: Jesus Christ is the epitome of a successful adman. "Every one of His conversations, every contact between His mind and others, is worthy of the attentive study of any sales manager" (Barton 72). Barton reminds us that Jesus is an expert in human resource development, possessed of a "keen knowledge of human motives" (73), and employs catchy, novel narrative approaches. With "a single sentence," Jesus is capable of "achieving triumph, arousing interest and creating desire. . . . With sure instinct, He follow[s] up His initial advantage" (68). Most important, he radiates charisma—he is "resistless," to use a term current among twenties' advertisers.[16]

This Christianity is also very much the purview of the heterosexual male, rather than the dominion of women and "feminized" ministers, as Ann Douglas (herself apparently too convinced by early-twentieth-century commentators like Barton) argues it had been in the nineteenth century.[17] Especially in his portrayal of the Reverend John Jennison Drew, who is "proud to be known primarily as a business man" and preaches a "Manly Man's Religion," Lewis satirizes exactly the sort of business-friendly, macho Christianity that Barton advocates (171). Throughout *Babbitt,* Lewis satirizes, too, business culture's anxious nationalization and gendering of cultural styles. To Barton, as well as Lewis's protagonist Babbitt, both spiritualist and Victorian Protestant religion are effeminate and lacking in vigor; so, also, are the debilitatingly Old World high culture, book learning, and artistic ambitions.[18] All of these are opposed by the macho gusto of the American profit motive, the prioritization of financial success: this economic robustness is coded as a physical, gendered, and heterosexualized health and virility.

Treated earnestly in advertising archives and by Barton, this gendered dualism is parodied by Lewis. His evangelical preacher, Mike Monday, slams "a bunch of gospel-pushers with dishwater instead of blood, a gang of squealers that need more . . . hair on their skinny old chests" (84). The local Chamber of Commerce, noting approvingly that Monday distracts workers from labor conditions and "thus avert[s] strikes," makes a point of inviting him (84). Lewis defines the rhetoric of masculinized, pro-business Christianity (the same that irradiates *The Man Nobody Knows*) as an economically based ideology, used by some as a tool of social control with a significant degree of conscious, even strategic intent.

This contrast between "a gang of squealers" and the "prophet with a punch" was common parlance among the liberal Protestant ministers so popular in Barton's day. Take, for instance, Harry Emerson Fosdick, whom Jackson Lears called "probably the most influential Protestant moralist in the United States" during the 1920s (Lears 1983, 13). Like Barton and contemporary psychological commentator G. Stanley Hall, Fosdick propounded a vigorous Jesus, potent and magnetic, convinced of abundance, not worried about scarcity. In his charting of the "therapeutic roots of consumer culture," Lears describes the modern hunger for vitality that fueled such depictions as symptomatic of widespread alienation from the workplace.[19] It is just this alienation that Barton aspires to counter with his lauding of business machismo. Lears does not focus on the gender politics of this yearning for zip: like Hall's, Barton's portraits of a vigorous Christ not only stress his ruddy good health, but also link it inextricably to his masculinity. Yes, "all His days were spent in the open air," and "He was an energetic outdoor man" (Barton 43). Yet this energy is exhaustively gendered . . . and eroticized: "Men followed Him, and the leaders of men have very often been physically strong. But women worshipped Him. . . . Women are *not* drawn by weakness. The sallow-faced, thin-lipped, so-called spiritual type of man may awaken maternal instinct, stirring an emotion which is half regard, half pity. But since the world began, no power has fastened the affection of women upon a man like manliness" (40–41). Though heterosexual appeal is underscored, the lure of Christ's magnetism is essentially unconfined by Barton's language.

In another scene, Jesus drives the animals from the temple with a rage depicted as masculine, potent, and captivating. Here and throughout the text, his erotic appeal seems by no means to be prophylactically heterosexual: "There was in his eyes a flaming moral purpose . . . but with the majesty of His glance there was something else which counted powerfully in his favor. As His right arm rose and fell, striking its blows with that little whip, the sleeve dropped back to reveal muscles hard as iron" (35). In a sense, because Barton's protagonist is a deity, and thus released from the closet paradigm that links spectacle and shame for mortal salespersons, his appeal is allowed to carry with it more open homoeroticism than one would encounter in a traditional sales manual. Still, Barton rushes to gird up the titillation of his prose with a quick show of strength. He follows up the peekaboo sexuality of the dropped-back sleeve with the swagger of the next sentence: "No one who watched Him in action had any doubt that he was fully capable of taking care of Himself" (35). Self-reliance functions not as autonomy but sheer spectacle, theater that persuades others to believe more efficaciously than could exhortation.

Adman Barton's invocation of manly energy was not at all rare among his fellow practitioners. Advertising archives burst with examples of copywriters borrowing masculine imagery—such as locomotive, hunting, and military metaphors—to physicalize their work, to make it seem vital, dramatic, and vigorous. For instance: "William Wrigley, Jr., the successful chewing gum magnate, . . . was talking to a smoking car audience the other day. . . . 'My friend, if I were to stop advertising, it would be just like taking the engine off this train. It would slow down and after a while stop. Advertising is the locomotive of business, and if you don't have it, business comes to a stop.'"[20] The art deco visuals favored by advertisers in the twenties lovingly rendered trains in innumerable ads as the indicators par excellence of modern progress; no wonder Wrigley called on the phallic power of the locomotive to make his point.[21] And then there is the hunting trope:

> Large numbers of the public are like rabbits. . . . Fire into a likely cover with any old shot-gun . . . and you may bring down a bunny. But . . . cottontails pall as a steady diet. If you want to bring in important amounts of game you must adopt more finished methods of pursuing the rabbits and then with better equipment go forth after the shyer, scarcer game. Bear steaks are found in the deep forests, mountain lamb chops cling to the high peaks, antelope cutlets travel on swift hoofs. . . . To the advertiser, media are the guns. It is only by skillfull use of media that he can reach all his prospects, including the shyer but profitable game unreached by scatter-gun methods.[22]

The author of this ironic passage comments openly on advertisers borrowing "thrill of the chase" machismo to invigorate their own notions about themselves. The dehumanization of the consumer in the above extended metaphor is most palpable in the author's de-*animalization* of the game described: like the gullible consumers-to-be, "steaks," "chops," and "cutlets" still race through natural habitats, but are staked out in advance for the butcher.

Military figures are, of course, a rhetorical staple throughout American business discourse: "The time to bring up reinforcements if we can get them is the time when the enemy is in the weakest condition and that we will be very lacking in strategy if we give him an opportunity to fill up his ranks before we renew our attack."[23] Such martial language is everywhere in the advertising archives, but in his utopian 1928 tribute to commerce, *Business the Civilizer*, advertiser Earnest Elmo Calkins formulates a lineage rather than a set of parallels, to empower business through an evolutionary as opposed to associative trope. Since this is an industrial age, he asks, "Why not books for a businessman? Business runs the world. The world gets civilized just as fast as men learn to run things on plain business principles. . . . It is useless for classic dodoes and Us cultured folks to protest. Business is here, and here to stay. And selfish, sordid, grasping, gross, material though it may be, it has, thank heaven, no such tales of woe to put into verse, drama, history, and essay as one finds on every page of the chronicles of war, politics, and religion."[24] Knight, statesman, priest: Calkins argues that the businessman surpasses them all in accomplishment, sphere of influence, vision, and decency. "Men were never so generous, so honest, so agreeable, so well worth acquaintance as they are today," claims Calkins (vii). And this commendation is for any man, Everyman, not just the king. Business, for Calkins, is a democratic meritocracy.

We just need to remember Calkins's rhetoric if we begin to worry that Lewis laid on his satire a bit too thick. Above, Calkins contends that business has supplanted religion, war, politics, and even romance to become the central, formative dramatic sphere of our time.[25] Babbitt agrees: the very first paragraph of Lewis's novel describes the lovely "towers of Zenith" as "neither citadels nor churches, but frankly and beautifully office-buildings" (5). And Babbitt "beheld the tower as a temple-spire of the religion of business" (15). "To George F. Babbitt, as to most prosperous citizens of Zenith, his motor car was poetry and tragedy, love and heroism. The office was his pirate ship but the car his perilous excursion ashore" (23). Calkins's book illustrates that the romanticization of American commerce as the new arena for testing and expressing (white) manhood was indeed current in just the form that Lewis employs.

Babbitt discerns masculinity inhering in many of his daily activities—except those that bind him to his family and the domestic sphere. Driving, drinking, smoking, playing poker, camping trips (mostly hypothetical), and the world of business are all reassuringly suffused with heterosexual masculinity. When sanguine, Babbitt celebrates the middle-class-specific mundanities of his day as proof of his potency: parallel parking is "a virile adventure masterfully executed" (30), a poker game at the home of Vergil Gunch summons into being a "bold man-world" (7), and semicrooked business negotiation is a "manly battle" (44). Cast as indices of his inclusion in an exalted masculine arena, even quotidian events become satisfactions, and enervation is averted or at least postponed.

Interestingly, enervation emerges at the outset in *The Man Nobody Knows*, as the first in an extended series of parallels between Christ and a businessman:

> It was very late in the afternoon.
>
> If you would like to know the measure of a man, that is the time of day to watch him. We are all half an inch taller in the morning . . . [b]ut the day is a steady drain of small annoyances. . . . The little man loses his temper; the big man takes a firmer hold.
>
> It was very late in the afternoon in Galilee. (15)

With his focus on tedium and frustration, Barton universalizes a class- and site-specific twentieth-century, developed-world experience of office life. As when Babbitt infuses the petty, repeated tasks of his workday with machismo, the capacity to tolerate endless small frustrations, which was the measure of a woman in many nineteenth-century conduct manuals, is presented by Barton as a sign of (divine) manhood.[26] Some of the vigor with which the rhetoric of the new man was voiced can probably be ascribed to the anxiety induced by this recouping/recasting of traits originally seen as déclassé because associated with the feminine; as Barton's text and Lewis's protagonist make clear, much bravura and heterosexual bluster seem to be required to camouflage the essential borrowing at the heart of this new portrait of masculinity.[27]

So Barton's Christ exemplifies the virtue of patience, which now wears a white collar and tie. Christ's other strengths, as they emerge in Barton's text, are all strangely coincident with the characteristics of an effective salesperson and business manager: he has "personal magnetism" (24), a "powerful gift of picking men" (26), an authority with his disciples of the sort that "every businessman, every leader in any field today knows—or should know" (29), great powers as a copywriter, as evidenced by the parables (91), "vast unending patience" (29), and the psychological savvy ("He knew His man" [30]) and "executive ability" that allow him to "mold" his coterie of followers into "an organization which carried on victoriously" (31). Barton masculinizes these skills both by showing their influence over others and coupling depictions of Christ's leadership ability with his physical vibrancy. Indeed, one chapter is called "The Outdoor Man."

Barton's emphasis on leadership (the book includes a long digression on the self-control and vision of "Abe" Lincoln), but his inclusion, too, of many references to more "middle-brow" (15) concerns like tedium at work and successful social gatherings, reveal that his targeted audience is George Babbitt. John the Baptist is labeled "the sensation of the season" among the "fashionable folk of the city" (21), and with the miracle of the wine at Cana, Jesus "makes use of His mighty power, not to point a solemn moral, not to relieve a sufferer's pain, but to keep a happy party from breaking up too soon, to save a hostess from embarrassment" (50). On the one hand, Barton invokes and pretends to address the truly elite aristocracy of business, the steely nerved, set-lipped executive class: "There are times when nothing a man can say is nearly so powerful as saying nothing. A business executive can understand that" (16). Barton softens this approach, though, with repeated references to Christ's easygoing geniality: this is the magic mix when your audience is the midlevel manager—what Lewis dubs the "hearty fellow . . . the salesm[a]n of prosperity" and distinguishes from the true "ruling class," the "aristocrats, the men who were richer or had been rich for more generations" (317).[28]

Shortly before the onset of his midlife crisis, Babbitt delivers the keynote address at the Zenith Real Estate Board's annual dinner. In a parody that only slightly outdoes the rhetoric of Calkins, this speech paints the "Regular Guy" as the "type of fellow that's ruling America today" (152), thereby rewriting corporate conformity as mythic dynamism. The machismo of these new heroes stems from their economic vitality, and extends to include a cheerful readiness to annihilate dissent: "Here's the new generation of Americans: fellows with hair on their chests and smiles in their eyes and adding-machines in their offices. We're not doing any boasting, but we like ourselves first-rate, and if you don't like us, look out—better get under cover before the cyclone hits town!" (154). Babbitt appropriates a rebellious, Wild West populism for the defenders of the status quo. He uses the imagery of heterosexual manly vigor to laud both a commerce-driven Christianity and the homosocial bonding necessary to ensure victory over those ever threatening on the margins. Babbitt's "two-fisted Regular Guy . . . belongs to some church with pep and piety to it . . . [and] any one of a score of organizations of good, jolly, kidding, laughing, sweating, upstanding, lend-a-handing Royal Good Fellows" (158). Moreover, this "Ideal Citizen's" "answer to his critics is a square-toed boot that'll teach the grouches and smart alecks to respect the He-man and get out and root for Uncle Sam, U.S.A." (158).[29]

Throughout *Babbitt,* this celebration of the potent American man of business is coupled with the characters' voicing of a consistent anxiety—gendered and sexualized—about sissified highbrows with "too much" culture and book learning, who seem to carry with them the threat of a contagious doubt about the merits of the status quo.[30] Babbitt's keynote address includes this diatribe against a suspect intellectual class: "The worst menace to sound government is . . . the long-haired gentry who call themselves 'liberals' and 'radicals' and 'non-partisans' and 'intelligentsia.' . . . Those profs are the snakes to be scotched—they and all their milk-and-water ilk!" (157). Mistrust of an overly educated elite has been a part of bourgeois ideology since the eighteenth century, when attacks on Old World aristocratic "refinements" were wedded with a more bourgeois linking of virtue to the practical world.[31] While the actual aristocracy no longer presents a threat to a twentieth-century ascendant American bourgeoisie, the vestigial notion of an aristocratic, decadent impracticality still helps give force to such critiques, as when Lewis has his Babbitt subtly invoke the homosexualized excesses of a Lord Bryon with the sexually ambiguous phrase "long-haired gentry." That "socialist" "grouches" are tainted with inferences of aristocratic debilitation is an incongruity that remains unexplored.

The same concern is readily discernible in advertising archives, where literary ambitions and college educations are treated as embarrassing liabilities that copywriters should suppress or at least disguise under all circumstances. Jennifer Wicke points out that by the 1920s advertising no longer leaned on literature as it once had.[32] Advertising's unmooring from fiction was not a clean break, though: the archival material is full of advertisers' anxious disavowals of their link to the literary realm. The industry's decoupling from this arena was a *gendering* activity, as advertisers eschewed the literary impulse on the grounds that it was effeminate and a distraction from the "masculine" emphasis on ultimate gain. Letters of recommendation that accompanied the job applications of two female copywriters eventually hired by J. Walter Thompson in the 1920s were typical in their assurance that the applicant would not be preoccupied by creative impulses: one explained that the candidate was "strong for business, has no desire to do literary work and is not of the artistic temperament, though she is a trained writer."[33] The gendered fear of "excessive" culture and refinement seems driven by the pressure to toe the bottom line without diversion, in the advertising profession as well as in Lewis's novel.

In *Babbitt*, popular society "artist" Chum Frink, who composes jingles and prose poems for ads and newspapers, is approved of by his friends as a creative sort who still manages to be a "regular guy"; in other words, he enjoys drinking and dining with the "set," and agrees to flirt rotely with their wives. The set rather thrills that he pays attention to them at all, hinting perhaps that their disdain for erudite, artsy types stems from their own insecurity. Frink's "regularity" is limited, though. One night, when Babbitt is wandering through a pea-soup mist in the grips of some troubling doubts, he spies an inebriated Frink, engaged in a tortured soliloquy. (That Frink appears to be of only limited talent as a writer is possibly Lewis's way of privileging his own status as an artist beyond the kind of encapsulated characterization he creates for his jinglist.) Like Babbitt himself—and Barton, for that matter—this seemingly eager proponent of middle-class American mores and aesthetics is secretly "irregular," full of doubts and hungers unanswered by the pop culture that he himself helps generate.[34]

Such doubts have no place in *The Man Nobody Knows;* Jesus Christ's virility seems founded on a rejection of the query, of bafflement. In its opening sequence, mentioned earlier, the little boy oppressed by the cohort of Christian ladies cathects not one whit to the "meek and lowly" "pale young man with no muscle and a sad expression" introduced to him as the Son of the Lord (12–13). Preferable by far is Daniel of the lion-felling sling and especially Moses, depicted here only via his startlingly phallic "rod and his big brass snake" (11). Later, Barton contrasts the effeminate, enervated standard Christ with his own masterful Lord: "All the painters have misled us. They have shown us a frail man, undermuscled, with a soft face—a woman's face covered by a beard—and a benign but baffled look" (38). Barton's Christ confronts his invalid supplicants with a machismo so penetrating that it transforms the moment of healing into a virtual seduction scene: "The calm assurance of those blue eyes, the supple strength of those muscles, the ruddy skin that testified to the rich red blood beneath— . . . It was as though health poured out of that strong body and into the weak one like an electric current from a dynamo" (39).[35] During this period, of course, the feminine ideal also moved increasingly toward tanned athleticism, but female good health was typically depicted as facilitating the modern woman's autonomy and independence as an individual unit, whereas in *The Man Nobody Knows,* the "rich contagion" of masculine vigor radiates outward like a gas or an infection; it persuades, invades, and transforms others, for "the health of the Teacher [is] irresistible" (39).[36]

While many of the "refinements" of nineteenth-century gentility are treated with mistrust by Barton, Babbitt, and many advertisers on record as effeminate, anti-American, and antiquated, as indicated earlier, Barton and Lewis's texts both illustrate the male appropriation of attributes previously represented as part of the female temperament. In Barton's passage about the gaseous, resistless health of the master, the notion of influence—a quality deemed quintessentially feminine during the nineteenth century—was being reinvented as the sort of masculinized "rich contagion" discussed above, and the American businessman's key to success. (Witness the work of Barton's spiritual descendant, Dale Carnegie.) Influence, the circuitous power of suggestion, once lifted from the realm of the feminine, added persuasion to the arsenal of a new machismo devoted less to the romance of an autonomous self than to success at any cost.

Barton points out again and again that nothing persuades like sincerity. This tenet, proffered repeatedly in many advertising manuals as well, opens up a conundrum, for how can sincerity itself be maintained once its benefits have been tabulated and are being strived after? Ultimately, the resolution of this quandary involves a shift in the way truth value itself gets figured and talked about. The notion of a fixed essence or inherent nature that shapes much discussion of authenticity and truth, whether absolutist or metaphysical, is not of use in this context. Instead, the truth value of a claim or performance resides in its bottom line impact, its effects on other people.

This commitment to exteriority seems an appealing approach, to one who deceives, and therefore, would like to deflect attention away from the disjuncture between the external and internal selves. In a tradition of masculine self-staging bracketed chronologically by figureheads Barnum and Carnegie, the ongoing emphasis on effect rather than essence could be viewed as the dissembler's shame-based strategy of self-protection. In Barton's contrast, quoted above, between the painter's false Jesus and his own portrayal, he rejects one external indicator of male vitality as a disguise ("a woman's face covered by a beard"), in favor not of revelation of some hidden inner essence, but of another external sign ("the ruddy skin that testified to the rich red blood beneath"). Barton offers no signifier of masculinity, but just a signifier more convincing than the fake beard donned by a cross-dressed Christ. The work of influence that the "ruddy skin" performs as an indicator of virility is more important than the richness of the actual blood beneath.

Imagine that you are an advertiser. You make a claim about the high quality of the chocolate that your client company used in preparing their pudding. The proof does not inhere within the pudding itself, but rather in the pudding's eventual purchase: Will someone buy it because of your claim? That's "proof" you can take to the bank. In *The Man Nobody Knows,* Barton builds up an illuminating relationship between this effectuality and "sincerity," connecting Christ's profound persuasiveness directly to his virility:

> What . . . were the principal elements in His power over men? . . .
> First of all, He must have had the voice and manner of the leader—the personal magnetism which begets loyalty and commands respect. . . . We speak of personal magnetism as though there were something mysterious about it. . . . This is not true. The essential element in personal magnetism is a consuming sincerity—an overwhelming faith in the importance of the work one has to do. Emerson said, "What you *are* thunders so loud I can't hear what you say." (25)

Barton's list of leadership qualities begins with the importance of a mesmeric voice, and only via this criterion does he introduce the notion of sincerity. Sincerity is desirable because it will provide you with the power of influence. Just as a sincerity sought after for its effects seems to present a paradox, so too, there is an unexamined slippage here between the efficacious theatricality of a magnetic voice and manner and the transparency posited by Emerson's quotation, whereby an inner "essence" is "thunderously" and unquestionably evident.[37]

Later, Barton examines the parables and tabulates the "elements of their power." The first two keys to the success of the parables, condensed narrative and simple prose with few adjectives, are strictly technical; "sincerity" comes in as Barton's "third essential" (95). Barton fuses the virtue of sincerity with the benefits that accrue from its semblance: this coalescence is replicated in the memoirs and manuals of many advertisers. For instance, in *My Life in Advertising,* Claude Hopkins repeatedly conflates being and seeming. In one of many examples, he instructs a well-known athlete to sign a testimonial campaign about "My Farewell Car," dismissing the man's comment that he is not yet retiring—a textual instant later, Hopkins remarks that the ads in this campaign "typified . . . the man of rugged honesty" (119). As Jackson Lears puts it in a related discussion, "despite the myriad invocations of sincerity as the sine qua non of all effective advertising, admakers continued to realize that the crucial task was '*the creation of a feeling of confidence on the part of the purchasing public*' " (Lears 1994, 217).[38]

In the following passage, Barton again traverses the anxious terrain between "sincerity" and the benefits of its by-products. There appears to be a challenge to Barton's object lesson on the level of chronology. The reader is being educated in the likely benefits of sincerity beforehand, but must unlearn this long enough to deliver the sales pitch "sincerely" and with "spotless" motives, only to discover and capitalize on his or her advantage as a happy, coincidental by-product after the fact: "It's hardly necessary to say that Jesus did not heal merely to stir, awe, and anger doubters. Yet His honest directness had a startling, far-reaching effect. . . . Once again we can be sure Jesus' purpose was single. But we can easily believe also that His instant winning of Matthew shook Capernaum for the second time that day" (85). Barton's point—that personal gain and altruistic service were not mutually exclusive—is one that he makes in different moments throughout *The Man Nobody Knows*. As Warren I. Susman explains, "In a society where the older ideal of the stewardship of wealth could no longer serve, a new idea evolved: business—all business—as service to others and something fundamental to the development of self."[39]

The development of this model is, of course, among Max Weber's central themes in *The Protestant Ethic and the Spirit of Capitalism*. Citing Benjamin Franklin's axioms of capitalist conversion ("time is money," "credit is money," and so forth), Weber comments that, "according to Franklin . . . virtues . . . are only insofar virtues as they are actually useful to the individual and the surrogate of mere appearance is always sufficient when it accomplishes the end in view."[40] Weber then makes a strange move. He neither condemns nor defends this analogue between sincerity and its simulation. Mentioning that some might call it hypocrisy to conflate the two, he explains that since it is motivated by the capitalist drive toward accumulation that is his topic, and not by "purely egocentric motives," such a conflation cannot be critiqued as hypocritical (53). Or at least, "the matter is not by any means so simple" (52). And then he presses on. By invoking the push for profit as a kind of cosmic force, and distinguishing it from the supposedly smaller, more petty "egocentric motive," Weber has helped foster the notion that the profit drive's investment in "mere appearances" is "not so simple," and therefore, beyond scrutiny.

Sometimes an incremental approach to persuasion can elide completely the distinction between "sincerity" and "seeming sincerity," as when Barton quotes a "splendid salesman" about influence and sales contact:

> "You must put yourself in the other man's place; try to imagine what he is thinking; let your first remark be sincere and honest but in line with his thoughts; follow it by another such with which you know he will not

disagree. Thus, gradually, your two minds reach a point at which small differences are lost in common understanding of a truth. Then with perfect sincerity, he will say 'yes' and 'yes' and 'that's right' and 'I've noticed that myself.' " Jesus taught all this without ever teaching it. (72)

The understanding is arrived at so seamlessly and indirectly that there is no express indication of a moment of persuasion. The seller and potential buyer enter a miasmic pool of influence together, emerging as one with an agreed-on sale. The newfound buyer alone speaks the agreement, and speaks "sincerely."

In this passage from a lecture given by one Mr. Kimball at a J. Walter Thompson staff meeting in 1930, the creative task of working with "facts and possibilities" is deemed the "Scientific Approach to Copy Ideas."

> The discovery of new merchandising angles . . . is leading more and more into territories formerly populated solely by . . . specialists in . . . science. The quest for selling points . . . now frequently leads to the modification of existing formulae in line with the latest findings of science, or even, itself, forces pioneer work. . . . This work is hard to define . . . an unceasing grind to acquire all possible relevant facts and a great many which seem, and may prove to be, irrelevant, along with an iconoclastic attitude dissatisfied with any existing facts where there is believed to be the slightest possibility of improving upon them by reorganization or invention.[41]

The terrain seems to be one of "dark dealings" couched in euphemism, shady ambiguities that border on deception, trickery charading as "invention." Implicit to such a critique would be a posited opposition to the brilliant clarity afforded by "plain speech" and empirical observation. Yet these two modes of gaining authority have often worked in tandem, and do so in key ways for the advertiser, as implied by Kimball's invocation of "science" above.

In her work on race, gender, and colonial imperialism, Anne McClintock explores the camera as a signal instrument of externally based notions of truth.

> The photograph . . . constituted a crisis in value between the aggressive empiricism of science, bent on achieving a "universal inventory of appearance" (a doctrine of externality) and the romantic metaphysics of inner, individual truth (a doctrine of internality). Again, the contradiction was displaced onto the feminized realm of empire. Colonial pho-

tography, framed as it was by metaphors of scientific knowledge as penetration, promised to seek out the secret interiors of the feminized Orient
and there capture as surface, in the image of the harem woman's body, the
truth of the world.[42]

The specular, cataloging revelations of the colonial photograph seem to unseat
the notion of an inner truth that cannot be excavated, that is given its very
definition by its interiority. Jackson Lears chronicles the participation of advertisers in the twenties in this empiricist "universal inventory of appearance,"
showing that they tapped both photography and the Calvinist "plain speech"
tradition to lay bare all facets of life for frank examination.[43] He points out that
in so doing, the industry attempted to expand its arena of influence, distance
itself from its carnivalesque roots among the patent medicine salesmen, and
take its place instead as part of the new managerial elite. This fact-based model
of externalized truth seems distinct from the performative externality relied on
by Barton in his depiction of Christ's power of influence.

In his emphasis on the effects of a calculated sincerity, Barton's Jesus appears
the perfect heir to the legacy of the carnival master himself, Barnum, for whom
the proof was inevitably in the pudding's *impact:* that is, if it works its effect on
its audience, it's as "true" as it needs to be.[44] The undeniable, bottom line truth
of its success overrides any other concern. This externality-based "truth" gets its
authority not from its "objective documentability," as with McClintock's photograph, but from its effects. For all the difference evinced between the "objective," regulatable, "scientific" truth of "plain speech" and the photographic
record, on the one hand, and the "sleight-of-hand" success rate of a seemingly
sincere master salesman on the other, one important similarity emerges: both
models reject what McClintock refers to as "the romantic metaphysics of inner,
individual truth." In each case, the proof of truth value does not inhere within,
but instead resides in the degree of mastery achieved over the external world as
a result of the truth claim.

Of course, this is not to imply that the notion of truth as inhering is
unconnected to the quest for authority. Where would the early modern mon-
archs have been, for instance, without the concept of an absolute sovereignty
fixed within the essence of their persons? It was just this notion of divine fixity
that early protocapitalist ideologists needed to incorporate and surpass in order
to make their effect. In the modern era, however, empiricism and influence
(reason and seduction) contradict one another less than they partner up as

modes of gaining authority. When Kimball invokes science as an arena with which advertising shares much, he uses the (imperialistic) language of conquest, referring to "pioneer" work, to "discoveries" and "quests" into "territories formerly populated solely by . . . specialists in science." In short, the essentially optical mastery achieved by the "laying bare" of the external world—its examination, documentation, and regulation—is augmented, not contradicted, by the persuasive mastery achieved by the salesman's understanding of psychology and exertion of influence.

In *My Life in Advertising*, "scientific" advertiser Hopkins attempts to distinguish the presentation of empirical evidence from "soft-sell," mesmeric persuasion, but instead only provides a further example of the indistinct lines between them. In one of many harangues against the suspicious embellishments of "fine language," Hopkins apparently prefers the "plain truth" of empiricism, urging the importance of "demonstration." He says he has learned this approach, though, from "street fakers," hardly the lab-coated rationalists one would expect from an advertiser claiming to have developed "scientific principles." And ironically, the demonstration of product that he apparently propounds is very specifically not offered to the public. Rather, Hopkins's strategy turns out to be the "free with purchase" deal, which supposedly manifests the principle of "demonstration" via the substantial materiality of the proffered bonus, its excess: the something else pictured along with the commodity in the ad is tangible, indisputable, and thus "demonstrable." Again, we are at work in the arena of almost gaseous "influence pools."[45] Through proximity in the material world, the bonus somehow verifies the product, lends it allure, and adds to its demonstrable presence.

Illustrative of the "miasmic" approach to influence was adman William Esty, who emerged in the last chapter as a key proponent of collaboration between the advertising and movie industries. Working at the J. Walter Thompson Company during the 1920s, Esty was a debonair, up-and-coming copywriter photographed for the agency's newsletter in an immaculate white suit, posing with a well-dressed woman in front of his cherry new car (see figure 1).[46] In the minutes from company meetings, Esty emerges as a particularly modern voice, especially flexible in his blurring of the divide between sincerity and the appearance of it. Esty sounds rather like the narrator's uncle, Edward Ponderovo, in H. G. Wells's influential novel condemning commodity capitalism, *Tono-Bungay*. Ponderovo relates the mysteries of a truth forever beyond our grasp:

Figure 1   Adman William Esty snapped on his
recent Hollywood trip with date Leila Hyams.

I never really determined whether my uncle regarded Tono-Bungay as a
fraud, or whether he didn't come to believe in it in a kind of way by the
mere reiteration of his own assertions. I think that his average attitude
was one of kindly, almost parental, toleration. I remember saying on one
occasion, "But you don't suppose this stuff ever did a human being the
slightest good at all?" and how his face assumed a look of protest, as of one
reproving harshness and dogmatism. "You've a hard nature, George," he
said. "You're too ready to run things down. How can one *tell?* How can
one venture to *tell?*"[47]

Using a not dissimilar strategy, in one contentious 1929 staff meeting, Esty
took on the rather thorny challenge of a cigarette advertisement. After all, he
argued, "most people who smoke cigarettes at all are inclined to wonder
whether they smoke too much and whether cigarettes affect them adversely."[48]
His proposed campaign asserted Tareyton's steadying effect on the nerves,
using "ordinary people—commonplace people" to "sound a note of sincerity"
(3). Based as it was on conjecture, the advertisement was countered vigorously
by colleague Stewart Lea Mims, who emerged from the archived minutes as the

Figure 2   Stewart Lea Mims.
Courtesy of JWT Archives.

company's vocal resident "grouch" (see figure 2): "I just feel . . . resentful of
our being willing to invent out of whole cloth the theme copy and then
manufacture the evidence. It depresses me to see us apparently adopt the
criterion of success as the only criterion. I say that the storm is going by and I
seem to be out of tune with what is accepted as the philosophy here" (4). Esty
defended his campaign with a lengthy invocation of "psychology" and the
placebo effect:

> There are hundreds of thousands of people in this world whose ills . . .
> are due purely to imagination. . . . Every doctor, at times, prescribes
> bread pills for disorders they know are purely imaginary. . . . Based on
> this, if people are told that this cigarette is better for their nerves, is it not
> entirely possible that that will actually take place? . . . [W]hen you have
> something as implanted as these cigarette prejudices, you are dealing with
> something over and beyond facts—a psychological factor. To get a person
> to change, you have to offer him something he will mentally accept. (5)

Advertisers' claims about consumer psychology can often be projections. Here,
Esty depicted his own proposed delusion (that Tareyton possesses a sedative

effect superior to that of other cigarette brands) as the "psychological factor," the self-delusion practiced by consumers at the mercy of imagination and prejudice, a self-delusion that is powerful enough to create beneficial changes in the real world: "If they think, 'Here's a cigarette which is more of a sedative,' won't it be a sedative?" (5). Thus, the persuaded customer *makes* the advertiser's claim true, thereby entirely exonerating the linkage between "seeming sincerity" and its effectuality. (The grumpy Mims was quick to interject, "I think you have given a very interesting explanation, but frankly I think it's ——, but I don't care to argue it out here" [5].)

The "psychological factor" of suggestibility had the power to turn advertisers' claims to truth, and hence, it was much posited in the profession. During a period of employee disgruntlement at J. Walter Thompson, for instance, a lively employee-produced newsletter was squelched, replaced with a management organ designed to boost employee morale and drown out the growing sounds of grumbling from the staff. One number of the "mouthpiece" newsletter focused on the benefits of life imitating ads, illustrating this "little understood by-product of advertising" with a story about some Lever Brothers workers. Much to the approval of the newsletter's editor, these blue-collar workers read fabricated advertisement claims posted in the workplace about their own skills, and were then drawn by discourse to approximate the fictive versions of their own work. This story of beneficial self-delusion and the publicity that induced it was exactly paralleled by the "faux" newsletter itself, which was an attempt to "use publicity to foster the morale of [the] organization," intended to rouse and recorral JWT employees, creating unity of mission after the fact by claiming it.[49]

In the case of the J. Walter Thompson newsletter, what's ultimately at stake is not inherent truth, but access to narrative voice, as management clearly realized when they appropriated their employees' periodical. An episode from Barton's own life contains the same conclusion. Apparently, Barton had an extramarital affair with one Frances King, a romance that he asserted lasted one month in 1928 (when she worked for BBD&O), and that she contended went from 1925 to 1928 (Fox 110–12). Barton paid King and her husband $25,000 after the husband threatened to sue him for alienation of affection; it appeared that was to be the end of it. Then, in 1932, King bobbed back up with a manuscript of a novel she had written, called *Roos Martin,* about a philandering adman. Using the threat of its publication, she demanded $50,000. Barton promptly sued her (successfully) for blackmail. Though it may have boosted his reputation for machismo, the trial endangered his public self-representation as a pillar of Christian virtue. To an extent, however, damage control was in effect. Because Barton had the power to withhold or place large advertising contracts, the tabloids proved uncharacteristically discreet about this particular scandal, and did not cover the trial. What a shame: in a wonderfully postmodern touch, King's manuscript was read aloud to the jury. Her account was avowedly fictive, with limited claims to truth value. This did not reduce its power of persuasion, as Barton knew. The fundamental question was not about who told the truth, but who got to control the narrative. Who was to profit from weaving tales? Despite their standard of noisy irreverence for those in the limelight, the tabloids proved themselves to be entirely at the service of their advertisers, while King's effort to seize the story-for-profit reins from below was criminalized and quashed.

Roos Martin was not the only novel from the period featuring a protagonist modeled after Barton. *The Virgin Queene,* by Barton's friend and fellow copywriter Harford Powel Jr., features a Bartonesque hero named Barnham Dunn (the Barnum allusion is intended).[50] This story, overall a warm portrait of the Barton figure and a paean to advertising itself, was published and disseminated to the public, unlike King's effort. *The Virgin Queene* is an extended attempt to resolve the intellectual adman's crisis of faith about the legitimacy of his own profession, culminating in his renewed commitment after an eventful sojourn in Britain.[51] In the book's first chapter, the anguished protagonist takes a sudden leave of absence from his position as "senior partner of New York's most distinguished advertising agency" (Powel 4). He is burdened by shame and fed up with his craft, which he has come to experience with increasing disgust as an unending chain of deceptions. His rebellion is instigated by concerns far more coherently articulated than the vague, wistful anxieties of Babbitt. Dunn feels that he has sold his artistic skills for an "indigestible" "mess of pottage" (30), and remarks ruefully to his secretary that, "All I've done for you . . . is to teach you to lie" (9). He leaves for an old aristocratic manor in the British countryside, ostensibly in "pursuit of the real," to invoke Jackson Lears's term for the search for authenticity that resonates throughout American culture in the 1920s (Lears 1994, 345–78). Yet during his stay so motivated by a yearning for the genuine, Dunn winds up—almost in spite of himself—promulgating a spectacular ruse (penning an "Elizabethan" drama and then foisting it off as a "found" work of Shakespeare's). Widespread, clamorous appreciation for this piece of concocted history finally teaches him that the inventions of the advertising industry, which he had been castigating as "deception," are better interpreted as "the finest hoax in the world" (182) and a gift to the delighted public. In this shift, he does not cease to categorize the advertiser's endeavor as a sort of purposive misrepresentation; he simply revalues this project, moving from self-censure to self-congratulation. Thus reinvigorated, he returns to advertising, once more a believer in the utopian powers of an industry of dream weavers.

The book opens and closes with Dunn's work on a particular advertisement. Developing testimonial copy, he impersonates a young woman: "I was about to become a mother, and I didn't want to be" (3, 255). We learn in the book's first chapter that the fictive speaker in Dunn's ad starts out "frightened and depressed," but thanks to her embracing of the commodity, winds up a "joyful mother of a son" (3).[52] Just like his imaginary mother-to-be, Dunn moves from mortified resistance to fecund acceptance over the course of *The Virgin Queene*, and when he returns to this professional impersonation at the novel's end, he is himself the "joyful" author of a play, "frightened and depressed" no more. Just as the "purity" of Jay Gatsby's dreams is not sullied by the vast performative apparatus these dreams engender, here too, the practices that feel like a shoddy "deception" to Dunn at the outset are revealed to be pure, transformative, and fecund because they are fueled by the impulse toward utopia.

Shame and the Man

Powel "manages" and resolves the shame and uncertainties of his principal character, Dunn, while Barton expels the issues of doubt and mortification from his text by selecting a suprahuman protagonist. Jesus Christ, a more-than-mortal adman, is unshaken by the sorts of questions that wracked Barton's own career. Some of this unease, however, was not so much palliated as deflected and projected onto the posited consumer. If we move from Barton to Lewis—and from the producer to the consumer—the terrain of hidden questions and drives that lurks beneath the performance of white-collar gusto can be examined. What *of* the role of the consumer—*Babbitt*'s "Regular Guy," Christ's disciple, the Tareyton smoker seeking to steady his or her nerves?

In *Babbitt*'s naturalist opening sequence, Lewis puts forth the notion that advertisers subtly invoked so regularly: individuality as flaw. The people in this first passage are depicted as workers, distinguishable only by social "type" or position. They are busy ants filling various professional niches, remarkable as individuals in one regard only: they fall short of the fancy modern buildings that are supposed to stand for progress, the "shining new houses, homes—they seemed—for laughter and tranquillity" in "a city built—it seemed—for giants" (5–6). Lewis problematizes a cultural environment where individual traits are perceived primarily as deficiencies that prevent workers from "living up" to modern capital's dream for society. Critics have often commented on the ironic distance between Zenith's gleaming towers and its stolidly marred inhabitants, but they do not seem to question Lewis's zest for the dwarfing cityscape itself; Lewis links that urban landscape so closely to the self-doubt and insignificance of its inhabitants that the portrayal borders on one of causality.[53] To cite Eve Kosofsky Sedgwick, for Lewis, the skyscrapers generate and presume the closet.[54]

Babbitt is the story of a midlife crisis induced by this disjuncture between a pinched psychic terrain and an epic cityscape. After all, Babbitt is a real estate agent dealing in pieces of that urban geography. His individuality manifests itself mostly as that which he must hide from others: his piercing tenderness for daughter Tinka and friend Paul, his erotic fantasies of escape with an unspecified "fairy girl," and especially his restlessness and angst. He seems anxiously aware of "exposure" and "vulnerability," those states that Heilbroner describes, as we saw earlier, as inherent to the process of capitalist production. When the vague, poorly defined malaise of his midlife crisis isn't asserting itself, Babbitt zestfully enacts a "standardized" personhood and set of standardized values. Catalogs of these values are inevitably capitalized in the book, achieving the comfortingly authoritative proper noun status bestowed on brand names. Throughout the novel, Babbitt raves, for example, about "Modern Appliances" (8), the "God of Progress," "Salesmanship," and the "Solid Citizen" (11), "Good Fellows" (12), "Cheerful Modern Houses for Medium Incomes" (15–16), "Society with the big, big S" (21), "Unselfish Public Service" (38), and "Vision" (42).[55]

Babbitt hides a lot in his eponymous novel: besides his erotic daydreams and poignant devotion to Tinka and Paul, he also struggles to hide his failings as an employer and family man, and his affair with Tanis Judique.[56] What our "man whom nobody knows" hides most, though, behind loud banter and an increasingly strained good cheer, are the restlessness and discontent that drive him through the various stages of his only partially realized rebellion. This branding of malaise as something shameful that probably indicates only an embarrassing lack of energy results in the suppression of all social or political diagnoses for discontent. To read one's doubts or desires through either lens would align oneself with the "grouches and smart alecks" it is safer to revile. Through this shaming, the sociological is made the physiological, even the pharmaceutical, and discontent is individualized—isolated as an individual's shortcoming. Lewis was addressing a ubiquitous strategy. Listen to Barton's reprimand to social critics in the final chapter of *The Man Nobody Knows,* and note its sexualized dig. Christ has been abandoned by the mass of his followers, "His best friend had died doubting . . . and His enemies had triumphed. . . . What was *His* attitude? One of complaint? Of faultfinding? Of *weak railing* at His own misfortunes or the willful wickedness of men?" (129–30; emphasis added).

In his consideration of the intellectual affiliations suggested by *Babbitt,* Sheldon Norman Grebstein compares H. L. Mencken's *The American Credo.* Mencken remarks on the American dread of condemnation that leads to the repression of idiosyncrasy; he argues that the fear of standing out results in a paralytic resistance to the process of questioning "ideas and institutions."[57] In *Babbitt,* clearly a portrait of Mencken's "Booboisie," the main tactic that characters employ to avoid looking dangerously conspicuous themselves is to bond with their social group by marginalizing others. Attacks against Jews, "reds," intellectuals ("woolly whiskered book-lice"), women, foreigners, and non-whites (the subjects of particularly virulent outbursts) all help the men in Babbitt's set feel closer to one another, secure in their own position (49–50, 85, 122–23). In a vicious cycle, one obvious result of this social tendency is an ever more entrenched fear of disclosure of one's own potential marginality, as when the book's most venomous anti-Semitism is voiced by an eager character named Finkelstein (50).

Watching a group of strikers during a period of labor unrest, Babbitt "hated them, because they were poor, because they made him feel insecure. 'Damn loafers! Wouldn't be common workmen if they had any pep!' he complained" (257). He invokes "pep" in an effort to distance himself: again, the pep paradigm individualizes analysis of both urban distress and its remedies, shifting the focus away from political and social analyses. Lack of pep, though, cannot account for a lively, well-organized strike; Babbitt is disconcerted by the workers' rechanneled energy and their atypical accessing of social voice, not by their enfeeblement.

Relevant here is Elizabeth Lunbeck's discussion of "modern manhood" and industrial psychiatry, which later was geared to make psychiatry indispensable to the corporate managerial class via the transformation of malcontents into work-ready males. Lunbeck explains that for those performing diagnoses, "the man vexed by his lassitude was at least playing the game," while the " 'queer guys, eccentrics, disturbers, querulous persons, unreliable and unstable fellows' who sullenly roved from job to job, leaving behind them trails of unrest" were the men targeted by such advocates of industrial psychiatry as most seriously in need of psychiatric rehabilitation.[58] The identified problem of these "disturbers"—pathologized and thereby not politicized—was certainly not enervation; rather, it was the failure to cheerfully acquiesce to the demands of modern industry.

Is anxiety about the profit motive itself a major source of Babbitt's unease? Doesn't that contradict the notion that he and his "good fellows" are ashamed of (and trying to hide) their doubts regarding the capitalist project? Could you be ashamed because you lack ardor for the status quo and simultaneously, on a more fundamental level, because of your own participation in that status quo? Sure. Trying to exude more zeal than you actually feel, squeamish and secretive about your doubts, you mistake those doubts for weakness, but *also and nonetheless* you feel tortured with guilt about your endeavor. Importantly, Babbitt's own unrest during his rebellious phase is profound enough that his effort at distantiation from the picketers fails. As Babbitt tumbles from one stage of his midlife crisis to the next, this citywide strike sparks off in him a short-lived political metamorphosis: though rather muddleheaded, this phase sees Babbitt reacting against the "ideas and institutions" that appear responsible for the inequities and sorrows around him.

Babbitt contains several explicitly political passages about the hegemony of business, and its characters level many attacks on "agitators" so absurd that they seem by contrast to indicate Lewis's own advocacy of radical activism (see, for instance, 317, 157). The book can be read with or without the fully leftist slant; its condemnation of conformity could be viewed as a companion piece to Randolph Bourne's mobophobic essays, or an antecedent to David Riesman's 1950 anticonformity study *The Lonely Crowd* and the (significantly canonized) literature spawned by its analysis: Saul Bellow's "Seize the Day," say, or John Cheever's "The Country Husband."[59] Indeed, as Thomas Frank notes, among Lewis's vast original readership, "Babbitts coast to coast bought the book in huge numbers," participating in what Frank describes as "bourgeois self-loathing as a literary force."[60] And though Lewis often eschewed the invitations he received to take his place as a spokesperson for the American cultural center, those invitations never slowed down, from 1920 until his death. Martin Light points out that in the thirty-one years from the publication of *Main Street* until his death, Lewis garnered 260 entries in the *New York Times Index,* and while he turned down a proffered membership in the National Institute of Arts and Letters in 1922 and a Pulitzer Prize in 1926, Lewis did go on to accept the Nobel Prize in 1930 and even to write a weekly column in that organ of American centrality, *Newsweek,* for a year or so in the late thirties.[61] But despite the decisive middle-of-the-road embrace of Lewis, his own engagement with socialism makes a more political reading of his book possible, as does his focus on a specific segment of the population; Lewis treats as his topic the "salesmen of prosperity," and does not pretend to address American subjectivity in toto, as his periodic departures from Babbitt's subcultural pool remind us (see, for example, 83). Furthermore, while the individualistic creed of a John Cheever typically blames women as the stifling enforcers of conformist strictures, Lewis does not (though Babbitt himself sometimes does).

Christopher P. Wilson argues forcefully that it was the New Thought psychosocial activism that Lewis rejected after 1920, while his socialist views, now unhooked from "the power of positive thinking," remained in his work not as a call to action but only as a dark, satiric, claustrophobic pressure.[62] But doesn't *Babbitt* contain positive references to the activism of Seneca Doane, Zenith's radical lawyer? Is Doane "entrapped" (96), too (to use Wilson's term for the characters' claustrophobia); does he share in the book's "sheer suffocation" (106)? When Babbitt chats with Doane on a train, the latter is described as "curiously kind" (247), and clearly possessed of far greater breadth of experience and perspective than Babbitt can lay claim to: on a picket line, Doane is "smiling, content" (257), in sharp contrast to Babbitt's persistent unease. In fact, Lewis explicitly privileged character Doane in his notes, and for years prepared to write a labor novel with the lawyer at its heart. Modeled on Eugene V. Debs, Doane was to be the "Christ-like" "great soul" and protagonist in what became Lewis's "phantom project" (Hutchisson 91–92). *Babbitt's* only dig at Doane comes from the Left. In the aforementioned social panopticon section, scientist Dr. Yavitch deflates Doane's zealous tribute to the benefits of standardization, interrupting him to retort, "You . . . are a middle-road liberal, and you haven't the slightest idea what you want. I, being a revolutionist, know exactly what I want—and what I want now is a drink" (86).

Perhaps Yavitch's puncture of Doane's "liberal" grandeur (otherwise admired in the narrative) is an indication of what letters from August 1922 reveal to be Lewis's ambivalence about labor heroism. Spending a few weeks with

Debs and a group of union activists in the month prior to *Babbitt*'s publication, Lewis records that Debs, with a face "molded of bronze," was a true "Christ spirit" (though Barton might object). And yet several days later, Lewis despairs of ever writing his labor novel, complaining how keenly "the sight of a group of lolling and ignorant rough necks, addressed by an agitator who is going immediately to supplant the capitalists—& who couldn't run a fruit stand—gets my goat. . . . [T]here's so few Debses!"[63] In *Babbitt*, the lionizing of labor—of both its "great men" and collectivities—coexists with the skepticism about leftist politics that would ultimately keep the envisioned Doane novel forever a "phantom." Lewis allowed this skepticism to underwrite his retreat from political engagement.

It would be a misreading, then, to categorize all Babbitt's agitation as clearly political in origin. In his normal life, Babbitt employs the rhetoric made available to him via mainstream media as a preextant form into which he can funnel his experience. Unsurprisingly, when he gets restless, he uses the leftover available rhetoric of officially marginal behavior to try to organize his period of revolt.[64] But what do we learn of the "curst discontent" itself (108)? In key moments, once his grumbling has subsided and subsequent efforts to enforce good cheer have failed, Babbitt's restlessness allows him to attain states of aesthetic apprehension normally precluded by the worldview and model of masculine subjectivity to which he cleaves. Lewis depicts Babbitt as possessed of "some genius of authentic love" (26) for Zenith, and at one point, his immersion in a "mysterious malaise" leads to a full engagement with that genius: "Conscious of the loveliness of Zenith . . . he lifted his head and saw" (29). Such vision is normally clouded, since the directives by which Babbitt is accustomed to living require that he be "strong for business," "with no artistic temperament" distracting him from ongoing business growth.[65]

Later, alone on a lake at night, and reeling with confusion and dissatisfaction over his life, Babbitt stumbles on an almost Wordsworthian apprehension of nature's sublimity: "Larger and ever more imperturbable was the mountain in the star-filtered darkness, and the lake a limitless pavement of black marble. He was dwarfed and dumb and a little awed, but that insignificance freed him from the pomposities of being Mr. George F. Babbitt of Zenith; saddened and freed his heart" (244). His attempt to respond to this dark, quiet awe in fact contains it. Worked up by his experience on the water, Babbitt rushes off to hire a completely indifferent woodsman to be his guide to "real living" (244).

This experiment, which proves a total failure, is in keeping with the message disseminated in a thousand advertisements of the period: that day-to-day life was *not* real, and that controlled bouts of outdoorsy leisure could provide access to a vibrant, authentic, manly inner nature, which would then inform and invigorate continued labor, until the next vacation. The masculinizing benefits of this posited "nature" are distinctly at odds with the sublime terrain of the romanticists that Babbitt seemed to have been apprehending on the lake, far more restorative of the nerves than shattering of perceptions. Again, as with Babbitt's effort to dismiss the strikers from his mind, Lewis portrays a suffusion of "improperly" directed energy (illuminatingly aesthetic) being reinterpreted by Babbitt as an indication of neurasthenic malady.

Babbitt's profound failure of communication with the guide-for-hire, Joe Paradise, suggests that the white-collar worker's fantasy about the woodsman's life is predicated on a vacation-based nostalgia for a preindustrial nobility that never existed. In a chapter entitled "The Pursuit of the Real," Jackson Lears describes Babbitt as a "victim" of "the wave of life-worship [that] surged across the coasts of bohemia and into suburban living rooms. . . . The feeling that one had somehow been cut off from intense emotional or physical experience spread among the comfortable classes as well as their avant-garde critics" (Lears 1994, 357). In this episode, Lewis has Babbitt retreat from an actual encounter with the sublime on the lake into a familiar avowal that he must, by all means, seek (through the hiring of an "expert") the authenticity of "real living."[66] The freedom devolving from perception is quickly replaced by the anxious desire for help, for augmentation, for prosthesis, that fuels consumption. A lifetime of training in consumer practices has taught Babbitt that desire is part of a repeating cycle: yearning is followed by purchase, which is followed by temporary satiation or relief, which is followed by renewed hunger, which is followed by another purchase, and so on. Desire, then, is a component of a closed energy conversion system, rather than the heart-palpitating outcome of perception.

Similarly, after Babbitt's rebellious phase is over, it appears to have functioned mostly as a "safety valve" release of built-up tension, only enabling the status quo to continue.[67] Lewis's novel succeeds where *The Virgin Queene* fails, though, to the extent that it isn't quite that. Nor is it a romanticized tale of transformation, spiritual conversion, and the rejection of inauthenticity. No bildungsroman, *Babbitt*. Babbitt's rebellion has left its mark, "weakened" his "moral fiber" (312; again, Lewis illustrates the recasting of change as enfeeblement) so that he can't exuberate in corrupt business practices or politics quite so much as previously, and gives his blessing to his son's downwardly mobile rebellion. Babbitt hasn't fully faced his own condition or culpability the whole time, but he has had the experience; it makes sense that his life should neither really evolve nor snap back tautly to its old form.

Babbitt's midlife crisis is a critical transition through which he must move alone. Nothing in Babbitt's world, except perhaps the solidarity and outspoken dissent of the picketers he observes, encourages him to think that this wrestling with internal doubts and shame could be anything else than a profoundly private one-man battle with his secret side. But was *Babbitt* actually a highly public rehearsal of this ostensibly hidden imploding nausea of the self? As mentioned, Thomas Frank claims that the best-selling *Babbitt*, well thumbed and chuckled over precisely by "Babbitts coast to coast," helped usher in an era of "bourgeois self-loathing," and that "smug self-satisfaction thrives in a strange symbiosis with self-loathing in the soul of the American businessman" (7–9). To arrive at a reason for this "strange symbiosis," one must ask: what might be enabled or precluded by these interlinkings of self-congratulation and shame?

During Lewis's era, many of the attacks on consumer culture that enjoyed greatest cachet revolved around the charge of "other-direction," a critique that began in the 1920s, but reached a sociological and literary heyday in the 1950s. Palpable in *Babbitt* as an attack against standardization, this denunciation of conformity still drives some analyses (see Lears 1983). Its central implication is that we all should be self-directed, and that it is the individual's right to self-direction that consumer culture most hampers. The painful irony here, to come back to Frank's "strange symbiosis" between bourgeois self-loathing and self-congratulation, is that the terms on which this critique rests actually validate and underscore the model of subjectivity that propels the commercial address. They each flatter the posited audience member with the injunction to individuate, to search above all for expression and indulgence of the desires that make him or her unique; simultaneously, they each berate the same audience for lacking the vigor to do so. In the meantime, they keep the focus squarely off interpretations that would place the individual in a larger social context. The "other-directed" critique of commodity culture, therefore, actually cojoins with the omnipresent celebrations of that culture to manage and channel the subjectivities of its participants.

This diatribe against conformity was as prevalent as it was, in part, because it was so readily employed in advertisements, paradox never being an enemy to the commercial project. *Babbitt* definitely reflects the twenties' concern about the perils of social "standardization": the motivating fear in this novel seems to be one of greater and greater consolidation of the powers that be, at the expense of individuality—an extremely modern source of malaise. Babbitt's yearning, like Chum Frink and Paul Riesling's, is to break away, to fly off and be free of the stultifying, enforced unity of conformity. In *Babbitt,* characters seem to form groups largely to soothe down and exile impulses toward resistance, and "primitive terror" is that which courses through someone when they are finally alone. Shivering in his bed on the brink of his rebellion, cognizant of his own capacity not to conform, Babbitt is "reduced to primitive terror, comprehending that he had won freedom, and wondering what he could do with anything so unknown and so embarrassing as freedom" (111). Lewis implies that the political and cultural powers that were consolidating during the first half of the twentieth century extended to include a mode of subjectivity that fought back terror—a terror that perhaps needed to emerge—kept it at bay, whether that terror erupted from some "primitive" wellspring or the modern conditions that inspired it.

Far more fearsome to Lewis, it seems, than the dread of apocalyptic disunity and social disintegration so characteristic of the postmodern era, was the idea that the dominant society *was* succeeding, all too well, despite its murderous lack of ethics and its brain-deadening insistence on conformity. This must have seemed especially depressing following the period during and immediately after World War I, when Lewis, like many socialists, had believed for a time that Americans were witnessing capitalism's moment of self-destruction, that it was "a thing attacked, passing" (Wilson 98).

In *Babbitt,* there is room to read more than a strangely implicated portrait of an ensnared modern individuality, too stunted to assert its distinction from the crowd. This claim does not contradict *Babbitt*'s attack on the dangers of conformity, conformity being an outcome less of community allegiance than of what Stuart and Elizabeth Ewen call "unity without solidarity." "If *economic* consumerism tends to organize disconnected individuals into coherent and predictable markets, it is *political* consumerism that defines the current state of western democracy seeking to create a vast patriotic unity—a unity without solidarity."[68] It was not unorthodox individuality so much as it was community-oriented "other-direction" that most threatened the period's new professional elites. We have seen the way that 1920s' advertising evoked shame and anxieties about social judgment, almost always reinforcing gender or racial polarities to do so, and that it thereby denaturalized impulses toward community allegiances. Can the self be understood primarily not as an individual psyche, nor as a manifestation of gender or racial hierarchies, but as a member of various larger groupings, ones not necessarily delineated by market profile? Such communal identifications seem a refutation of advertising's first move, which is to evacuate or refunnel all nonconsumerist motivations (and allegiances) from the subject it addresses.

Perhaps just such impulses and bonds are the outcroppings of the doubts and hungers that circulate troublingly in *Babbitt,* and that Barton exiles as weak and unmanly from his portrait of *The Man Nobody Knows.* Unmanaged, these could lead not only to individual lassitude, but more profoundly, to the development of alliances and perceptions unlinked to and uncircumscribed by the consumer experience.

Chapter 3

"Complex Little Femmes"

Adwomen and the Female Consumer

The average woman. . . . Is there some way to stick her on a pin like a butterfly and to put her under a microscope? We've got to know more about her.

—Christine Frederick

"We've Got to Know More about Her"

Advertisers of the 1920s speculated unceasingly about their prime target and ultimate object of scrutiny, the female consumer. In this chapter, I have no plans of my own to "stick" the "Average Woman" under a "better" microscope than that wielded by Christine Frederick and her colleagues. Rather, I look at one fiction that animated a fiction-making industry and chart the zealous efforts of an influential profession to shape a working definition of an "essential" female nature.

Theorists in the advertising industry wanted to figure out what makes female shoppers tick. The fierce hunger to plumb and predict the female shopper's psyche hints at a real dependency on consumer compliance, a vulnerability inherent to marketplace relations that the producers of commercial discourse might prefer to keep veiled—or as discussed already, project onto the consumer herself. To present-day readers, the declarations from advertisers about the heart of the female consumer seem dizzyingly self-contradictory and adherent to the agenda of the instant. This failure to fix a portrait of woman's "essence" suggests neither incompetence nor deceit on the part of these professionals, but instead, that gender roles are always more constructed than intrinsic—slippery, maddening, if your goal is to control through definition. These efforts to define the feminine target were shaped by industry-wide anxiety, both about the consumer's freedom to withhold her dollar and the ethics of advertising as a profession.

The women working in advertising brought an additional strange tension to this endeavor: for the presence of women in the profession profoundly challenged the symbolic divide between the savvy salesman and gullible consumer, between the scientific analyst and instinct-driven subject. When women began to generate advertisements, the men in their midst seem to have often grown nervous, wary of the threat leveled against this extremely gendered sucker-and-the-salesman model that helped organize their world. For a *different* gendering of persuasion predates P. T. Barnum by almost two millennia:

> Of course, advertising work is the rightful heritage of women. Look at the bill of goods Eve sold to Adam. He didn't want an apple, had never heard of an apple, wasn't even hungry. But he got an apple! Eve sold him the idea that he had to have one. So I say, women, go to it—you're natural advertisers![1]
>
> Eve was the first advertiser. She held the apple rosy side out and Adam bit![2]

This chapter reads the archival records from the J. Walter Thompson Company along with the manuals and memoirs of female copywriters Christine Frederick, Dorothy Dignam, Helen Woodward, and Ruth Waldo to delineate their theories of the female consumer. At the same time, consideration is given to both the disruption of the adman/consumer relation and the eventual destabilization of modern gender identity brought about by women's penetration into the predominantly male advertising workforce.[3]

These women's careers are marked by a certain doubleness: a straining between strategy and goal, between what the women said around their male colleagues and what they said to one another, between the adwomen's professional triumphs and the ideological codings in their copy.

The self-contradictions that proliferate in all industry theorizings of the female consumer seem in the work of adwomen to stem from multiple identifications. These women vacillate between manipulating the woman shopper and serving as her advocate. Some of the women discussed in this chapter were conscious feminists, pioneers in a masculine field. Their feminism could translate into a sense of allegiance with and responsibility to the women they addressed, or, contrarily, an embrace of a widely maintained professional posture of disdain for the consumer in the name of their own right of access to full-fledged professionalism. In many instances, this split seems systemic and, thus, beyond the control of the advertiser; sometimes, though, it asserts itself as a strategic, ironic distance. This detachment bears similarities with the "disjunc-ture from utterance" or ironic gap noted as the marker of the adman's authority in chapter 1. In the case of adwomen, authority is exactly the question, as their presence in the workplace, and ready manipulation of gendered language and imagery, challenge the gender divide that supposedly justifies the authority of the advertiser's expert voice. For these industry women, then, often enough the irony extends to code and color the women's collegial as well as commercial address. When Frederick advocates sticking the average woman on a pin, she seems to caricature and highlight the anxious violence of the scrutiny to which her own sex is being subjected. Waldo commented, late in her career, that adwomen "*had* to be shrewd, to get around the men, women have always had to be."[4]

"Women are, indeed, the shoppers of the world," declares the foreword to Carl Naether's *Advertising to Women,* "buying 96% of the dry goods, 67% of the foodstuffs, 67% of the automobiles."[5] To the adman, woman is the everyday, the great ordinary, that paradoxically proves the most pertinent mystery. As Claude Hopkins points out in *My Life in Advertising,* when a 1920s' market researcher canvassed door to door in order to get his finger on the national "pulse," it was a housewife who greeted him.[6] Both mythically and statistically, a woman was and is the primary consumer, and so holds considerable eco-nomic power. "All the maker can do is to beg the consumer to buy what he makes; the consumer can *force* the maker to make what he buys, or go out of business," a J. Walter Thompson Company editorial groaned in 1926.[7] As such, she must be read, examined, hailed, and mimicked in address so that she will relate to the pitch, and then respond with a purchase. This response was seen as emerging directly from her unconscious; allegedly, advertisers had, by the twenties, a well-theorized leverage over the psyche of this posited con-sumer, whose will could be directed—or bypassed—if the unconscious drives beneath it were adequately understood.[8]

In trade journals and industry manuals, advertisers extended varying degrees of autonomy and partnership to the feminine consumer. She could be figured as anything from judicious selector to passive sheep, from ruler of a micro-cosmic domain to a rampant id, driven by instinct, purse in hand. Perhaps guided by a centuries-old feminizing of inconstancy, the analyst of female nature often passes along his or her own self-contradictions, incorporating them as a pivotal component of femininity. In the commercial arena, too, claims about the paradoxical female helped justify what appears over and over in the industry manuals: not paradox, but self-contradiction, especially when claims are made about the feminine consumer. Naether's *Advertising to Women,* for example, vacillates between assertions of the female consumer's savvy, discretionary use of advertising's information, on the one hand, and her suggestibility and slavish obedience to her own instinctual drives, on the other.

A case in point: in an extended discussion of various advertising buzzwords, Naether considers the use of the word *smart.* First, he writes admiringly that the woman who is "smart . . . expresses her individuality to the best advantage, through the choice, the construction, and the wearing of her clothes, for all of which she is individually responsible. Above all else, her dress shows her individuality, not, however, to an extent to make any part of it seem loud or otherwise extreme in the eyes of others" (78). But then, on the same page, he undercuts this respectful portrait of both the term and the woman who would exemplify it: "How gullible, how dull, the feminine reading mind must be to accept . . . [the overuse of the word *smart* in advertising]. 'Smart ' to me always implies 'conspicuous' and I am sure there must be many women who dress well who care little for conspicuousness" (78–79). Naether conflates the advertiser's unease about the truth function in his or her own work with a gendered anxiety about the spectacle of feminine display and its links to female agency, choice, and intellect. The term *smart* is already ambiguous. In this context, it means chic, of course, but embedded in this is its double valencing, a synonym simultaneously for "intelligent" and "saucy and presumptuous." Is the "smart" woman tasteful and in control, or is she "gullible" and "overconspicuous"? What is it about this topic that makes such contradictions possible? The question of an advertisement's "essential nature"—is it information provided or a trap?—is raised in an implicit, projected fashion via Naether's dual readings of the "smart" consumer.

Though she invokes the modern woman far more believably than does the almost dyspeptically misogynistic Naether, Frederick also engages in constant self-contradiction along the same lines that Naether's work lays out. Unlike Naether, though, Frederick seeks to reconcile the seemingly oxymoronic traits she ascribes to "Mrs. Consumer." A home economics expert who applied Taylorian efficiency principles to her study of kitchen work, and who contributed to *Ladies Home Journal* and other women's magazines for thirty-six years, Frederick also cofounded the League of Advertising Women of New York in 1912 with her husband, ad executive Justus George Frederick. Her

Selling Mrs. Consumer became an industry bible.[9] In a move typical of this postsuffrage decade, Frederick attempts to resolve the contradictions in her portraiture of the female through a popularized feminism co-opted in the service of nation.

In "Advertising Copy and the So-Called 'Average Woman,' " Frederick careens back and forth between speaking as a woman and a woman's analyst, between ridiculing men for mythologizing her and then doing the same, between saying that women are too diverse to be generalized about and then claiming that sometimes "women may be bunched together like so many asparaguses."[10] "A woman who comes out of the head of a man rarely is a woman! . . . [T]he picture, finally, resembles in its incongruity, something of a beautiful but highly wicked Parisienne knitting socks for father" (228). Frederick digs wittily at a contrived portrait of feminine inconsistencies, yet in the very next paragraph covers similar ground: "The cardinal principle by which to explain womankind is *paradox.* . . . [H]er 'yesses' are 'noes,' her retreats are advances and she is both kind and cruel, highly practical and other-worldly" (228). And similarly, Frederick declares that both "metaphysics" and "lump averages" must be avoided by analysts of the feminine consumer, as "ten women will be a great deal more varied than any ten men" (230). Then, blithely, she proceeds to disregard her own counsel:

> Every woman has about the same reactions when she is in love, when she has a child, and when her feet hurt. Also, she is "average" in her tight economy for all things useful and her lavishness on things decorative of herself. She is a born bargainer; she will not be fooled by inferior goods, no matter how successfully trademarked or camouflaged. She likes to feel she is different than other women; yet she likes to be doing and wearing what is "the mode." She likes to imitate the "best people"; she accepts authority readily. (233)

The "asparagus" Frederick "bunches" here is simultaneously undupable and readily accepting of authority. Again, unlike Naether, Frederick attempts throughout *Selling Mrs. Consumer* to reconcile the conflicting pictures she has presented of the shrewd and suggestible consumer, the hypnotic and helpful advertisement. She argues that advertising offers "an intelligent invitation to compare values," but she is careful to justify its more seductive function as well. This is accomplished, in part, by linking woman's supposed pliancy with her alleged liberation and modernity: "Women have a greater *suggestibility* than men; they are more receptive; men being more stubborn and unadaptable. . . . Mrs. Consumer in America has a very volatile character. . . . She is a new race-mixture without fixed social roots or traditions in a new and democratic country. . . . [T]he reason she is more [suggestible] than man is that there are more male traditions to bind the man. American women feel far less bound" (49). The industry has branded women gullible; Frederick attempts not a new analysis, but to remove the onus of the sucker from feminine credulity by redefining it as an American liberation from the shackles of rationality and training.

An erstwhile feminist, Frederick validates the modern woman's sense of her own contribution to society, leaving us, however, with the paradox of agency posed by the consumer's participation in her own duping. Frederick presents the consumer's consent to this addressing of her unconscious as patriotic participation in the economic vitality of the "modern age":

> The average woman consumer . . . does not want to visualize herself as an automaton told what to do by advertising. . . . But nevertheless the American woman has struck up a closer *entente cordiale* and co-partnership with industry and trade (even if it is so largely unconscious), than has ever been known in the history of trading. . . . [S]he has developed a "consumer acceptance" spirit,—a readiness to follow where she is led, that has had an immense bearing upon American industrial prosperity and standards of living. . . . We women simply adapt ourselves to an advertising age as men adapt themselves to a machine age—because it is an important element of modern life. (334–37)

The woman suffused with the spirit of "consumer acceptance" participates in the Hooverian commitment to business growth at all costs by agreeing—out of patriotism—to check her discretion at the door.[11] Frederick typically links women's supposed instinctual love of change to the national economic benefits of what she calls "creative waste" or planned obsolescence. The "distinctive characteristic" of "creative waste" is "looking to a larger end, beyond the draining of *the last bit of utility*" (82), she explains, taking the hatchet to the nineteenth century's endless lauding of thrift.[12] Frederick adds, "The cumulative effect of [Americans'] free-spending, creative wasting policy has been to raise wages and standards of living" (82). In a book dedicated tellingly to Herbert Hoover, guru of American business expansion, Frederick urges us to avoid being "merchandise hoarders" (81), clinging as do the Europeans to tradition and the antiquated. "The American housewife, perhaps more than any other in the world, can be said to be 'open-minded' and unshackled by tradition" (123). Liberated by the culture of progress, she is set free to shop, desire, and spend her way toward abundance.[13] Early in her career, Frederick's model kitchen experimentation at Applecroft had combined a feminist concern for women's domestic exertions with a Taylorian industrial vision. During this phase of her professional trajectory, an up-to-date Frederick forges a similarly capitalist alignment between her feminism and Hoover's notion of national growth through business expansion.

But what is the relationship between Frederick's "bunched asparagus" and the experiences of actual female consumers? Naether promises his readers that examination of "the pictures and words which have been printed upon costly space for [the female shopper's] eyes to see and her mind and heart to follow" will "reveal . . . the mind of woman . . . and so give us a glimpse of her personality" (vi). Naether's guarantee notwithstanding, advertising's address of the female consumer does not, of course, give us an accurate portrait of actual consumers. The burgeoning research departments of the twenties' ad agencies understood this; they claimed as their raison d'être the quest for the heart of the female consumer. Energetic in their pursuit, market researchers simply took to the roads. As Jackson Lears has pointed out, the industry's adulation of statistics notwithstanding, resultant surveys indicate that early market researchers understood the object of their study at least as much in terms of individual psychological probing as demographic profiling. The early work was "energized by the researcher's eagerness to catch the consumer unawares and penetrate the inner sanctum of his [her?] motivation" (Lears 1990, 22). Such itinerant surveyors asked questions of women from a wide variety of ethnic, class, and geo-social contexts. In a 1963 interview, advertiser Margaret King Eddy commented that, "I think I've rung doorbells across this country. . . . Now, they wouldn't consider that research, you know. That's not 'professional' enough. But I think it gives you better ideas for copy than the professional research does. . . . You talk to hundreds of [women] and you hear what they say."[14] Though perhaps in the sixties Eddy enhanced her depiction with the glamour of hindsight, documents from J. Walter Thompson's Research Department of the twenties bear out her sense of the specificity of the individual women interviewed by Thompson staff.

One traveling researcher at J. Walter Thompson conducted a survey on Woodbury soap products in 1923. He preceded findings with vivid, belletristic introductions that painted portraits of the women being interviewed. Some of these depictions, followed by the women's replies to queries about magazine reading and preferred facial soaps, do allow the present-day reader to apprehend not only the narrative stylings of a talented young advertiser but also a vast population of specific women out there, most of whom resembled not at all the women posited in ads, even when they felt amiably toward these conjectured "women."[15] In what was perhaps a frustration for the JWT surveyor, none of the interviewees he described so painstakingly used Woodbury products or seemed at all concerned with the issue of their skin. Standing in darkened doorways with unbathed toddlers clutching their skirts, or "receiving" the researcher in tiny, immaculate parlors, the objects of his survey maintained again and again that, "there's nothing wrong with my complexion," "I am not interested in the French appeal," or "I don't have time to read magazines."[16] In 1932, having spent a day interviewing New Haven, Connecticut, housewives, Edith Lewis and Aminta Casseres at J. Walter Thompson were struck by the women's "lack of understanding of points that seemed so clear to us and their indifference to some of the things that we had hoped to make important to them."[17]

How should we think about the relationship between the female consumer and the adwomen who tried to train her in the fine art of needing, wanting, and buying? Casseres and Lewis seem fed up here, alienated by the disjuncture between the posited "you" in their ad copy and the women they found at home in New Haven. These housewives apparently stalwartly refused to prioritize their concerns along lines desirable to the marketer. The women are still improperly educated, the remark from Casseres and Lewis implies, and these potential shoppers must be brought more closely into alignment with the female consumer constructed in their ads. And yet, despite the discursive and cultural chasm that seems to yawn between consumer and adwoman in this instance, the women who worked in advertising during the first decades of this century squeezed their way into the industry only by mythologizing an ostensibly unbreakable bond of gendered solidarity between themselves and the female consumer.

"Eve was the First Advertiser"

Female copywriters played a peculiar role in the early ad industry, as a result of its hunger for the feminine tone. If the archival record is any indication, admen preferred to see their female colleagues not as professionals but as visiting ethnographic subjects, as "real wom[en] who lend . . . a helping hand whenever it is necessary to inject a woman's touch into the copy" (Naether 38). Representatives of their sex, women supposedly lacked the "vital selling punch" crucial to actually lead a consumer's "straying thought into the straight and narrow path of final—buying—action," but nonetheless proved invaluable for their knowledge of "intimate details" and their feminine "point of view" (Naether 18). The thought of the feminine "point of view" being, in essence, mimicked on demand by women themselves apparently threatened the essentialist reliance on that discourse's authenticity. Daily indications that women had the power to don and doff that "femininity" at will were an unsettling revelation of the Irigarian "mimesis" that makes up so much of women's self-presentation in commodity culture.[18] Whether they complained about it and militated for change, or negotiated with it more conservatively, women in the industry were required to confront this limited notion of female professional capacity. In 1928, advertiser May Heery reviewed Roy Durstine's *This Advertising Business,* charging that he "does not appear to take woman in advertising very seriously. He does not mention her as executive or client but he gives her very grave consideration as the reader and judge of advertising."[19]

Acknowledging that adwomen gained professional legitimacy by behaving as "visiting consumers," J. Walter Thompson Vice President Ruth Waldo advised in 1931 that the "good taste" of a shopper is an "especially important" prerequisite for women entering the advertising field, although "men in advertising seem to get along nicely without it."[20] Presumably, males in the industry were seen as manipulating public opinion rather than personifying it. Waldo continued: "This covers taste in general—what it is 'nice' to say, do, ask people to do or take for granted about them—as well as good taste in wording, illustration, typesetting, clothes, interior decoration, and so on" (Fleischman 14). Ironically, the "authentic" feminine discourse mimicked by copywriters of both genders concerned itself almost invariably with the *artifice* of dress, ornamentation, decor, and manners (Waldo puts "nice" in scare quotes). Meanwhile, the adwomen took advantage of their status as representative females to move into delimited but indisputable prominence in their careers.[21]

Dorothy Dignam—twelve years a copywriter with N. W. Ayer and Sons, and longtime historian for the Chicago League of Advertising Women and the

Frederick-founded Advertising Women of New York—describes what a young woman should do to prepare for an advertising career, winding up:

> In short, she has to know as much as any *man* in a similar job . . . plus why it is that women like blue better than red for a floor covering!
> And so, in ten years, perhaps, we see Mary Edith as an advertising woman. Poised, confident, able to stand on her feet and defend her decisions before a masculine board of directors. She has married perhaps and built an admirable home. She may have a baby and know more than the doctor! It is women like this . . . living in homes, shopping in stores, driving their cars, entertaining their friends, going to church, loving their neighbors . . . who write advertising. And that's why, for the most part, advertising is sensible and believable.[22]

Note that in this passage, the adwoman's value, prowess, and knowledge are linked exclusively to her representative female status; it is her biological womanhood that allows her to "know more than the doctor," for instance. Dignam's language creates the patently false sense that most advertisers were women—and married women, suburban women, Christian women at that.[23] Their expertise—which they turned into professionalism—stemmed directly from their cleaving to the newly "traditional" profile of the All-American consuming female. This obfuscating formulation was helpful to advertising, an industry with a permanent image problem, and to the adwoman, who might otherwise be seen as suspicious in her entry into a male-dominated world.[24]

Helen Brown Beckett, who worked for the J. Walter Thompson Company from 1924 to 1948, was not alone in stressing her status as a typical consumer in her job application, even to the point of downplaying the considerable professional skills and education evidenced in her letters of recommendation and job history.[25] In fact, Beckett held an M.A. and had tackled not just copywriting, but also merchandising, sales, and production. Yet asked if she has the ability to concentrate, she replied, "Yes. For instance, after selecting the three test ads [in the *Saturday Evening Post* as part of the application procedure], I did not yield to the impulse to stop and read a story!" Asked whether she considers herself impulsive, she responded, "Yes, in small things. For instance, I enjoy little bargains in handkerchiefs, stockings, etc." The modern reader may wince at Beckett's self-promotional efforts to suppress her own professionalism, but we must not forget that Beckett wanted, got, and held the job; this should remind us that Dignam's summoning of the iconic, moral wallop of the patriotically shopping wife and mother must not overshadow completely her enthusiastic description of the adwoman as "poised, confident, able to . . . defend her decisions before a masculine board of directors."[26] Dignam wanted to paint an attractive portrait of professional women succeeding in the public sphere, as she herself had done.

Waldo took a different tack, swiping sidelong at the "representative female" model, in her contribution on advertising to Doris E. Fleischman's 1931 anthology of career options for women. She described the status quo: "In the main women fill the lesser and run of the mill positions, working under men department heads" (Fleischman 14). This condition she attributed both to business' bias against female judgment and woman's lack of training in the realm of business and commerce, arenas which she depicted as warmly welcoming to men.[27] Sounding like a proponent of Lukácsian standpoint theory, she pointed out that this strangeness, though, this lack of familiarity "with the terms and the usages of commerce," makes the woman in advertising singularly equipped to "question and investigate . . . dicta generally accepted by men" (15) that may well need a fresh overhaul. Having made this vigorous declaration, Waldo seemed by contrast decidedly noncommittal when she went on to comment that "the commonly given reason why women are in advertising is that their intimate knowledge of women's habits and desires suits them unusually well for writing advertising on distinctly women's articles" (15). Waldo herself chose not to capitalize on the "intimate knowledge" her sex supposedly afforded her. She wound up the first female vice president of her agency, and along the way, avoided gender specificity by addressing all coworkers by their last name without the addition of a courtesy title. She also famously insisted that the female writers working in her department wear their hats in the office, so that there was no chance of their male colleagues "mistaking" them for secretaries or receptionists (see figure 3).[28]

The J. Walter Thompson Company, where Waldo made her career, was the industry's most successful during the twenties. And it was distinctive for the strong presence of women among its employees, including department heads.[29] A house advertisement published in 1918 bragged that "among the members of its creative staff [are women] holding degrees from Barnard, Smith, Vassar, Wellesley, the University of Chicago and Columbia."[30]

This group included Edith Lewis, lifelong partner with Willa Cather, who graduated from Smith University in 1903 and worked at J. Walter Thompson

Figure 3   Ruth Waldo, sporting a chapeau,
circa 1940s. Courtesy of JWT Archives.

for twenty-nine years. Whether because of temperament or the pressures of the closet, Lewis was quite retiring on the job; the "head" of a "group" whose only writer was herself, she handled several large beauty accounts entirely on her own. Her 1919 job application gives the impression of great intelligence and professionalism: its only "proof" of her status as a representative female is to list children and housekeeping as two of her hobbies, and this, perhaps, served a preventive function of warding off surveillance of her personal life. Lewis's personnel file shows her a steady, distinguished employee over the years, insistent only on her extended beachside holidays every summer with Cather. Her J. Walter Thompson memoirists mention her link to Cather with decorous pride, and seem more concerned that she had spent decades writing about radiant skin while herself suffering from blemishes, than that she had spent the same period helping to create and foster heterosexist subjectivity when she herself was a lesbian.[31]

Helen Resor shares with the elegantly hatted Waldo much of the credit for the company culture specific to J. Walter Thompson. Helen Landsdowne had joined the company in 1908 as Stanley and brother Walter Resor's only writer in the tiny Cincinnati office. (They moved to the New York office in 1911.)[32] Stanley went on to become both her husband and president of the company. Mrs. Resor was openly committed to the feminist movement. Agnes Court, her secretary at J. Walter Thompson for forty-six years, described enthusiastic company participation in a suffragette parade in New York in 1915: "I marched with her in the big parade. Mrs. Resor got us all big campaign hats. . . . Peggy King and Mildred Ashland [marched, and] I helped carry the big banner. Augusta Nicoll [a group head handling seven writers and eighteen accounts] rode a white horse! . . . After the parade, Mr. J. Walter Thompson gave us a big dinner at the Savoy Hotel."[33] A number of the applications of women who became longtime presences at the agency cite extensive participation in the feminist movement.[34] This probably indicates both that feminist activists were drawn to the company's reputation as amenable to women and that those who applied for work at J. Walter Thompson may have thought it advisable to include reference to such activism, knowing that Helen Resor might be the one reviewing their file.

Mrs. Resor did not limit her activism to her leisure hours, though company archives present her as at least superficially deferent to her husband. Despite her prominence in the company, executive Sam Meek (rather reprehensibly) "took the responsibility himself for keeping much of Mrs. Resor's history out of the obits when she died . . . because throughout her J. Walter Thompson career she always remained subservient in *name* to Mr. Resor, although her contribution was undeniable. . . . [S]he never took credit, it was always 'Stanley.' "[35] Actually, public relations at the time certainly extended credit to "Mrs. Stanley Resor," represented in a lavish *Ladies Home Journal* spread as "an executive in one of the largest agencies in the world. Her influence extends over many fields and in shaping policies not ordinarily referred to in connection with women in advertising."[36] Helen Resor insisted from early on that the women copywriters should work separately, in charge of their own department. Over the years, some women grumbled that it was their right to work alongside the men, but in this company, departmental segregation apparently functioned to consolidate female employees. An elderly Waldo explained it this way in the 1960s to a company archivist:

> When a woman works for a man or in a men's group, she becomes less important, her opinion is worth less, her own progress and advancement less rapid. Then she does not have the excitement and incentive to work as hard as she can; nor, in a men's group, does she get the credit for what she has done.
>
> But with the knowledge and confidence of Mrs. Resor's support, a woman at Thompson could advance in her own group without having to compete with *Men* for recognition of her ability. She has greater indepen-

dence and freedom; a woman's ideas could be judged on their value alone. It was one less handicap [since women were frequently accused of being devious]. . . . They *had* to be shrewd, to get around the men, women have always had to be.[37]

Shrewd indeed, intense, impeccable, and a "hard taskmaster," Waldo was not active in the women's movement, though she was concerned about peace and joined the Society of Friends in 1953. "She wasn't a suffragette or anything like that, but as far as I'm concerned, she did more for the cause of women's rights—and opportunities—than practically anybody else I can think of," said Ruth Downing in an obituary column published in the J. Walter Thompson newsletter.[38]

What do we make of this, when the advertising copy and professional gender politics in the life of the copywriter seem so disparate? Increasingly, it is a misleading exercise merely to analyze the language and images in individual ads without contextualizing their production. But the challenge here is not only a matter of reconciling the creation of sexist copy with the evolution of professional gains for women within the ad industry: we must also consider the coexistence in individual women of wildly contradictory expressed attitudes.

Sometimes, such apparent contradictions stemmed from the desire to promote women in the industry. For example, at a 1930 staff meeting, J. Walter Thompson adwoman Aminta Casseres tried to steer a group of twenty-eight men and three women away from a "cheesecake" approach to a Simmons mattress ad about sleeping positions. The projected campaign featured a man in black pajamas shifting in his sleep. Some had asked Casseres, "Why don't we have a pretty girl pose in these postures? I am against having a pretty girl [she explains,] because I think the pictures we have are very scientific, really laboratory pictures; they have a scientific significance that a pretty girl in pretty pajamas will not have. *I am willing to grant that the male of the species is the species and the female is just a variation.* I feel that we should show men in the illustration if the advertising is to be sincere and true" (emphasis added).[39] Her kowtowing to the "thirteenth rib" notion of gender difference shows, on the one hand, a troubling dislocation between her own womanhood and her positing of an implicitly secondary and aberrant female "variation," and on the other hand, a strongly focused, strategic effort to militate against an objectifying ad, something that easily dovetails with a feminist advertiser's professional agenda.

At times, professional gains for women in advertising coalesced with attempts at reforming advertising content itself. In a 1920 speech, "Woman as Bait in Advertising Copy," Christine Frederick, predicting mistakenly that the use of the "P.G." (or "Pretty Girl") in advertising would soon disappear, described in detail exactly why she thought the advertising anachronism failed to reach the actual target for the ad. "This type of picture girl is drawn by men and appeals to men, but it does not appeal to the type of woman who must buy these prosaic commodities. It repels her" (17). Her argument, put with such "insider's" authority, is in large part a call for more women in the industry, which may well have been its primary motivation. Dignam listed gender integration of the industry as the key achievement of Frederick's career, certainly more central than any truth function in her analysis. "*Selling Mrs. Consumer* was the book that woke up or nearly broke up a lot of agency copy departments. What it told about women and their buying habits made menfolk more tolerant of girls hanging around on the staff. If women really were like Christine's complex little femmes—hard as nails and fluffy as kittens—advertising had better be revamped from end to end!"[40] Notice Dignam's ironic detachment from "Christine's complex little femmes." Whether or not such women exist, she implies, Frederick, by summoning them, pried open the industry's doors.

Cross Copying

IS THIS ACCOUNT MASCULINE, FEMININE OR NEUTER? WHAT ACCOUNTS ARE ESSENTIALLY FEMININE? OR, FOR THAT MATTER, MASCULINE?

IS THE FEMALE OF THE SPECIES A BETTER WRITER, FOR EXAMPLE, OF COPY FOR FOOD PRODUCTS? AND THE MALE OF COPY FOR MOTORS, SHOCK ABSORBERS, OR GADGETS?

THE NEWS LETTER WILL BE GLAD TO RECEIVE YOUR OPINION!!

—J. Walter Thompson *Newsletter,* November 1927

The J. Walter Thompson Company, perhaps more than other agencies because of the strong presence of women on its staff, took up and worried the issue of gender distinctions and their constructedness. Selling itself was coded as implicitly masculine, despite the constant gender crossings and engagements with femininity involved in the commercial address. In an agency history, one staff member marveled over copy for JWT's Lux account that "effervesc[ed] in the most feminine way while still doing a wonderful job of real selling."[41] By the same token, female advertisers were often praised by their male colleagues for being "swell advertising men" while still managing to maintain their womanliness.[42] Of course, ads themselves frequently championed the businesswoman who managed to retain signs of femininity, implying by extension that the painstaking care required to keep up the gender performance while at work was her price of entry into a "man's world." This copy was generated in 1923 by J. Walter Thompson's women's department:

> There was a time when everybody said that of course the woman who gave up the calm and the leisure of her home for the rush and the worry of business would just lose all her charm. But they were fooled. Women have found a way to sit at their typewriters or in their private offices as dainty and roseleaf as ever! In spite of their new rushing, tearing life that should bring lines of worry, in spite of stuffy, sooty trains and the daily trips in any weather, . . . the woman in business has been obliged to find the *right* way to care for her skin.[43]

This ad calls for gender performance on the level of toilette; ironically, the copy exemplifies the kind of textual performance of gender that made up so much of a copywriter's duties. The ad indicates that working women were "obliged" to keep their complexions "lovely," and while J. Walter Thompson employees may not have been especially "dainty and roseleaf," that they felt the pressures of this duty will become clear.

Copywriter Helen Woodward was open about her alienation from this obligatory construction of femininity. Once, she tried to imitate the style of *Women's Home Companion* articles:

> I could not. It was too gentle and soft and words were used too loosely. In handling words in such a style one gets the feeling of contact with something smooth and round and slippery. Ideas slide off, slip away, and disappear. Women's magazines are often written in this fashion so exasperating to one who writes advertising to be paid for at $168 per inch in those same magazines. When you pay $12,000 for one page to appear in one magazine for one time, your words are made of radium to you. . . .

When this sample advertisement was finished, it was really a translation from the harsh, masculine style of mail-order book copy to the gentle femininity of its prospective readers. But I did keep it clear and definite. . . . [Women] want facts, provided the facts are stated simply and gently.[44]

Though Woodward highlighted the constructedness of "female" copy, which she thinks far too vague and diffuse, it is key that she also denaturalized the campy swagger of "male" copy, saying that she had written much "bullet-like, raucous, over-emphatic" advertising targeted at men. The impersonation of a "feminine" style went hand in hand with an equally artificial mimicry of the "masculine" in copy directed at men.

At least at J. Walter Thompson, women were not consigned solely to writing about women's products. In 1932, one Miss Walker wrote an almost parodically "rugged" Lux ad for insertion in "Our Navy":

Swab the personal decks with Lux Toilet Soap if you want to keep them in condition for the next close-up. This Lux Toilet Soap costs only a dime, but believe you me, it's as good as any savon that costs a buck in Paree. Makes a Lulu of a lather . . . goes after dirt, grime and oil by dead reckoning. . . .

And do the port-side dames go for the Lux-washed? Are you asking me! Lay in a supply before you ship. Convince yourself![45]

In another ad in a related military series, a Miss McDonald wrote copy to accompany a photo of two "particularly tough-looking troopers" (8). The advertising of toiletry articles to males was always seen as a dangerously effeminate proposition, requiring energetic macho posturing as compensation. McDonald had these gritty guys lay on the manliness with a trowel:

"Yea, Bo. The Army knows beaucoup about routin' out dirt and grime. That's why you'll find Lux Toilet Soap top hole with the boys, from Major General to buck private." . . .

You owe it to the Ladies, Buddy, not to hide that he-man personality behind a weather-beaten beezer. . . . The Janes'll think you're the berries.[46]

Not only do the women in advertising create "drag" copy, assuming male voices, but of course, admen mimic the feminine. For example, the last section of Naether's *Advertising to Women* is devoted to the "personal" sales letter, a mailed advertisement constructed as a letter from a "friend" and sometimes even typeset in an imitation cursive; "In appearance and general make-up, [these letters] approach very closely [women's] own habits of personal correspondence" (284). He urges that these letters, though penned by a man, should always be signed by a woman. "Frequently, business letters to women are prepared by men who inject into them the needed selling force and are then feminized where needful and sent out under a woman's signature" (289). Note his phallic call for "injection" of masculine "selling force," and his elision of the female copywriter's labor through use of the passive phrase "are feminized." Throughout his manual, Naether attempts to masculinize, even eroticize, the adman's textual cross-dressing—his stylistic penetrations and impersonations of feminine expression and perspective.[47]

In a chapter about an ultimately unsuccessful venture she undertook with some male colleagues, Woodward rather provocatively suggests that in their desire to establish a line of cosmetics, the admen were driven by a deep-seated hunger for beauty in their lives, masked by their loud, forceful surface noise about the profit imperative. Her anecdote, like Naether's book and its compulsive renderings of the "feminine" style, infers an almost transvestic yearning for the "feminine"—this, at a time when admen were expected to assert their business dominance by masculinizing the bottom line.[48] But Woodward places the flexibilities of such simulations within the far more rigid gender politics of lived business relations: "It was unbearable to them that a woman should know more about anything, *even her own business,* than they did—they, masters of mankind. . . . Do not speak to me, you captains of finance, about faithful and loyal service—it is nonsense of the first water," she concludes bitterly (326).

In this account of her failed beauty line, "Selling Beauty," Woodward's identification with the female as consumer seems vexed—alternately disingenuous and profound. Seemingly eager to deflate the hype of the advertising address, she openly doubts that cosmetics work at all, and jokes about the gulf between a cosmetic's retail cost and the value of its ingredients. In this debunking, she speaks more as a cynical copywriter, beyond seduction, than a consumer advocate engaged in exposé. But then, in the next passage, she lavishly depicts her own sensual love of the whole line, ostensibly aligning herself with the seduced feminine consumer, and thereby distinguishing herself from her comparatively insensible male cohorts, the "captains of finance" with whom she was in dire conflict.

Every woman will understand how much I liked to plan these cosmetics and their little packages. It was fun to examine little jars of cream sent by the chemist—some white as milk, some rosy, and some yellow as sweet butter, some perfumed with mimosa, others with clover, and others with elusive, undiscoverable scents. Some were heavy as narcissus, and some delicate as yellow tulips in May. There were gold liquids for the face and green ones for the hands. It was easy to forget the sophistry and be seduced by smell and touch into believing what one was selling! (313)

Playing out her own, gendered sensuality and aesthetic pleasure, perhaps Woodward engages in the kind of feminine veneration of lovely things that Emily Apter calls "a subversively erotic practice, thoroughly 'perverse' in its own terms."[49] But this extravagant passage also sounds like the generation of copy—self-seduction, not "by smell and touch" here, but by words. Is Woodward expressing solidarity with the female consumer or selling her(self) something? Her descriptions of the products even make a virtue of their huge price markup. "Thus the woman seeking loveliness pays for the sense of luxury, the advertising, the show. . . . She is buying a little confidence" (306). Completely aligned neither with the female consumer, from whom she automatically distances herself as does a performer from the audience, nor the admen whom she finds so intransigent, greed bound, and oppressive, Woodward here shifts uncomfortably between the two positions. When she dupes herself almost autoerotically with seductive prose, does she prove her distance from her hard-bitten male colleagues as a wide open sensualist or her kinship with them as a manipulator of desire?

One might argue that Woodward's capacity to slide between identifications with admen and female consumers should be read as ludic mobility, as a benefit peculiar to her interstitial position. "Shifting positionalities" are not *structurally* imbued with the pleasure of subversion, however.[50] Woodward's marginality is uneasy because despite the (modest) inroads made by women in advertising, the workplace remained a contested site. In 1935, Frances Maule's advice manual for female job seekers appeared, its author an advertiser at J. Walter Thompson throughout the twenties and into the thirties. Entitled *She Strives to Conquer: Business Behavior, Opportunities, and Job Requirements for Women,* the book begins with a foreward that emphasizes the burgeoning business opportunities for women, using the all-too-familiar advertiser's explanation: women do 85 to 90 percent of the shopping, so manufacturers and retailers—and even bankers, insurance brokers, and realtors—want the "woman's point of view."[51] And "it is realized that service is of great and increasing importance . . . [a]nd here, of course, is right where women shine" (3). The whole book is weighted quite shockingly toward tips on appearance and physical decorum. The foreword, too, includes a warning about the importance of appearance that seems oddly topsy-turvy:

> Time was when all a girl had to do was to produce her references and her school records, and if they were good enough, she got the job. But—no more! Now her landing the job may depend upon the way she walks, or talks, or does her hair, or the quality of her complexion or the immaculateness of her manicure, or her ability to say "no" in a manner perfectly delightful. (5)

In a text informing the contemporary young female professional that "OPPORTUNITY is knocking," one would expect modernity's working climate for women to be depicted as an improvement on the "bad old days" (3). Maule surprisingly reverses this, emphasizing exactly the fears of bodily excess and impurity that advertisements incited and insisted on throughout this period—a period when jobs were, in fact, elusive for reasons unrelated to personal hygiene.

But Maule devotes *four chapters* to the modification, presentation, and restraint of the physical self: a chapter on "voice culture," one on the importance of all-around health and stamina, one on dress that reports that 90 percent of business employers would prefer to hire "an exceptionally well-groomed woman who is only passably competent" than "an exceptionally competent woman who is passably well-groomed" (125), and an astonishing chapter treating "Things Your Best Friend Won't Tell You." This latter reads like an amalgam of contemporaneous ads for mouthwash, deodorant, shampoo, laundry soap, and feminine hygiene products.[52] Maule notes that "the particular things about which we have to be most careful are: first, ODORS; second, irritating and unpleasant NOISES; third, irritating and unpleasant MOTIONS" (142). Her discussion of body odor pathologizes and medicalizes bad breath and perspiration odor ("halitosis" and "bromodrosis" could bespeak serious medical trouble, she reminds us), thereby keeping perfect step with the era's advertising approach to "hygiene" products. As the paragraphs reel by, each taking issue with a new form of "b.o.," her frequent, euphemism-laden apologies for indelicacy seem more and more strained: "Excuse us please if at this point we offend any delicate sensibilities, but here we simply must remark . . . " (146). Such declared contrition notwithstanding, something or someone is quite zealous here. Apparently, we are dealing with a boisterously recalcitrant body indeed: garlic breath, oozing oil glands, vaginal discharge, phlegmy nose, fatigued intestines, and underarm perspiration—all must be warded off with vigilance and expertise.

Once Maule's advisory battle against the businesswoman's secretions and effluvia gives way to discussion of "NOISES" and "MOTIONS," she seems to be calling not merely for decorum, but feminine self-erasure. "We" must ascertain whether we "drum or tap with fingers or toes or pencils, hum or whistle under our breath, sniff, snuffle, breathe noisily, snort when we mean merely to laugh, chew gum audibly, blow the nose with a stentorian blast, clear the throat with a raucous rasp, or cough or sneeze . . . oftener, or louder, than is absolutely unavoidable. . . . The ideal woman employee is noiseless" (152). With a similar call for self-censorship, Maule goes on to catalog vulgar motions, such as fussing, fiddling, adjusting, scratching, face picking, nail biting, foot swinging, gum chewing, and doodling. Again, "the ideal woman employee is not only noiseless, but motionless" (153). Unfortunately, "not even our best friends will tell us about [offensive personal traits]. There are things that people just cannot bring themselves to talk about" (153). These unspeakable crimes of the body, with daily contact, "seem almost worse offenses than grand larceny or embezzlement" (153). The chapter's fantastic, almost Swiftian enumeration of the body's abundant, disgusting excess, and its vehemently worded calls for women to rein in such excess by any means necessary, suggests an embattled relationship to the professional sphere, an assumption of shame, apology, and self-condemnation on the part of the women entering this sphere. We have seen, in the last two chapters of *Living Up to the Ads,* that the psychic economy of the commercial endeavor is always strangely shame based, but here that shame is gendered, even sexualized, via a remarkable emphasis on physical excess. Jackson Lears has argued that the thirties' obsession with "bodily purification and control," and the eradication of "alien filth" as manifested and propagated by the period's advertising, can be partially linked to a search for social "purification and control," to "the eugenic dream of perfecting Anglo-Saxon racial dominance in the United States through judicious breeding and immigration restriction" (Lears 1990, 33). Perhaps in Maule's text, the interloping immigrants are Maule herself and her female readers, would-be businesswomen attempting to penetrate an arena previously closed to them and coping with the "filthiness" that comes along with the status of "alien."

Unsurprisingly, the other bodily excess incessantly cautioned against by Maule is that of female sexuality. "After all, a man wants to keep his mind on his work *when* he is working, however much he may enjoy and appreciate the candid display of feminine charms in his hours of relaxation" (128). Hence, it should be "a point of honor" among women at work "to refrain from turning loose their feminine allurements upon defenseless and susceptible males" (155), Maule warns, making men sound the innocent victims of unreined, almost predatory charms. Maule handles sexual harassment as a tragic happenstance that occasionally leaves no alternative but flight. "The one thing a girl absolutely cannot do is carry troubles of this sort to anybody higher up. Unjust? Yes. But that is the way it is" (15). She provides a positively grisly test case about a "girl who was just too beautiful, too lavishly endowed with the life force, to be allowed around a business office" (158). This "girl" is badly and extensively harassed by one of the company's highest executives, and when she reports the behavior to the manager who had hired her, he tells her "that she [is] a very vain and silly girl, who had mistaken mere fatherly kindness for evil intent" (159). Maule explains that "poor little Jocelyn" had put the manager in an embarrassing predicament by informing him of the trespasses of his superior. Jocelyn leaves the job. The section has a tragic ring to it, as it details the suffering Jocelyn endured and vetoes reporting as a reasonable response to such illtreatment, yet does not offer any more "appropriate" means of dealing with persistent abuse on the job. Instead, Maule segues abruptly from this unsatisfactorily concluded harassment tale to a vigorous, lengthy denunciation of women foolish enough to fall in love with their superiors and to expect reciprocity. One detects shame and also a clearly stated sense that the rest of the women, all those who actually do have strong feelings about the work, are hampered in their endeavor by the presence of those women with such "frivolous" priorities, as dictated by "the movies and the popular romantic novels about 'skyscraper souls' and 'office wives' " (159). In a stance reminiscent of the rigorous Waldo's, Maule assumes that it is women's work to correct against the stereotypes that lead the men in their midst to infantilize, patronize, and even harass them at work.

In her classic text *Purity and Danger: An Analysis of the Concepts of Pollution and Taboo,* anthropologist Mary Douglas defines "filth" as the label with which people are quick to dub any "alien" element that challenges the structuring categories in a constructed system, through either indeterminacy or the traversal of borders.[53] In the field of advertising, from which Maule operated, the unspoken association of professional women with an endangering "filthiness" seemed to stem not only from their gendered incursion into an all-male work world, but also from the blurring of boundaries effected by the female copywriters' facility with variously gendered speech. A 1930 profile of Aminta Casseres, highly paid J. Walter Thompson copywriter and group head, is scrupulously careful to commend her office's feminine furnishings and retiring style, yet still ends by citing a male coworker's remark that "she is a swell advertising man."[54] This perceived "manliness" may have instigated the men's discomfort, since the insinuations of the advertiser's influence were increasingly sexualized by the industry as the new machismo of persuasion. After all, "every ad inserted in a woman's magazine is a silent salesman," as Carl Naether rather graphically put it (v).

In this climate, the women who took on this more "masculine" agency were often seen as sexually threatening, requiring the retaliation of ridicule. J. Walter Thompson's Stewart Lea Mims, described earlier as the agency's resident grouch, was among those who were uncomfortable with the women in his professional life (although it should be said that he appeared uncomfortable with almost everyone). A full professor of contemporary history at Yale, he sacrificed his academic career (and his entry in *Who's Who*) for the opportunity of a job in advertising. A company archivist remarks that Mims's "battles at J. Walter Thompson must have been fierce, as he decries the effeminizing presence of women in business, and maintained intense prejudices against Mencken, Personality advertising and Harvard men."[55]

In her chronicling of women in the industry, adwoman Dignam details the belittling attitudes expressed in the "amusing" industry coverage of the first mixed gender advertising convention, held in June 1931 after the men's club became too impoverished to continue without female attendees.[56]

> We were called "Women Boosters" and said to give color and perfume to the meetings, and in another clip they were kind enough to say that our pretty summer hats with the flowers on looked very gay. . . . The story in the Sun said that we came late to meetings, forgot our pocketbooks and rushed off to our ad-women's "boudoir" between sessions, but not one of us was reputed to make less than $5,000 a year, and one [female] delegate was reported to have turned down $25,000.[57]

This rather biting reportage is typical of the tone struck by advertising women amongst themselves. The "bottom line" financial success enjoyed by many adwomen provides Dignam with the only possible triumph over the condescension the women encountered there.

A more compressed and coded irony can be seen as helping them militate for change among their male colleagues. Here's an example. Addressing the 1920 World Convention of Advertising Clubs on the overuse of attractive women in advertising imagery, Christine Frederick remarked,

> It seems odd that nobody supposes that I may like to look at *pretty men!!* . . . I think that the "appeal" which would be strongest with me would be to see the picture of a handsome gentleman, like our chairman of tonight, immaculately attired in a dress suit, and smilingly operating the "Lily White" washer without once dampening his glossy vest! (12)

Especially with her personal dig at the chair, Frederick employs sarcasm as the kind of shorthand "radium" of expression available to her without endangerment to her professional position. Waldo's irony, too, is condensed when she advises that the "good taste" of the born shopper is an "especially important" prerequisite for women entering the advertising field, while pointing out that "men in advertising seem to get along nicely without it" (Fleischman 13). As discussed above, her remark here, seemingly a rather merry gibe at male lack of refinement, at the same time cuts more deeply to imply that admen, unlike adwomen, did not have to impersonate "Mrs. Consumer" in order to claim a place in the profession. The allusive impact of the wry dig becomes crucial to consider among women who were occupying a vexed, multiply identified position. The disjuncture from utterance that served as a cathexis point for many advertisers—proving mastery, is here brought into play as a stance that can allow adwomen enough detachment to sustain them in their relationships with their work and their male colleagues.

Perhaps the requisite shrewdness that Waldo cited earlier animated the adwomen's work itself as well as their professional style in the workplace. Perhaps adwomen's tongues were in their cheeks as they wrote their copy and designed their campaigns. Gender essentialism was certainly tried to the breaking point in the milieu of the mixed gender ad agency. One hopes wistfully that maybe the female consumers who glanced at these women's ads somehow sensed an undercurrent of irony, and felt freed by the sense of distance, humor, and survival that it implied. But maybe they didn't. Such claims for the subversive power of subtexts can easily be overstated by the critic hungry for signs of resistance. When consumers held themselves at an ironic remove from the commercial address—or openly resisted it—they were probably impelled by other sources than the ad's own subtext. At the least, though, acknowledgment of the irony with which adwomen generated both masculine and feminine gender stylings in their work while building their own professional lives can provide a new depth to the modern-day analysis of advertisement, allowing it to extend beyond "New Critical" readings of the ads themselves. When we consider those end products that wind up the constitutive landscape of a marketized United States, we should consider, too, the strains and contradictions that inhered in their production.

In their copy and workplaces, female advertisers performed gender work. Generating ads that told stories about gender, advertising their own "feminine touch" to colleagues, and selling, simultaneously, the notion that a feminine presence was essential in the workplace, they negotiated continuously with prevailing notions about gender. In its ambiguities, pleasures, and frustrations, its cojoined benefits and liabilities, this work was not dissimilar to that performed by women engaged with gender spectacle more generally in 1920s' commodity culture. To approach this larger issue, we will move from Waldo, Maule, and their sisters in the industry, to the women featured in the ads they generated, posing all aglow with the starring commodity.

Figure 4   Saks Fifth Avenue Vida Shoes ad, *Vogue,*
15 December 1926

Chapter 4

"Lending an Air of Importance"

Vehicles at Work

The thing that made you first notice Gay was that manner she had, as though she was masquerading as herself. All her clothes and jewelry were so good that she wore them "on the surface." . . . She could do that because she, too, was awfully good quality. . . . [S]he had unquestionably the best figure in New York, otherwise she'd never have made all that money for just standing on the stage lending an air of importance to two yards of green tulle. And her hair was that blonde color that's no color at all but a reflector of light.

—Zelda Fitzgerald, "The Original Follies Girl"

Often enough, a beautiful woman poses next to the product in an ad. Her job there is to represent and augment the commodity's appeal. She represents, too, the potential consumer's fixing or hiding—through purchase—of his or her inherent lack. This "Carol Merrill" figure draping herself across the proverbial car hood in an ad can be viewed as the "vehicle," looking to linguist I. A. Richards's 1936 designation of the parts of a poetic metaphor. Richards explains that the "tenor" is the "underlying idea or principal subject which the vehicle or figure means."[1] In other words, in a metaphor the tenor is the thing that needs describing, and the vehicle is the term introduced to help do that. While being, ostensibly, the "principal subject," the tenor is in need of some augmentation and color—and this the vehicle provides. The advertisement model, then, plays vehicle to a commodity tenor, making meaning about its desirability with her presence. Already doing metaphoric work in the ad, the ad model presents us, too, with an illuminating metaphor for woman's symbolic and performative role in commodity culture.

In an ad, the augmentation of allure moves in two directions: the commodity and advertising model piggyback on each other's appeal, leaving us in a world of eroticized things and commodified women. (In the epigraph above, Gay, like her clothes and jewelry, is of "awfully good quality.") In *Advertising to Women,* Carl Naether instructs his fellow copywriters in this process of transferal:

> In such phrases as "alluring shades," "entrancing colors," and "beguiling stockings," the meaning of the adjectives used to describe such lifeless, commonplace things as hosiery, shades, and color is . . . transferred almost in toto to those parts of the feminine figure on which the color, shades, and stockings are to be displayed. . . . "[A]lluring shades" become "alluring ankles," "bewitching shades" become "bewitching ankles," and so on through the whole category of words whose meaning is to attract or to make attractive.[2]

Like the "two yards of green tulle" that need Gay's body to lend them importance, here a commodity designed to lend magic to the consumer's body is revealed to be "lifeless, commonplace." As Stuart Culver remarks, "Goods can't be made to go if they are simply and transparently displayed."[3] For the ad to work, the commodity needs first to borrow the magic of the vehicle's "body" (here entirely textual), and then offer it back again. Note the vital function played by the vehicle, the life that her presence breathes into the commodities around her.

Most female consumers know that some of that vehicular power belongs to them. Despite the belief in her own deficiency, a (supposed) deficiency that motivates her to shop, the consumer understands that she doesn't need to be an advertising model for her "work" as a woman in commodity culture to be partly vehicular. Rachel Bowlby has described the window-shopper's experience of her own lack when she sees "herself" outside of herself, augmented by the commodity displayed on the other side of the pane.[4] Commodity culture's rewrite of the Lacanian mirror stage becomes, with this model, the "window-shopping stage." This analogy, parallel in some ways to Laura Mulvey's linking of the Lacanian mirror and movie screen, needs to be complicated, though.[5] More than a sense of lack or deficiency marks the space between projected identification with the externalized object and the window-shopper's own body image. Treating the phenomenon of the show-window mannequin, Sara K. Schneider asserts that "women, simultaneously the targets of arguably male-produced merchandising images and the objects of male visual consumption, may have a particularly intense relationship to mannequins: they may both sympathize with them, as both are objects of a gaze judged according to

male-defined standards of beauty, and critically assess such beauty in mannequins that they define as 'other.' "[6] Perhaps Bowlby's browsing consumer, staring longingly through glass at the well-dressed mannequin, would see her own
reflection in the store window, superimposed on that mannequin within. And,
being female and thus cast as an object of desire, what the woman would see in
the window would be not only herself augmented by the commodity, but also
the commodity being augmented by her. There is a contradiction here and for
now it must stand: the consumer's belief in her own lack and own plenitude
coexist. As a woman, she's "got the goods," though they never seem to be
good enough.[7]

When Richards first coupled the term *vehicle* with its partner, the *tenor*, in
his discussion of metaphors, he defined the tenor as originary, fundamental.
Using language of adornment happily suggestive in the present context, Richards hastened to point out, though, both the liquidity of this metaphoric
hierarchy and the vitality of the vehicle in actual use:

> The vehicle is not normally a mere embellishment of a tenor which is
> otherwise unchanged by it but . . . vehicle and tenor in co-operation give
> a meaning of more varied powers than can be ascribed to either. . . . At
> one extreme the vehicle may become almost a mere decoration or color-
> ing of the tenor, at the other extreme, the tenor may become almost a
> mere excuse for the introduction of the vehicle, and so no longer be "the
> principal subject."[8]

Richards celebrates the fecundity of meaning that seems born from the very
process of metaphoric yoking. His description of this back-and-forth meaning
swap as one of mutually enhancing "co-operation" appears tested, however, by
his portrayal of a "principal subject" whose preeminence is endangered by
proximity to an overly vivacious vehicle.[9]

At least in theory, however, the vehicle has been "hired" to represent the
appeal of something else. In an ad, the "something else" is the commodity next
to which she stands, the big prize that Carol Merrill gestures winningly toward
on *The Price Is Right*. Like Richard's textual vehicle, Carol does representational work that is overdetermined. She is a metaphor, in part. The prize is as
beautiful as she, and her presence "proves" it (as slipshod a proof as is any
textual metaphor). Also, she is what will follow if you get the prize, that is, she
will be its corollary, a prize herself. Further, she impersonates a potential you,
ecstatic owner of the prize.[10]

For women at large, the "something(s) else" that they find themselves representing can shift and multiply. In the twenties, it remained the vehicular duty of the middle-class American wife to "stand by" the man in the marketplace, and through her proximity, to both represent and augment his and its desirability. With her carefully consumed and constructed personal image and domestic microenvironment, the middle- or upper-class wife was supposed to "advertise" the husband's abilities as a marketplace player, and even to advertise, in a more diffuse way, the viability of the marketplace in toto.[11] Thorstein Veblen grouped the wife and servant, emphasizing the performative, trophylike function of each: "In order to satisfy the requirements of the leisure-class scheme of life . . . [t]he servant or wife should not only perform certain offices and show a servile disposition, but it is quite as imperative that they should show an acquired facility in the tactics of subservience—a trained conformity to the canons of effectual and conspicuous subservience. . . . [This skill is] one of the chief ornaments of the well-bred housewife."[12] A sort of metaornament, wives should also look good, and actual advertising vehicles could perform the task of training them in this arena, as Frank Presbrey gratefully explains in his 1929 *The History and Development of Advertising:* "Many a husband owes the trim appearance of his wife at breakfast to the suggestive power of the good-looking woman who is pouring coffee in the advertisement."[13]

The period's "new woman," at least as received and posited by the media, did a related job for modernity itself, or the particular brand of modernity most amenable to commodity production and sale: her modish, uninhibited style representing and augmenting the appeal of the modern era more completely than could the modern male's. *Our Modern Maidens,* 1929, starring Joan Crawford, illustrates this. Like its 1928 predecessor, *Our Dancing Daughters,* the entire movie revolves around the task of proving that the "modern" (an ultimately feminine adjectival noun in the film's vocabulary) can and should be read as wholesome, morally safe, and chaste, her dabbling in marginal and tabooed behaviors implying only high spirits.[14] Consider, too, the "skyscraper clothes" presented in 1928: long, narrow frocks modeled after the Brooklyn Bridge, the Paramount Building, the Ritz Tower, and many others, these outfits gave women the mannequin task of "express[ing] twentieth-century] America as she should be expressed."[15] Using the verticality of her own form (exaggerated with the breast binding and diets so heavily marketed in commercials of the period), the wearer of the "skyscraper frock" could advertise the increasingly vertical urban landscape—and the approach to commerce that

that landscape represented and facilitated. After all, as one 1928 Pond's Cold Cream ad reminds us, "to look attractive [and] to retain the charm of youth as long as she can" is "a woman's first duty to the society in which she moves."[16] (Later, when the United States became involved in the Second World War, the link between feminine self-presentation and civic duty normally felt as an undercurrent would be stated overtly: "Woman's desire to sublimate her natural charm [in wartime] is a matter of concern to her government," since "an unsightly female . . . plays hell with morale," Dorothy Dignam ghost-wrote for Walter Neuberg, president of Coty Cosmetics, in 1943.)[17] Other vehicular work that a woman might find herself taking on is to augment the image of the social caste with whom she associates, of the professional who has photographed her, of the executive or store owner in whose name she greets the public. There's even a term for the work that makes the commodification as specific as one could want: *window dressing*. Of course, during the twenties, a huge number of women were flocking into (relatively low paid) retail positions, as the urban and economic landscapes generated more and more spaces for public, commercial interaction. Susan Porter Benson cites a sales training article: "Every merchant should remember that his clerks are his personal representatives and that the public only know him, and pass their judgment upon him, from their CONTACT WITH HIS SALES FORCE."[18]

What does it mean to be a representational vessel "farming out" one's appeal as if it were so simply channeled? Is the vehicle's presence a destabilizing one, simply because so fluid? A speech given at a J. Walter Thompson Company staff meeting in 1928, by famous fashion, art, and advertising photographer Edward Steichen, seems to suggest that this is the case. Steichen began an otherwise lucid "list of problems" with the following extended, incoherent splutter about models and their intractability:

> Models. The most difficult problem that is directly outside of ourselves, is undoubtedly the question of models. . . . I don't think there is any one department of *Vogue* that gets as much of Mr. [Condé] Nast's time, as this question of models. Not one particular item. He has been working on it for years and has not solved it—and that's the answer. I don't think it can be solved. We have tried everything. It is just simply one of the things we have to muddle along with and make the best of it.[19]

Steichen is rendered unintelligible by the disparity between the incorrigibly flesh-and-blood, extrametaphorical models and their desired end as sleek, impermeable representational vehicles. Hopefully, the discussion that follows will illuminate exactly that disparity, that insoluble problem that Steichen found so very difficult to define, and link the problematics of gendered representation specifically to the idea of class crossings and female *labor*. The cultural performances examined in this and the next chapter reveal both the strains on this social system of metaphor and the burden on the vehicle herself, as she negotiates her spot on the axis between "mere embellishment" and "principal subject."

"This Fantasmatic Place"

"For beautifying themselves, [American women] spend nearly $2 billion a year," wrote advertiser Kenneth M. Goode in 1927.[20] As the rather sneering Goode might say, women's fascination with spectacle makes them, allegedly, frivolous—easy marks, more hungry than men for commodities because of their sheer love of show. But, in another way, their (socially enforced) expertise at spectacle-making means that these self-beautifying women are canny, as directors always are. A part of them must oversee their own image making, peer at their own unfolding self-portrayal. As one advertiser put it in a 1937 article pitched toward copywriters, "A woman's eyes are forever turned in upon herself . . . critically."[21] Exactly this psychic bifurcation, as required by woman's daily performance of the gender spectacle, complicates her status as a spongelike recipient of the sales ploy.[22] Mary Ann Doane's comments on masquerade are relevant: "I was searching for . . . a contradiction internal to the psychoanalytic account of femininity. Masquerade seems to provide that contradiction insofar as it attributes to the woman the distance, alienation, and divisiveness of self (which is constitutive of self in psychoanalysis) rather than the closeness and excessive presence which are the logical outcome of the psychoanalytic drama of sexualized linguistic difference."[23] Doane goes on to argue that by no means is mask play inherently liberating or empowering (despite what Camille Paglia may say to the contrary), as it evolves out of and is normally circumscribed by a "logic dictated by a masculine position" (47). Also, she warns, the masquerade performed by women in their mode of self-presentation is "an anxiety-ridden compensatory gesture," at least as it is laid out by Joan Riviere in the much referenced 1929 piece that Doane explores (47).[24] Indeed, the "cooperation" between masquerading women in commodity culture and the forces with which they swap representational meaning is often strained, just as is that between textual vehicle and tenor. No metaphoric vehicle is strictly at the service of its tenor. If it were to conform itself totally to that tenor and simply become a blank screen or mirror, it would instantly lose the distinct life and color that the tenor needs to borrow from it. Suddenly a synonym, it would cease to exist.

"The woman does not exist," Jacqueline Rose asserts, in her introduction to Jacques Lacan's *Feminine Sexuality;* "What the man relates to is this object and 'the whole of his realization in the sexual relation comes down to fantasy.' . . . As the place onto which lack is projected, and through which it is simultaneously disavowed, woman is a 'symptom' for the man. Defined as such, reduced to being nothing other than this fantasmatic place, the woman does not exist."[25] How to consider women's metaphoric endeavor without actually mistaking women themselves for blank lacunae? One must look at the *work* entailed.[26] Obviously not, in fact, unattainable figments of a desiring and itself flimsy imagination, women recognize the representational chores being handed them, and they become rather expert at approximating such figments. Feeling both the allure and the compulsion of this performative labor, women engage their own desire and imagination in the endeavor.

And it is hard work to play the vehicle, hard work to "reduce" yourself to a "fantasmatic place," performed under the perpetual menace of possible termination: "*No* woman is so highly placed that she can afford to neglect her beauty," Queen Marie of Romania warned readers in the most popular of all the society testimonials that Pond's ran in 1925.[27]

Hard work often comes with perks: the rewards seem to revolve most around the "piggybacking" already mentioned, whereby the vehicle can herself borrow the appeal, acceptability, or entitlements of that which she "advertises" with her feminine charm. In her study of the several versions of *Imitation of Life* (a novel by Fannie Hurst and films by John Stahl and Douglas Sirk), Lauren Berlant has contended that both Anglo- and African American women have been at a disadvantage in the twentieth-century political sphere, because the Enlightenment's model of supposedly abstract and bodiless citizenship enjoyed by males is barred from women due to their presumed excessive embodiment, an extreme material presence that only proves their disentitlement.[28] Berlant goes on to suggest that women "ameliorate" this limiting restriction by "borrowing the corporeal logic of an 'other' and adopting it as a prosthesis. . . . This is how racial passing, religion, bourgeois style, capitalism, and sexual camp have served the woman" (132–33). The prosthetic borrowing depicted by Berlant is, in fact, a two-way process; as we shall see, the specific effects of that process and work help constitute the identities of the female protagonists under examination here. Below is a job description—or a symptomology—for the vehicle, as the texts discussed in this chapter conjure it.

1. The vehicle's persona represents and enhances the appeal of something else:
   a. her image helps to sell products or tickets;
   b. she herself is a commodified woman "worn on the arm" of a man, thereby accessorizing his own act of self-presentation; or
   c. more generally, she experiences self-presentation as a business.

2. Either in the private or public realm, she is the site for projection of male and female "consumers'" fantasies.

3. She may disappear behind the instant-recognition familiarity of a "brand name" (that is, stage name, public name) or may "become a trademark"—her most broadly evident traits being perceived as familiar, expected, and marketable—and she is impossible to apprehend outside of such "recognition."[29]

4. She will exude and be veiled in "atmosphere." The back-and-forth borrowing of allure between commodity and commodified woman creates a mist of "indefinable" glamour.

5. Along with her disappearance into thing status, the obverse is true: commodity animism. Increasingly, the things around her take on agency.

6. She will experience vertigo, fatigue, and kinetic discontent. Importantly, these were just the complaints worried over in much advertising of the period that propounded the indispensability of pep, and the profound social and physiological dangers of lassitude.[30]

My investigation begins, naturally enough in light of the vehicle's status as a symbolic vessel, with other's impressions of women in the vehicular role, and moves slowly in toward the vehicles' perceptions themselves. The two F. Scott Fitzgerald stories, "The Freshest Boy" and "Jacob's Ladder," focus on *men's* experience of women as representational vehicles for the men's sensations, and on the struggle between public and private "ownership" of these women's representational powers. "Our Own Movie Queen," a collaboration (of sorts) between F. Scott and Zelda Fitzgerald, depicts and then hedges in a working-class woman's use of the vehicular role for her own purposes. The narrative distances the reader from the heroine with its broadly applied humor, but this same slapstick also tests the limits of vehicularization by showing what can happen when an "unruly" vehicle refuses to rein in the exuberance of her performance. Finally, Nella Larsen's *Quicksand* deals extensively—and often rather painfully—with a woman's impressions and sensations as she engages in acts of self-presentation that bring into collision "types" of gender and of race.

Male Projections

The work of the Fitzgeralds provides rich fodder for someone investigating the issue of women's performative and representational labor during the twenties. In part, this is because they participated so energetically and successfully in the popular culture of the day as writers and celebrities, but more specifically because Zelda's own relationship to performativity as a female was apparently highly vehicular. "Muse" to Scott and the quintessential modern to the public eye, she had a harder time staking a claim to being a "mouthpiece" for an age than its "embodiment." The conflicts between Zelda and Scott about authorship, collaboration, and bylines, and the contested intermingling of their written voices, make their textual record as much a terrain for gendered struggle over representation as were their celebritized lives. These stories, then, bespeak interesting resonances between their explicit content and the contestations that informed their production.

Two stories by F. Scott Fitzgerald, "The Freshest Boy" (1928) and "Jacob's Ladder" (1927), feature vehicular women whose images and stage names function as trademarks and brand names are supposed to, conjuring up (for the heroes and probably the readers as well) a complex of associations and identifications intricate enough to pervade, to become "atmosphere."[31] These stories provide nuanced examples of commodified women representing and enhancing men's experience, thereby occupying the "Carol Merrill" position even though there is no literal commodity next to them. The protagonist of "The Freshest Boy," Basil Lee, is a fifteen-year-old, middle-class, Midwestern youth at an exclusive eastern prep school, suffering from mysterious and extreme unpopularity. At his lowest moment in the story, Basil receives a package that he had ordered some time previously: "color reproductions of Harrison Fisher girls 'on glossy paper, without printing or advertising matter and suitable for framing'" (335).[32] Each girl is named; as he puts up and admires the pictures, Basil gradually singles out "Babette" as his favorite. The sound of her name, "so melancholy and suggestive, like 'Vilia' or 'I'm happy at Maxim's' on the phonograph, soften[s] him" (336) to the point where he can weep and name his griefs.

In the thick of it, he calls out, " 'Oh, poor Babette! Poor little Babette! Poor little Babette!' Babette, svelte and piquant, looked down at him coquettishly from the wall" (336). With his crying reiteration of her name, Basil projects all his experience of rejection onto the pinup girl; he means "poor little Basil," doesn't he? As represented by her, however, his suffering becomes lovely and worth mourning, his fragility not shameful but "piquant." Babette returns his gaze, "svelte" and "coquettish." Fitzgerald's modifiers here, so cool and un-wounded despite Basil's pity, suggest that Babette somehow eludes the boy's attempt at appropriation and possession of her image. But perhaps, like all pouting "calendar girls," she ultimately complies because her gaze, no matter how blithe, doesn't work: sheer representation, she doesn't really *see* anything when she "looks down." This "woman does not exist."

The promotional insert "quoted" by Fitzgerald trumpets the pictures' lack of printing or advertising matter. This lack only diffuses Babette's vehicular work. The invisible commodity that she so emphatically is not selling persists as a highlighted absence, and this very absence is supposed to enhance the picture's value; perhaps its textlessness makes it "art," unsullied by crass commercial-ism.[33] Or possibly, as Basil's story implies, the offer is this: you purchase and post this ad-minus-a-commodity, and the girl and her "brand" name will become vehicles exclusively for your experience, allowing you to detach your emotions from your own shame and hinge them onto an object that has been deemed to have value. Through this act of projection, tragedy becomes possi-ble, mutating and exalting your quotidian sorrows.

In "Jacob's Ladder," the protagonist is a grown man, a thirty-three-year-old failed opera singer who feels at least as sorry for himself as does Basil Lee. Jacob, Pygmalion-like, "discovers" a young woman, names her Jenny Prince, and assists her on the way to stardom.[34] Throughout, he pulls a "poor Babette," associating Jenny's beauty with the poignancy of his own smashed dreams in order to feel a tenderness and hope about her that seem to originate in his yearnings about himself. Jacob's lost hopes for his own "destiny" are linked with the childish Jenny when they are described as "the love child of a wish" (359). "Once he had possessed a tenor voice with destiny in it, but laryngitis had despoiled him of it in one feverish week ten years before" (353). Jenny is connected with Jacob, but with a redemptive difference: her "destiny" will not be squandered; it remains latent in her eyes even when she treats it lightly. "Seventeen—[Jenny] was as old as he; she was ageless. Her dark eyes under a yellow straw hat were as full of destiny as though she had not just offered to toss destiny away" (358). Jacob "projects" his lack onto Jenny (and thereby "disavows" it) much as did Basil onto Babette (another alliterated pairing).

The vehicle, however, is not a photographic representation, but a character come to life, and her autonomy outside of Jacob's head becomes the central theme of the story. Jenny Prince not only accepts, but very much benefits from Jacob's symbolic appropriation of her as a vehicle for his wistfulness. This is just the prosthetic borrowing that Lauren Berlant describes as serving women well: by fitting herself into the logic of his emotional drama as if she were donning some sort of garb, she can compensate for the rather considerable liabilities of her position. Like a dress model, she plays the cipher and muse; finding her way into his borrowed frock, she fits all her life and loveliness to the task at hand—and is remunerated. Over the course of the story and with Jacob's help, she moves from sordid scandal and underclass mien (she is the estranged sister of a murderess going through a messy trial) to "radiant" fame and tasteful sophistication. As his lessons take hold and her success blossoms, Jacob begins to fall in love with Jenny. His passion for her is exactly coterminous with her maturation as a discrete individual. Inevitably, she resists his eventual efforts to possess her. Jenny pulls away from him decisively when she herself becomes a desirer:

> "The one thing I want in this world is to make you happy."
> "I know," she whispered. "Gosh, I know!"
> . . . "What do you mean—you know?"
> "I get what you mean. Oh, this is terrible! . . . Listen, Jacob, I fell in love with a man." (368)

It is the painful cognizance of her capacity to desire (another) that forces Jacob to experience her as autonomous. As the story draws to a close, Jacob must acknowledge the limits of his appropriative power over her and content himself with her movie persona. But what is the nature of the autonomy that Fitzgerald grants to Jenny? One could argue that her resistances to him are signs less of independence than of her status in the story as an object of desire: that object needs to elude in order to represent the lack that proves desire. The conclusion suggests that what Jenny gains, above all, is the mobility necessary to move from the private to the public domain of representation, a shift figured in the story by her literal move to Hollywood.

In this final stage of the story, after she has both become a star and rejected his advances, when Jacob must buy a ticket to enjoy Jenny and her transformation into a commodity is complete, she is "radiant. A communicative joy flow[s] from her and around her, as though her perfumer had managed to imprison ecstasy in a bottle" (369). The subtly kinky language of captivity Fitzgerald employs was almost stock in the perfume advertising of the time. To cite one: "the entrancing odeur held prisonniere in this scintillating globule thrills the nostrils." Another ad, for "Parfum Cappi," described a "strange new sweetness lately wrung from the reluctant flowers" by masters of floral sadism who had devoted "lifetimes [to] forcing the flowers to yield their deepest, rarest secrets."[35] Jenny's glamour is atmospheric, pervading, a perfume. Strangely, the achievement is not hers. Like the "inexhaustible charm" of Daisy Buchanan's voice in *The Great Gatsby*, which is due to its being "full of money," Jenny's radiant elegance is proven by her ability to find and procure the services of an unsurpassable perfumer.[36]

Jenny's attainment of true vehicular status is indicated even more by her disappearance into her stage name than by her scent. Compare the conclusion's reiteration of her pseudonym with the litanizing focus on Babette's "suggestive" name in "The Freshest Boy":

> In great block letters over . . . the Capitol Theater, five words glittered out into the night: "Carl Barbour and Jenny Prince."
> . . . He stopped and stared. Other eyes rose to that sign, people hurried by him and turned in.
> Jenny Prince.
> Now that she no longer belonged to him, the name assumed a significance entirely its own.
> It hung there, cool and impervious [like Babette's image], in the night, a challenge, a defiance.
> Jenny Prince.
> "Come and rest upon my loveliness," it said. "Fulfill your secret dreams in wedding me for an hour."
> Jenny Prince.
> . . . She was there! All of her, the best of her—the effort, the power, the triumph, the beauty.
> Jacob moved forward with a group and bought a ticket at the window.
> (370–71)

As a child's entrance into the linguistic realm is contingent on loss of preverbal oneness with the no-longer-possessed mother, Jenny's attainment of stardom is linked to Jacob's loss of her. In other words, once she has left his sphere of influence to become a "big name," a trademark public persona, her coined name assumes the freewheeling power of an animated, unleashed signifier. Jenny's fame would have been unfairly hoarded were Jacob to have continued to claim her as a vehicle solely for his own frustrated longings. Though Jenny's perfumer may be intended to "imprison ecstasy in a bottle," her Pygmalion must uncap and (democratically) distribute the "ecstasy" of her essence.

Working-Class Women: Status and Performativity

Was the quality of this essence itself predetermined? Is this an aristocracy of sentiment, where some sort of inherent, buried value provides Jenny with the liberty to circulate upward (with proper tutelage), while her damned, sleazy sister must remain forever "cheap"? Little Jenny, who starts out screaming "Geeze!" whenever she's displeased, turns out to have a substantial storehouse of latent classiness, ready to manifest itself under the proper conditions:

> He watched in her the awakening of a sharply individual temperament. She liked quiet and simple things. She was developing the capacity to discriminate and shut the trivial and inessential out of her life. He . . . brought her into contact with a variety of men. He made situations and explained them to her, and he was pleased, as appreciation and politeness began to blossom before his eyes. (358)

This movement, depicted by Fitzgerald as a flowering both moral and aesthetic, is primarily a rejection of one set of class indicators (devalued) for another (privileged). Mythologized in many a piece of "makeover" magazine fiction, this "blossoming" of refinement apparently cannot be counted on. In his diatribe against models, directed to advertisers at J. Walter Thompson in 1928 and quoted earlier in this chapter, Edward Steichen's inability to define the insoluble problem that these models create finally gives way to a hint that the concern is one of class: "I have advocated for a long time at *Vogue,* that more effort be made . . . to get society women to pose for the photographs . . . [since] they wear clothes more logically. A great many models are very lovely girls, but when they are dressed up . . . they don't feel into the clothes."[37] Some clarity returns to Steichen's rambling speech as he remarks, in essence, that the trace of one's origins is indelible, and typically, one simply cannot masquerade social status successfully.

The pivotal question about beautification's impact on status was this: was its promise one of democratic class leveling or merely of a more or less effective imitation of the upper class? Ads from the twenties propound both a slavish mimicry of the rich (posited in the ubiquitous society testimonials as an inborn yearning in all but the elite), and a more populist insistence that "it is not so much a matter of beauty with different classes of girls as it is how they are fixed up."[38] In a positively valenced study of working-class fashion in the 1930s, Angela Partington argues that class positioning does indeed impact the way women dress and adorn themselves, but not always along the classist lines that Steichen presumes. She notes that fashion modes (like cultural praxis more generally) have often trickled *up*, and that working-class women have frequently chosen not to select a "poor (wo)man's" approximation of upper-class tastes, but have consciously, and knowledgeably, followed another aesthetic path in their adornment and personal affect.[39] While Fitzgerald's "Jenny Prince" is pleased to accrue the benefits that her "remake" proffers, not all working-class women considered fashion or self-fashioning as processes of simulating the rich.

"Jacob's Ladder" first appeared on August 20, 1927, in the *Saturday Evening Post,* a tremendously popular journal that Roland Marchand terms "the nation's advertising showcase" (7), and that was bulked up with advertising copy by the mid-twenties to over 200 pages per issue. The classic "makeover" progression that Fitzgerald depicts in "Jacob's Ladder" was fitting for magazine fiction that itself rubbed shoulders with cosmetic ads. "Our Own Movie Queen," a story by Zelda and F. Scott Fitzgerald published four years prior, asks questions about the limits of such cross-class traversal, and invokes an antagonism about social power that does not dissolve into "atmosphere" as the story progresses. This story, which first appeared in the *Chicago Sunday Tribune,* was a somewhat strained collaboration, and it is included in anthologies of each of the Fitzgeralds' work. As Matthew J. Bruccoli explains in Zelda Fitzgerald's *Collected Writings,* "Movie Queen" was originally "published as by F. Scott Fitzgerald, but Fitzgerald's *Ledger* notes: 'Two thirds by Zelda. Only my climax and revision.' "[40] The broadly comedic quality of this story could be read as a painfully elitist "buffooning" of its working-class protagonists, but partly because of this boisterous humor, it can also be viewed as a transgressive commentary on commodity culture's "business as usual."[41] As heroine Gracie Axelrod moves from the normally unattended role of consumer to the public visibility of the vehicle, her performance evokes with unusual clarity the fissures in the fabric of commodity culture, particularly those strains where gender and class dynamics intersect.

Squeamishly, parodically, but without question, the story places Gracie in the "lower classes." She works in her father's "tumbledown shanty" of a fried chicken joint, surrounded by the "sodden bad taste," stockyards, and railroad yards of New Heidleberg, Minnesota.[42] The story pits this "full-blown," "flaxen-haired" (274) young woman against "Mr. Blue Ribbon" (275), owner of the Blue Ribbon Department Store and one of the richest men in town. From the start, her mode of taking in the spectacles he produces suggests that hers will not be a blank, generic consumption of myth, entirely in accord with the advertiser's intentions. In *The Practice of Everyday Life*, Michel de Certeau discusses the difference between "the production of the image and the secondary production hidden in the process of its utilization" by the consumer, heralding as a form of "poaching" the "dispersed, tactical, and makeshift creativity" of consumption as it is actually practiced.[43] Such creative and energetic reception is practiced by Gracie even prior to her memorable experience as a "vehicle," which becomes the focus of the tale. Apparently, Mr. Blue Ribbon is well versed in the marketing philosophy initiated by P. T. Barnum, who used both home and holiday—in fact, any site or occurrence—as a possible means for publicity.[44] Blue Ribbon is introduced into the narrative through a description of his ornate home, wheich boasts "a huge electric sign" declaring "Merry Christmas" (275); Gracie's father is introduced as he sits draped in a full-page newspaper ad for the Blue Ribbon store, which uses its holiday greeting as a venue to announce a sale. When Mr. Axelrod comments that the magnate "must be worth a good lot of money," Gracie displays a vigorous skepticism, "demand[ing], . . . 'Who says so?'" (275). On reflection, she waxes strategic: "B'lieve me, I'd just as soon marry a man like that. Then you could just walk in the store and say gimme this or gimme that and you wouldn't have to pay nothing for 'em" (275).[45]

"Our Own Movie Queen" articulates the normally unmarked "poiesis" of consumption because it deals with a consumer who has been turned vehicle, and thereby allowed a more overt—and unruly—expression of her interpretive stance.[46] Gracie's brush with fame begins with an image of border crossing that intimates the violence of her eventual, transgressive move from the consumer to vehicle position: "No wonder Gracie was as surprised and disconcerted as if she had been caught breaking his huge plate glass window when Mr. Blue Ribbon himself walked into the shack, demanding, in a loud and supercilious voice, chicken that was all white meat" (275). This figurative crashing of the store window as a foreshadowing of the consumer's impending crossover to the role of vehicle can fruitfully remind us of Rachel Bowlby's window-shopper. Again, Bowlby's gazer endures a gnawing sense of lack as she identifies with the mannequin through the glass, fully aware that the mannequin is augmented with commodities that she herself has (not yet) got. Gracie looks to annihilate that lack, that longing, that gap; she goes to work at the Blue Ribbon, planning in advance to take advantage of the wealth there without conscripting herself to the confines of business fealty. She declares to her stodgy supervisor: "I'd get what I wanted cheap and then quit. . . . How do you know I wouldn't quit . . . ? I guess I can quit if I want to quit" (276). Her insistence that her will is neither fathomed nor subsumed by the Blue Ribbon enterprise leads her manager to dub her "Miss Quit" (278), and this "anti-title," arising so completely out of her own resistance, provides an ironic counterpoint as the plot unfolds.[47]

For Gracie's addition to the floor staff of the Blue Ribbon comes serendipitously just as elections are being held for the new "Grand Popularity Queen," a contest hosted most centrally by the Blue Ribbon Department Store and designed, like all true "pseudo-events," to garner publicity for the companies that back it.[48] Mr. Blue Ribbon has declared behind closed doors that "the jane that represents this store wins the whole contest" (277). Through a voting process that the Fitzgeralds depict as more flukey than democratic, Gracie wins the store vote, and thus, Miss Quit becomes Popularity Queen.

But will this lucky break bring Gracie the kind of gain and advancement she hopes for? Her social rise would require a marshaling of sexual and vehicular agency toward her own ends. Is this considered "punishable" hubris according to the class logic of the Fitzgeralds' narrative? Since they involve a class crossing, such endeavors are generally dismissed, laughed away as ungainly. A 1922 J. Walter Thompson newsletter prefaced a letter from a would-be testimonial model with the jocular headline, "All This for $50!" The letter writer, a bit of a Gracie Axelrod herself, had seen a testimonial campaign about the complexion benefits of Fleischmann's yeast.[49]

> Gentlemen: Seeing your ad in the post and being considered a Louisville beauty with complexion like a baby's skin . . . I offer you one of my photos for fortune's sake to use as Calendars sent broadcast, throughout

the U.S.A. They are of a "wonderful marked personality seldom seen critics declare," strength of character, and sweetness of expression both instantly seen and great intelligence. . . . Few people seem to know about your yeast that I have spoken to. . . . The picture if retained will cost you $50 only, a modest sum for such a picture. . . . I await your reply.[50]

The writer parrots back many of the advertisers' own moves, attempting, just as do they, to alchemize desire and image into cash. Clumsy but plucky, she (or he?) differs from the advertisers more in finesse than strategy. The heroics of the spirited climber, Horatio Alger–style, are less likely to be celebrated in American popular narratives when the striver is a woman, especially if her bag of tricks includes the self-marketing of feminine charm. By contrast, as we have seen, when that charm can be "coaxed to the surface" by some Svengali-from-above (a lab-coated cosmetician with a product line to sell or an intuitive highbrow lover), popular discourse applauds the process as a "makeover."

In "Our Own Movie Queen," the newly crowned Popularity Queen soon learns the limits of her carnival reign. Humiliating technical difficulties and a decided lack of adulation from the crowd plague Gracie's participation in the winter festival parade. Her real disappointment, though, comes at the preliminary screening of her movie debut, when she discovers that her work as "an early Queen of New Heidleberg" (284) only appears in the prologue, and that Miss Virginia Blue Ribbon, daughter of the magnate, is the picture's true star. Described as "a modern young girl in a fur coat" and listed in the movie titles as "representing the Queen of Today" (285), Virginia is this story's "New Woman," heralded throughout twenties' popular discourse as the harbinger and symbol of modernity.[51] Since Fitzgerald herself wrote some laudatory (but, as we will see, multivalenced) magazine pieces on this figure of the modern age, it is interesting to note that here the modish young woman is entirely a servant and an extension of the hegemonic powers-that-be, and not at all a challenging or liberating force in the story. Gracie feels furious that the ineffable "je ne sais quoi" of class positioning should hold sway over the election process, furious that, after all, Virginia and not she is to be the "movie queen." "Then rage [gives Gracie] dignity, [gives] her abandon" (285), and she creates an "event" of her own in the crowded foyer, by loudly confronting Mr. Blue Ribbon, zeroing in with deadly accuracy on his primary motivation: the economic. She yells out, "I think the picture was rotten and I wouldn't pay a cent to see anything so rotten as that" (286).

Later that night, with Joe Murphy, the young movie assistant who helps her realize a monumental revenge, she puts her verbal revolt explicitly in terms of consumers' rights and political process: "Wait till the people who elected me queen see what they done to that picture! . . . They'll all get together and never buy nothing more in his store" (287). (Consumer rights organizations led by activists like Stuart Chase and F. J. Schlink that created quite a splash by the early thirties were still only fledgling presences when "Our Own Movie Queen" was penned.)[52] Rather than organize a boycott, however, they join forces with the high-strung, creative, and dissatisfied director of the picture (who probably symbolizes what Scott feared for himself if he continued to work in Hollywood), and sabotage/recreate the film.[53] At the public performance of *New Heidleberg, the Flowery City of the Middle West,* the audience slowly discerns that the movie has been tampered with, wildly, and that Gracie has been made its star. And the Blue Ribbon Store, so far an enterprise that has monopolized access to media production for its own interests, has been made the movie's target, its laughing stock. Hilariously makeshift new pioneer scenes have been spliced in, shots of Virginia's face have been sliced out, and new titles have been added, such as

MISS GRACE AXELROD LOOKS THINNER HERE

BECAUSE SHE'S GOT ON A BETTER CORSET

THAN YOU COULD EVER BUY AT THE BLUE

RIBBON STORE. (290)

This vehicle's uproarious, revolutionary grasping of the reins of production revivifies an audience of popular culture that is normally encouraged to watch in mute passivity. As they watch, the astounded audience "gasps," "snickers," "whispers," "buzzes," "roars," and finally engages in the "pandemonium" of a "crazed howl" for "More Gracie!" (290–91). This giving of voice to the usually silent consuming class from which Gracie herself has sprung may be the coup de grâce (as it were) of her vehicular insurrection.

"Our Own Movie Queen" ends just a paragraph or two after this climactic scene. We learn that the film director ultimately continues with a lucrative career, that Joe Murphy marries Gracie, and that Gracie herself sinks back into the role of consumer, maintaining an energetic and "cynical" interpretation of all that she so avidly consumes. Essentially, the status quo reestablishes itself. But in their portrayal of the crowd's eruption during Gracie's forcible grab at stardom, the Fitzgeralds invoke the lively though hidden work of "poaching," or creative reception, that their protagonist personifies and that is part of everyday consumption.[54]

"Something Special" and Self-Commodification

Nella Larsen's 1928 novel, *Quicksand,* provides a far more ominous view of commodity culture's impact on gendered and racial identity. The protagonist of this story seems readier to question and reject the various communities through which she moves than the material culture to which she so earnestly cathects. Helga Crane is a restless young woman of mixed Scandinavian and African American descent, casting about unsuccessfully for a context that will anchor her, traveling from the Deep South to Chicago to New York to Copenhagen, and finally, to the South and an enveloping maternity that approximates death. Often (and appropriately) considered in the light of the Harlem Renaissance movement from which it sprung, this book can also be grouped fruitfully with the texts discussed here, and read, as Hazel V. Carby proposes, as "a conscious narrative of a woman embedded within capitalist social relations."[55] Helga consumes (even when she cannot afford it), self-commodifies, and interprets her own drama and subjectivity through the lens provided by commodity culture.

There are valuable linkages between *Quicksand* and Zelda Fitzgerald's *Save Me the Waltz,* treated in the next chapter. Both texts were received, to a degree, as "failed" novels, marred by weak endings[56]—and both authors had lives also commonly interpreted in the same manner. (Zelda Fitzgerald struggled with mental illness from 1930 until her death in a fire at an asylum in 1948. Larsen, shocked by a well-publicized 1930 accusation of plagiarism, left both writing and the limelight behind, and resumed a nursing career, dying in obscurity in 1964.)[57] Each book's project regarding commodity culture and subjectivity illuminates and recasts these "failures" as social commentary. Ann duCille has remarked of Larsen's (and Jessie Fauset's) work that it deserves recouping, as it treats "some of the most significant social contradictions of the modern era, including the questions of black female agency, cultural authenticity, and racial and sexual iconography."[58] As we will see, both *Quicksand* and *Waltz* shed much light on the connection between shame and pleasure. In a related vein, each book handles the topic of female rivalry with great subtlety, in a way that speaks directly to advertising's simultaneous manufacture and incitement of sexual desire and anxiety.

Perhaps most obviously, *Quicksand*, like *Save Me the Waltz*, is a novel studded with eroticized descriptions of commodities, and of the women who buy and utilize them in their gendered performance. The textual character of Helga Crane could be said to be forged in part out of those fetishized descriptions, though Larsen also inscribes Helga's uneasy negotiations with the problematic of self-commodification. Larsen's language seems to disperse Helga's subjectivity: it resides simultaneously and refractedly in her accumulation and display of gendered commodities, her various acts of presentation, and her resistance to them. Importantly, when the novel comes closest—in moments—to epiphany, it is via a mutation, rather than a rejection, of the aesthetic sense and female rivalry that have most typified Helga's immersion in commodity culture.

As Hazel V. Carby states, Helga "define[s] a self through the acquisition of commercial products" (172). Larsen's novel, however, like Fitzgerald's, goes on to thematize and critique the consumer culture approach to identity construction in which it participates. For one, *Quicksand* hooks Helga's aesthetic refinements rather firmly to an economic framework: the issue of money, not candy coated as it is in ads, is worried to the bone here, with Helga struggling variously to acquire it or discount its impact on her life and identity.

Also, *Quicksand* problematizes commodity culture's domination of the principle of desire. Over and over, the text repeats two litanies: Helga loves and must have "things, things, things" (67), and she is plagued perpetually by the nagging conviction that a "nameless" "something" is missing from her life (10).[59] As Deborah E. McDowell has pointed out, it becomes increasingly clear that the "something" that eludes Helga so maddeningly is her own sexuality.[60] The "things" she yearns for less inchoately are commodities. These two desires intertwine and stand in for one another in a way that suggests both the shaping influence of commodity culture and desire's own laboring against the economically structured confines that may have helped to formulate it.

Helga is not just a consumer; she is a vehicle as well, playing carefully with racial and sexual self-presentation in the face of various groups' expectations of her. Supposedly a synecdochical representative for, alternately, "the top tenth," "African exotica," "scarlet" womanhood, and Christian virtue, Helga searches in vain for a good fit. Her restlessness, which stems partly from unresolved feelings about race and sexuality, and partly from the unsatisfactory nature of the various communities open to her, is also due to the "burdens of reflecting":

the detachment, vertigo, fatigue, and kinetic discontent that so often accompany the vehicular performance.

This discontent triggers the rebellious departures around which the book is structured. The rebellions are doomed, though. The hegemony of the commercial is above all one of cultural definition. As a result, Helga's "uprisings," her struggles against the restrictions of the communities through which she moves, are themselves confined: the language and vision of individuality available to her are born of commodity culture, what Stuart Ewen describes as "mass-produced visions of individualism by which people could extricate themselves from the mass."[61] Advertising having largely cornered the market on key concepts like "beauty," "desire," and "self-expression," both Helga's yearning and her sense of self are circumscribed to the arena of the commodity. The book's fleeting glimmers of an alternate view of both individuality and racial community, never fully realized in Helga's life story, seem dependent first and foremost on an unmooring of both aesthetics and desire from the consumeristic base that normally defines them for her.

The first two paragraphs of *Quicksand* make clear Helga's love of objects and her (self-) objectification. In the first paragraph, Larsen describes Helga's lodging, "furnished with rare and intensely personal taste," with a sensually fixated attention to the details of color.[62] The second paragraph places Helga's beauty on a material and qualitative continuum with that of her furniture and clothes, encouraging not subject identification, but a voyeuristic objectification:

> An observer would have thought her well-fitted to that framing of light and shade. . . . In vivid green and gold negligee and glistening brocaded mules, deep sunk in the big high-backed chair, against whose dark tapestry her sharply cut face, with skin like yellow satin, was distinctly outlined, she was—to use a hackneyed word—attractive. (2)

Advertisers, always eager that the set of commodities intended to radiate information about their owner's character should proliferate, theorized to one another and in their copy about a woman's home being an extension of herself. A 1937 article directed at copywriters explains that the typical female firmly believes that she "must *improve herself.* As she grows older, 'herself' will come to mean not only her person, but her 'setting' . . . her home."[63] In *Quicksand*'s opening passage, Helga is "set" in her room, but she is "well-fitted" to it, rather than vice versa. From her spot "deep sunk" in the upholstered chair, the "yellow satin" of Helga's skin finds its place amid the "vivid" greens, the "glistening" brocades, and the "dark" tapestries around her, providing one more shade and texture to complement the rest of the decor.

Immediately, the book has "sunk" us "deep" into a discourse of fetishized commodities, as well as commodified race and femininity. Some of the novel's readership (past and present) are themselves likely to experience the strange splitting off of subjectivity so familiar to females in commodity culture, a splitting off that also troubles Helga throughout the book. Envying the clothes, the furniture, the "rare" taste and "sensuous," "delightful" physical features of the heroine, about which the text lavishes such meticulous praise, a portion of such a reader's attention peels off from the plotline. Whether taking in descriptions of "a shivering apricot frock" (60), "pale yellow pajamas of *crepe de Chine*" (56), or curls that "stray in a little wayward, delightful way" (2), this segment of the reader's attention, with a covetous hunger, applies itself to sheer yearning.[64]

Again, this opulently layered, seductive portrayal of "things, things, things" (and of a "thingified" Helga) seems to participate in the aesthetic lexicon of the advertising industry, whereby myriad commodities stand guard around the feminine consumer, each revealing facets of her unfathomable personality and assisting her in her endeavor toward beauty.[65] This is from a Pond's ad that ran nationally in *Harper's Bazaar* in the year of *Quicksand*'s release:

> Lady Lavery, famous beauty, has a gorgeous dressing table with a priceless Venetian mirror hanging over pink ruffles, quaint Chelsea candlesticks and jars of Pond's Two Creams and Skin Freshener. What dressing table does not reflect the personality of its owner? It mirrors her taste, her discriminations, her little indulgences. . . . It is eloquent of her very self![66]

It is safe to presume that "Lady Lavery" is white. Helga, too, is apparently well-versed in a cultural vocabulary that presupposes a white consumer-citizen, and suppresses or insults any other racial presence. For the most part, *Quicksand* does not overtly depict Helga consuming mainstream popular culture; we certainly never see her reading *Harper's Bazaar*. It is through Helga's oft-stated hunger for commodities, and Larsen's own reverential copylike catalogings of beautiful "things," that we come to understand Helga's engagement with that culture. In one passage, however, advertisements are mentioned, their rosy promise linked explicitly to Helga's cyclic, heady hopes for a refurbished future: "With her decision she felt reborn. She began happily to paint the future in vivid colors. . . . [L]ife ceased to be a struggle and became a gay adventure. Even the advertisements in the shop windows seemed to shine with radiance" (36).

But are these ads supposed to be shining for Helga? Roland Marchand describes trade journals manifestly excluding Black Americans from "consumer citizenship," due to their assumed lack of purchasing power.[67] Opinions like these led to minimal national advertising in Black newspapers such as the *Chicago Defender* and *Pittsburgh Courier*, Marchand says. Still, African Americans were living with and responding to advertising and its claims about reality, both to national advertising that was part of the landscape of their lives even when it implicitly "overlooked" them, and to the more localized Black-directed advertising campaigns that Kathy Peiss details.[68]

Paul K. Edwards's 1932 attempt to identify (and advertise) an undertapped market, *The Southern Urban Negro as a Consumer*, charts comprehensively the shrewd disdain felt by African American consumers of all classes for stereotypic slurs against Black figures in national ads.[69] With the greatest eloquence, Edwards's participants reject images common to advertising like the "Black mammy" housemaid, the shuffling old handyman, and the grinning "pickaninny." Seen by these consumers as sexless, undignified, unattractive, and powerless, these characters are dismissed out of hand as insults.[70] Not at all gullible or complacent about representations of African Americans in ads, Edwards's respondents seem more ready to accept advertising's founding correlations between happiness and consumption. Edwards quotes them as preferring ads that feature African American models embarking on a Black-inflected version of the same odyssey toward consumerist "self-improvement" that the white-directed ad campaigns depict for their readers.

> The comment made by the majority who found [the two approved advertisements] particularly pleasing was that here were illustrations which pictured the Negro as he really is, not caricatured, degraded, or made fun of; that here the Negro was dignified and made to look as he is striving to look, and not as he looked in antebellum days; that here was the new Negro. (251)

Ironically, one of the two advertisements is for a skin bleach, and the other features a woman with straightened hair and a heavily powdered face. Larsen reveals a similar contrariety in her description of upper-middle-class, African American socialite Anne Grey: "She hated white people with a deep and burning hatred . . . [b]ut she aped their clothes, their manners, and their gracious ways of living. . . . Theoretically, however, she stood for the advancement of all things Negroid" (48–49). Larsen's passage illustrates rather bitterly the paradox of Anne's rejection of African American culture. Yet it also evokes Anne's solid support for the "advancement" of her race. Likewise, one of the two "pleasing" ads lauded by Edwards's respondents is for a skin powder produced by the Black-run Madame Walker Company; this exemplifies that category of ads featuring Black "vehicles" who represent not only African American beauty, but also African American business. Here, respondents mingle the hunger for consumerist "self-improvement" with a rather different drive for community advancement.

Kathy Peiss details the emergence of a Black beauty culture "in which profit-making was intertwined with larger ethical and political purposes" (Peiss 1998, 90). For Madame C. J. Walker, beauty entrepreneurship meant a reliance on and strengthening of alliances and networks between African American women. Her vision of commerce was aligned with a race aesthetics that countered the equation of white features and skin tone with beauty: she refused to sell skin bleach (89). By the twenties, though (Walker having died in 1919), her company had joined the many, both Black- and white-run, companies that sold skin bleach to African Americans. During this period, "cosmetics and toiletries, including bleaches and straighteners, accounted for 30 to 40 percent of black newspaper advertising" (210), and the ads themselves increasingly employed "perfumed language" and glamorous images of beauty consumers that were largely "interchangeable with those of white women's beauty promoted in mass-circulation magazines" (217–18).

It would appear that both Anne and the respondents in Edwards's survey "buy" the aesthetics of the dominant culture. This stance, so irritating to Helga in *Quicksand,* was only one part of a vivid, prickly, and complex dialogue in the Black press about race, gender, commerce, and beauty. Peiss argues that ultimately "African-American manufacturers, newspapers, tastemakers, and consumers defined hair and skin preparations in ways that limited and resisted the charge of white emulation" (210–11). Significantly, understanding a "white"-coded aesthetics as an avenue for economic betterment for the Black community, the Black audience could respond to the (Althusserian) "hailing" of the individual consumer-subject along different lines than had been anticipated, honoring an allegiance alluded to in Black-produced ads, but never purposefully invoked by the dominant culture.

In distinction to Anne and most of the other people around her, Helga finds community allegiance stressful and beyond her grasp. Her search for community may be as frustrated as it is because her model for individual participation is vehicular: all Helga's efforts to "fit in" entail her not merely joining a social group, but inhabiting a representational role within it. At Naxos she is a teacher, and implicit in her position at this Tuskegee-like institution is that she must function as a role model for her backwoods students. In Harlem, she joins the model household of activist socialite Anne, and must enact her participation in "the talented tenth." In the pivotal, late scene at the storefront church where a desperate Helga converts to Christianity, she is perceived by all the churchgoers as representative of fallen womanhood. The conversion of "a scarlet 'oman . . . a poor los' Jezebel" provides the climax to the narrative flow of the evening service (112). And finally, in the Alabama town to whence she repairs with her new husband to make a home, Helga, of course, finds another showcase where she is expected to exude all the seemliness and Christian propriety that is appropriate for the wife of a reverend.

But it is in Copenhagen that Helga's social "work" seems most completely vehicular. She flees to Denmark midway through the book, imagining that "the race problem" will no longer "creep in" (52), that there she will be "appreciated" and "understood" (57).[71] With this attempt at escape from race itself through the rejection of one race, Helga makes her most concerted grab at the mode of individuality touted by consumer culture, a "personality" that is disengaged from the identifying marks of community and can be "reflected" instead in one's (theoretically idiosyncratic) display of commodities.[72]

In Denmark, though, Helga's own penchant for showy self-presentation is caricatured and made grotesque. Called a "decoration" (14) back at Naxos, in Copenhagen, Helga feels like "a curiosity, a stunt, at which people came and gazed" (71), an eye-catching advertisement for her relatives' social cachet. These white relatives, who hope her presence will increase their mobility in society circles, cast Helga as an "exotic," dressing her in garish costumes designed to resonate with local mythologies about the erotics of difference. In fact, Helga's physical self—in particular, the characteristics that mark her racially as "other"—"become a trademark," those traits being perceived by her white family as "marketable," and her self becoming less and less apprehendable apart from the recognition of those traits.[73]

Larsen portrays all Helga's social encounters in Copenhagen as staged performances. Helga's initial revulsion against the overdone outfits and incredulity about the theatricality of her "posing" gives way, for a time: "She was incited to make . . . a voluptuous impression . . . to inflame attention and admiration. She was dressed for it, subtly schooled for it. And after a while she gave herself up wholly to the fascinating business of being seen, gaped at, desired" (74). These are the perks of the vehicle's job, presented by Larsen with the tropes of seduction.

If Helga sees her vehicular performance of Blackness as sexually charged, so do the Danes. They chalk the eros up to the characteristics they project onto her because of her race. In Copenhagen, Helga's relatives dress her not only in "barbaric bracelets" (70), but also in risqué outfits designed to expose as much of her flesh as possible. They see her social capital as fundamentally erotic, as becomes more than obvious when her suitor, artist Axel Olsen—intermittently dashing, laughable, and repugnant—shocks Helga "with an admirably draped suggestion" (84) not of marriage, but an affair.

Crucially, Helga also sees her sexuality through a racialized lens. Horrified, she describes Axel's painting of her as "some disgusting sensual creature with her features" (89). This response indicates two things simultaneously. First, as is made clear by his objectifying survey of her appearance at their first meeting, Axel is influenced by the racist stereotype of the sexual Black female. His aestheticization of this stereotype intensifies rather than mitigates its offense, allowing him to reflect on Helga as a series of amputated body parts: " 'Superb eyes . . . color . . . neck column . . . alive . . . wonderful.' His speech was for Fru Dahl . . . he lingered before the silent girl, whose smile had become a fixed aching mask, still gazing appraisingly, but saying no word to her" (71). Second, Helga is influenced by the same mythos. She siphons her own sexual energy into the vessel of that stereotype in an attempt to excise and exile it. Giving voice to Helga's thoughts, the novel twice repeats that "anyone with half an eye could see that [the portrait] wasn't at all like her. . . . Yes, anyone with half an eye could see that it wasn't she" (89). As becomes increasingly evident, *half eyes*, which Helga tries so hard to cultivate for herself, are exactly the problem in this book about suppressed longings and splintered identity.

I link Helga's function as vehicle to the rather confusing correspondence the novel sets up between her repressed sexuality and racial identity. The "lack somewhere" that Deborah E. McDowell attributes to the realm of sexuality, critics like Lillie P. Howard ascribe to Helga's inability to "approve of her Blackness."[74] Both are right: the novel thematizes the challenges in identity formation for a middle-class African American woman steeped in a popular culture that conflates Blackness and sexuality, projecting both onto the figure of the "primitive."[75] Accustomed to understanding herself in terms of her representational and decorative function, Helga is particularly apt to perceive her own unarticulated longings through such an external lens.

During the period of gradual disenchantment with her life in Denmark, Helga goes again and again to a vaudeville house, "the Circus," to see two African American men singing ragtime, "prancing," and "throwing their bodies about with a loose ease" (83). She feels ashamed by her strong sense of association with their physicality, even as she reviles the performers' caricatured depiction of their race and the distasteful connoisseurship of the "pale pink and white" (83) spectators, to whom she is as connected by "blood" as to the dancers.[76] The (rather vile) erotics of this situation, as with her own social performances in Copenhagen, stem more from the fact of the spectacle of minstrelsy—performativity and masquerade itself—than from any of the qualities being presented as inherently "African."

As discussed by Lawrence Levine in "Jazz and American Culture," "jazz" functioned in the twenties as a cultural node that encapsulated the "dark" halves of all sorts of "high/low" binaries.[77] One overblown contemporaneous treatment of the equation between jazz and primitive sexuality was Lynn Montross's story, "Bass Drums," from the best-selling 1923 collection of white, middle-class "fluff" tales, *Town and Gown*. In a move typical of the period, this story suppresses the issue of racial difference by replacing Negroes with "Negroid" passion, by making the binary one of head/groin, or elders/youth, rather than white/Black.[78] When Helga responds with pleasure to the jazz she hears at a Harlem club, she brands the pleasure as an illicit one and recoils from her own sensual delight:

> She was drugged, lifted, sustained, by that extraordinary music. . . . The essence of life seemed bodily motion. And when suddenly the music died, she dragged herself back to the present with . . . a shameful certainty that not only had she been in the jungle, but she had enjoyed it. . . . She hardened her determination to get away. She wasn't, she told herself, a jungle creature. She cloaked herself in a faint disgust. (59)

Here, clothes "cloak" rather than seduce, protecting her from the "jungle" as would "hardened" armor, or disguising the jungle in her, at any rate, from the scrutiny of others. Of course, the racializing of sexuality (and the sexualizing of race) behind this censure of jazz is a cultural conflation deeply rooted in

American history.[79] McDowell reminds us that even in this "Jazz Age" notorious for its permissiveness, Black women authors were not at all forthcoming about sexuality, precisely as a cautionary response to tenacious and damaging racist stereotypes about the lasciviousness of the African American female (xiii).[80] By treating the theme of a Black woman's sexual desire, Larsen broke rank with more than a generation of prominent African American women who had insisted on their right to respectability and the privileges of citizenship that come along with it. Larsen's book suggests that the suppression of sexuality that had begun among the women activists of the post-Reconstruction era, though linked to a claiming of public voice, bore its own cost.[81]

Insistent that she is not "a jungle creature," Helga tries to dissociate herself from her sexuality. When a sole kiss with Robert Anderson—now married to Anne Grey—finally topples Helga over into cognizance and acceptance of her own sexual desire, for a brief period, the "something" that has been plaguing her throughout the story is coming to consciousness and even being welcomed as "special" (108). Significantly, Larsen breaks with the conventions of the romance by having her protagonist think "not so much of the man whose arms had held her as of the ecstasy which had flooded her" (105). The essential event in her mind is not the winning of male attention, but the unleashing of her own "voluptuous visions" and "irrepressible longing" (106). Even after the rebuff and the mortified "self-loathing" it induces, she is not attracted to the total annihilation of suicide, as she does not want to be "reduced to unimportance" (108–9).

This hint of an emergent celebration of sexuality is too ephemeral and unsupported to withstand Anderson's rejection of her, and his retreat into conventional morality and a "successful" yet passionless marriage. Itself shaped by the paradigm under discussion, this rejection has the effect of driving Helga toward the less tolerable, more "bestial" responses to the "something" that comprise the book's last third, responses that Helga winds up judging as inherently "lowly" even while indulging them. Having lost the possibility of "real" love with someone her intellectual equal who works for advancement of her race, she moves instead toward the "Bacchic vehemence" (113) of storefront Christianity, a marriage lacking in communication, and an insulated life of pseudopropriety, all because of its legitimization of sexual praxis.

The dominant culture's ideas about decency and refinement—as energetically disseminated by the advertising industry—have influenced both Helga's choices and the values of the African American "uplift" communities that Helga finds so confining.[82] Painfully, Helga's attempts to reject the restrictions of these communities that disappoint her are inevitably disappointments themselves, also governed by an equally restricting circumscription of both yearning and selfhood to the arena of the commodity.

Although her vehicularization reaches its dehumanized nadir in Copenhagen, Helga finds restrictive and inadequate the other roles that she takes on over the course of the book. Forced to understand her own identity in terms of representational capacity, she is restless. Throughout *Quicksand,* Helga comes detached from the spheres into which she enters; in fact, the book is structured by these disengagements. Each getaway and new beginning exhilarates her. And yet, each community that admits her winds up seeming like a quagmire (her upper limit is about two years). Deepening attachments and demands for commitment fill her with dismay, as at Naxos when she first feels stirred by Anderson's calls for her service.[83] As a vehicle who would otherwise be seamlessly synchronous with her representational work, Helga experiences her detachability as the surest manifestation of her individuality. The novel depicts this conviction as serving her poorly, making intimate relations impossible for her. In Copenhagen, "she managed . . . to retain that air of remoteness which had been in America so disastrous to her friendships. Here . . . it was merely a little mysterious and added another clinging wisp of charm" (74). Note that she doesn't even hope for real intimacy, just the deployment for gain of her isolating techniques.

On several occasions, the text articulates the discourse of individualism that informs her wrestings loose from social grips: Naxos, "a machine," "tolerated no innovations, no individualisms" (4). She explains her resignation to Anderson by saying that the spirit of their work there requires the "suppression of individuality and beauty" (20). And later, in Copenhagen, Helga's aunt rather disingenuously argues that racial restrictions, like those that make miscegenation inadvisable, don't apply "in connection with individuals" (78). Hazel V. Carby suggests that this strain in the book is a prerequisite of the romance, one which *Quicksand* shows to be inherently lacking through its portrayal of Helga's resultant restlessness and suffering: "Helga's [lone] search [for individual selfhood] led to the burial, not the discovery of self. . . . The question that remains is, to what social group does Helga attach herself in order to be saved?" (Carby 1987, 173).

Something is wrong in *Quicksand,* and the community solutions that present themselves, Black and white, can't help Helga. Significantly, nor can an isolated search for selfhood, as Carby claims the romance would dictate. In light of the novel's copious borrowings from the language of "copy," Helga's search "for individuality and beauty," though, seems as determined by the discourse of advertising as the conventions of literature. It is this quest that advertisements insist is the feminine shopper's first mission, as she hunts for commodities "eloquent of her very self."[84] And, as Frank Presbrey wrote in his laudatory history of the industry, "advertising is probably our greatest agency for spreading an understanding and love of beauty in all things" (611).

Over the course of *Quicksand,* Helga makes various efforts to unhook her own strong aesthetic sensibility—her variant of "individuality and beauty"—from its consumeristic, economic base. Some of these efforts, ultimately failures, appear one with advertising's suppression of the fact that consumer choice always involves *expenditure.* In cahoots with the advertising address, Helga would like to "look the other way" while she makes her purchases. "Knowing full well that [money] was important, [Helga] nevertheless rebelled at the unalterable truth that it could influence her actions, block her desires. With Helga it was almost a superstition that to concede to money its importance magnified its power" (6). Yet, after a spree, Helga is "frightened" by "the fact that she had spent money, too much money, for a book and a tapestry purse, things that she wanted, but did not need and certainly could not afford" (32). Helga's "superstition" has by no means reduced the centrality of the economic in her life; it has only made it possible for her to spend first, and regret later.

Helga's initial denial of money's impact actually facilitates consumerist practices; an eventual repudiation of "things" in toto is far too sweeping to last. With her final dramatic lifestyle shift, Helga attempts her most comprehensive rejection of material acquisition. After her conversion experience and marriage to the Reverend Pleasant Green, Helga moves to her husband's parish in a "tiny Alabama town" (118). Explaining this shift to herself, she declares: "All I've ever had in my life has been things—except just this one time. . . . Things, she realized, hadn't been, weren't enough for her" (116). Two aspects of this rejection mitigate its force. First, the ostensible claiming of Christian virtue that structures this relinquishment of the material is subsumed within another claiming—of access to sex. Helga leaves behind "things" in return, not so much for "godliness" (108), as for the "something special" (122) that is her own sexuality, spat on by Anderson, but allowed legitimate expression every night in her marriage to the reverend. Second, her renunciation fails. The book concludes with her longing in vain for "clothes and books, . . . the sweet mingled smell of Houbigant and cigarettes . . . all these, agreeable, desired things" (135).

But if the novel finds her options for community identification genuinely lacking—*and* her chase after "self-expression" intolerably isolating, materialist, and lonely—what does it offer as an alternative? Nothing for Helga; her story is a tragedy, as has been duly noted. In its depiction of this chain of events, the novel details the effects of commodity culture on constructions of gender, race, and subjectivity, and the effects, too, of society's mythic equation of sex and Blackness in the lived lives of its characters. Deborah E. McDowell has criticized the novel for its ultimate failure to "escape" the "repressive standards of sexual morality" it analyzes (xxii). Yes, both character and writer are impacted by the wider cultural confluence of animality, race, and sex (and in general, the economic and cultural forces at work around them), and this impact structures Helga's life story. As Ann duCille submits, we should not fault Larsen for failing to shrug off this confluence. She is inside it, and she does not feign the sort of pseudo-objective stance that would allow her to assert a "transcendent" subjectivity or to stand authoritatively aloof from the structuring paradigm.

There are, however, glimmers in the book of another kind of "individuality and beauty" that Helga, in passing moments, sees as betokening another kind of racial identity and solidarity, one less judgmental and restricting than are the communities Larsen critiques in the novel. During these brief epiphanies, Helga strives to reshape an aesthetics less rooted in the economic and status quo than that which motivates her elsewhere. To the extent that Helga thereby arrives at a positive theory of community—transient and unrealized as it may be—it is one that is linked not only to a re-visioning of the aesthetic realm, but also to a disengaging of the principle of desire from the rubric constructed for it by commodity culture. It is based on "oppositional" cultural practices, to employ Raymond Williams's term, and an aesthetics that could be called polychromatic, as an answer to the construction of race as a Black/white binary—a construction that makes Helga a "tragic" mulatto.[85]

Her love of colors and clothes, extravagantly tabulated in the book, sometimes comes unmoored from the refined, middle-class Black context in which

Helga so often lives, informing instead an expression of "the inherent racial need for gorgeousness":

> One of the loveliest sights Helga had ever seen had been a sooty black girl decked out in a flaming orange dress. . . . Why, she wondered, didn't someone write *A Plea for Color?* These people [working for "uplift"] yapped loudly of . . . race pride, yet suppressed its most delightful manifestations, love of color . . . [h]armony, radiance, and simplicity, all the essentials of spiritual beauty in the race they had marked for destruction. (18)

But despite the vehemence of this plaint, Helga's own taste is reactive, seeming to shift between the refined and bohemian, depending on whom she's identifying with or reacting against. At Naxos, her taste had appeared outlandish: "[The rest of the faculty] felt that the colors were queer. . . . And the trimmings . . . seemed to them odd" (18). When forced to personify savagery à la Copenhagen though, Helga reacts against the garish excess with a retreat to the "impeccably fastidious taste in clothes" (45) that typified Anne Grey. Indeed, she sometimes seems eager to "suppress" the "delightful manifestations" of race. When she first arrives in the Reverend Green's hometown, Helga shares the aesthetic philanthropy of Carol Kennicott, protagonist of Sinclair Lewis's *Main Street,* hoping to "subdue the cleanly scrubbed ugliness of her own surroundings to soft, inoffensive beauty. . . . Too, she would help them with their clothes" (119), which later she describes as gaudily beribboned and bright.[86] Here, Helga embraces the visuals of "uplift" as practiced by the cultivated Anne, at variance with the more sensual hunger for beauty that she expresses elsewhere. Her plans, that would rein in not only the townspeople's aesthetic vision but also Helga's own, quickly evaporate, leaving her at book's end, as we have seen, once again articulating a deep longing for color and "gorgeousness."

These reactive aesthetic swings are symptomatic of the false and unsatisfactory choice with which she is presented throughout the book. Advertising, as the main organ of a dominant culture inextricably tied to the capitalist project, succeeds quite handsomely in monopolizing the definition of concepts like beauty, desire, and selfhood. Should Helga align herself either with commodity culture's version of those things, which binds the sensory pleasure of "personality" with luxury items, and leaves Black community expression out of its mix? Or should she take her place in the "top tenth," which fades Black culture to "grey" as far as Helga is concerned, and (in the universe of this novel) offers her not unconditional membership in a community, but the "burden" of its "reflection"? Are these her options?

Resisting the role of human synecdoche, Helga experiences brief bursts of clarity that enable her to think through her own, quite visceral racial identification. This identification is crucially linked to both her "something" sensuality and a forgiveness of her African American father, whose ancient desertion of her Scandinavian mother has set the stage for the book's predicament. "For the first time, Helga . . . understood . . . [her father's] rejection . . . of the formal calm her mother had represented. She understood his yearning, his intolerable need for the inexhaustible humor and the incessant hope of his own kind. . . . [S]he longed for brown laughing [faces]. . . . [I]t was as if in this understanding and forgiving she had come upon knowledge of almost sacred importance" (92–93). Such moments unfetter desire and sensuality from consumerism, with which they are "intimately connected" throughout most of *Quicksand* (Carby 1987, 174).[87] The "better class" of African Americans with whom Helga is supposed to associate is depicted by Larsen as underimbued with these things (103); again, this is probably largely due to the defensive posture essentially demanded by a dominant society so unwilling to extend respectability to African Americans at all. Anne's "impeccably fastidious" world possesses at least the degree of "formal calm" Helga knew in the home of her white mother.

Helga deeply admires and pays homage to the beauty of Anne and her "things," yet limits her appreciation by articulating a sense of the chilly, nonsensual correctness and rigidity of her tastes. She is disappointed most keenly by Anne's tendency to "ape" white culture, to reject alternative cultural practices in the name of "taste." Anne's very surname hints that her hypocritical commitment to the false divide between races (despite her own cross-cultural borrowing) leaves her neither Black nor white, nor richly redolent of any color—only coolly "grey," an ultimately damning nomenclature in this prismatic novel. Equally or even more unacceptable to Helga is the Danes' "aping" of what they perceive to be the "primitive" through their dressing and painting of her: "Helga felt like a veritable savage" (69). Either masquerade she finds extreme and intolerable; both mark the permeabilities of these large cultural binaries in the very act of denying them, with groups staging unending mock-ups of what they view as "the other side." By contrast, Helga's moments of revelation celebrate the kaleidoscopics of cultural and racial interpenetration.

Color factors into all of Larsen's descriptions of beautiful "things." The first two paragraphs of the book list twelve colors. We hear, for instance, of a black and red lampshade, a blue Chinese carpet, "many-colored" nasturtiums in a "shining brass bowl" (1–2), and a green and gold negligee. Later, still in the throes of jazz appreciation, Helga

> marveled at the gradations within this oppressed race of hers. A dozen shades slid by. There was sooty black, shiny black, taupe, mahogany, bronze, copper, gold, orange, yellow, peach, ivory, pinky white, pastry white. . . . She saw black eyes in white faces, brown eyes in yellow faces, gray eyes in brown faces, blue eyes in tan faces. Africa, Europe, perhaps with a pinch of Asia, in a fantastic motley of ugliness and beauty, semi-barbaric, sophisticated, exotic were here. (59–60)[88]

The sheer proliferation of color names, especially in the context of a book that *loves* color, reveals how Helga's aesthetic sense, once disengaged from the consumeristic base that normally contextualizes it, winds up pointing her toward a vision of community unrealized by the middle-class Blacks, Copenhagen whites, and Deep South Christians with whom she socializes.

The thoughts of a "tragic mulatto," this passage implies that identification with her "oppressed race" is dependent not on bloodlines, but on any touch of hybridity, a "fantastic motley" that retains cultural specificity—this is clearly Harlem—while beginning to seem redolent of the entire globe, of humanity itself. In another revelatory moment of racial identification, she emphasizes, above all, a *multitudinousness* that links race to species, as she expounds on the ties that bind her "forever to these mysterious, these terrible, these fascinating, these lovable, dark hordes. . . . Ties [deeper than] mere outline of features or color of skin" (95). In this brief celebration, Larsen presents a significant challenge to the blunt, exclusionary, artificial, and numbingly pervasive binarization that has structured so much of American thinking about race.

Unfortunately for Helga, her epiphanies never erupt at moments or in forms adequate to the task of transformation. *Quicksand* ultimately immures its heroine in a smothering maternity that promises to be fatal. To some extent, the closing down that occurs at the end of this novel (much like that at the end of Fitzgerald's *Waltz*) could be read as punitive—both the protagonist and reader are chastised for taking too much pleasure along the way. These chastisements and frustrations do not indicate an outmoded Puritanism or a failure of artistic vision so much as a cognizance on the part of Larsen (and Fitzgerald, as we shall see) that pleasure is dangerous, especially the eroticized pleasure of notoriety, and especially for the notorious woman. Larsen, however, does counter Helga's tragedy with an almost flirtatiously tantalizing glimpse at a triumphant, rather than tragic mulatto. In two scenes, Larsen presents Audrey Denny, a risqué, "alabaster"-skinned woman who throws integrated parties and dances with "grace and abandon, . . . [and] obvious pleasure, her legs, her hips, her back, all swaying gently, swung by that wild music from the heart of the jungle" (62). Again, access to the "jungle" apparently depends less on "pure" bloodlines than on an ease with the alternative and hybrid. Anne, claiming that "Negroes ought to stick together," paradoxically wants to "ostracize" this "disgusting creature" (61); Audrey's mixed parties are rendered particularly "obscene" in Anne's eyes because this pale woman who could easily "pass" chooses open integration instead, thereby challenging the integrity of the racial divide along with the binary model of race that it polices, constructs, and upholds. Anne "trembles with cold hatred" (61) in the face of this, while a "greatly interested" (61) Helga passionately defends Audrey and yearns to meet her.

Larsen's descriptions of Audrey are seductive enough to indicate that Helga is drawn not only to the license to sensuality and interaction that Audrey gives herself, but also to Audrey's own person.[89] Ostensibly as a feminine rival, Helga "studies" this iridescent, maverick woman in a "shivering apricot frock," with a "brilliantly red, softly curving mouth," and skin of a "delicately creamy hue, with golden tones" (60–62). They are rivals in feminine spectacle. Both Audrey's appearance and Helga's own grooming and ornamentation for the evening are documented at length, and the two women "compete" for a particular man: it is with the magnetic Anderson that Audrey sits and dances. But her defense of Audrey, tabulation of her appeals, and almost helpless sense of Audrey's draw all suggest that Helga is feeling openly the sexual attraction and piercing connectedness that normally stand unacknowledged behind feminine rivalry. When Audrey and Anderson begin their slow dance, and Helga finds herself gripped by a "primitive emotion" that sends her flying into the night, this dizzying feeling seems triggered in large part by the "envious admiration" for the woman she has "studied" the evening through. Helga's apprehension of her entails a (only partially realized) revaluation (queerification) of the identificatory compulsion that leads Helga to such an absorbed, invested "study."

In this depiction, Larsen portrays female rivalry as laced with and driven by a specific, engaged though covert desire. Anxious, yearning, women watch and imitate one another. According to Judith Butler, when a woman behaves "like a woman" or performs "femininity," she is participating in an act of mimeticism impelled by a sense of loss and separation. Butler usefully connects the impulse toward gendered masquerade with the identificatory impulse of the melancholic (whereby the griever takes into herself and assumes as persona certain identifying elements of the beloved figure): "Identifications are always made in response to loss of some kind, and . . . they involve a certain mimetic practice that seeks to incorporate the lost love within the very identity of the one who remains."[90] Butler suggests that gender performance can be understood as rooted in a merging of identification and desire, arguing that the impulses to *have* and to *be* another person have been artificially segregated by a heterocentric psychoanalytic tradition.[91] By the same token, it is helpful to extend Diana Fuss's comments about fashion photography and homospectatorial looking to Larsen's depiction of the watchful, hungry rivalry between two women:

> Any identification *with* an other is secured through a simultaneous and continuing desire *for* that other. . . . [T]he desire to be like can itself be motivated and sustained by the desire to *possess:* being can be the most radical form of having. Identification may well operate in the end not as a foreclosure of desire but as its most perfect, and most ruthless fulfillment.[92]

It is not merely some primal loss of intimacy with the mother (phallic or otherwise) that structures these identificatory engagements, so threaded with both desire and aggression. Forced into "free market" competition, and away from the possibilities of both lesbian eros and personal intimacy in general, women engaged in "the fascinating business of being seen" must normally swallow and endure the loss . . . *of one another.* Helga yearns to meet Audrey.

In the second of Audrey's scenes, Helga almost does. This failed meeting, aborted by the arrival of the smug, naive James Vayle, could mark the story's true tragic turn. Audrey's color as a character comes from the "assurance" and "courage" that allow her to enact just the things that Helga has struggled with and wondered about throughout the book. Audrey appears to be openly sexual, and even more liberating, "placidly" unconventional. She hovers on the brink of two worlds racially, and refuses to honor a divide that her very being (as a mulatto) belies as false. Apparently, she incurs costs: she has a "deathlike pallor" and a mouth that is "somehow sorrowful" (60). Yet she is triumphantly, "coolly" independent and engaged. With this loss present as an absence in the book, Larsen's "peekaboo" look at a woman embodying the hybrid and committed to alternative cultural practices is the closest that *Quicksand* comes to realizing Helga's epiphanic vision. Diversity, idiosyncrasy, difference, would be givens in the polychromatic community imagined in snatches in Larsen's novel, and for women, membership in such a community would not be predicated on the burden of its reflection.

Chapter 5

In the Tutu or out the Window

Zelda Fitzgerald and the Possibility of Escape

On the cocktail tray, mountains of things represented something else, canapés like goldfish, and caviar in balls, butter bearing faces and frosted glasses sweating with the burden of reflecting such a lot of things to stimulate the appetite to satiety before eating.

—Zelda Fitzgerald, *Save Me the Waltz*

In my new studio you may have a tutu. . . . In its folds, who knows what you may find.

—Zelda Fitzgerald, *Save Me the Waltz*

My mother entered, pale with rage. "We'd just sat down at table," she said, "when that thing sitting in your place got up and shouted, 'So I smell a bit strong, what? Well, I don't eat cakes!' Whereupon it tore off its face and ate it. And with one great bound, disappeared through the window."

—Leonora Carrington, "The Debutante"

Rather like Nella Larsen's *Quicksand*, Zelda Fitzgerald's semiautobiographical novel of 1932, *Save Me the Waltz*, is most often received—and summarily dismissed—as a "flawed" work, interesting not as literature but as a biographical companion piece to Nancy Milford's 1970 *Zelda*. Its first published edition only sold 1,392 copies, and it wasn't rereleased until a small British run came out in 1958.[1] When noticed at all, this novel has been approached as an emblem of feminine subjugation and frustrated artistry rather than an investigation of them.[2] In this chapter, I will argue that the "shortcomings" of *Save Me the Waltz* are not grounds for its dismissal. Instead, they correlate in interesting ways with its thematics. Furthermore, in this novel written largely from a mental hospital, Fitzgerald did succeed in bringing her artistry to the issue of subjugation itself. She created, with remarkable textual effects, a detailed and rather sinister examination of the impact of 1920s' commodity culture on female subjectivity, self-presentation, and desire.[3] And in so doing, she thematizes the sheer physical and psychic work that goes into feminine self-presentation. In the insistent and frequently surprising materiality of her prose, Fitzgerald writes that which is "supposed" to hide unarticulated behind a veneer of leisure and elegance. She engages, in the novel's most exciting moments, in a Bataillean surrealism, writing furiously against the naturalistic determinism that defined much of her husband's literary project. Unlike Georges Bataille's, however, Fitzgerald's "visions of excess" are inextricably linked to her analysis of female subjectivity.

In brief, the book treats the troubled marriage of Alabama and David Knight—two creative, dissipated American expatriates—charting Alabama's ultimately failed attempt to become a serious dancer. Fitzgerald initially toys with a discourse of animated commodities and "thingified" women coined by the advertising industry, illustrating the physical and psychic effects of this objectifying inversion. In the universe of the book's first half, women are expected to "farm out" their appeal, to augment and represent the value of something or someone else. Then, with Alabama's turn to dance midway through the novel, the kinesis of bodily effort strains almost to the breaking point the artificial stasis of the objectified feminine body. Female desire, lurking in the book's first half behind an array of sumptuous, "vivified" commodities, finally becomes explicit at Madame's ballet studio, as the dancers sweat, bleed, curse, and soar, hungering for some kind of alchemy of form. Can a woman thus exert control over her "burden of reflection," the second half of the novel seems to ask, and carve out a space where that performative labor itself can be transmuted into something that feels (dare I use the word) real?

In an attempt to answer Fitzgerald's question, perhaps more hopefully than she does, it is fruitful to turn to the surrealist movement during the twenties and thirties, centered in France, where much of this novel takes place. Despite her cultural and social distance from them, Zelda can be seen as a fellow traveler. Fitzgerald employs elegant, bizarre imagery, at once rococo and fragmentary; as do the surrealists, she relies on dream pictures, distorted perspectives, and startling juxtapositions to engage and unsettle her audience. If their work is a reliable record, Fitzgerald and the surrealists both apparently found commodification and the representation of women two of the most unavoidable themes in the face of modernity.[4] Familiarity with madness also links Zelda and the surrealists—from André Breton's *Najda,* a self-absorbed celebration of feminine insanity as a form of poetic inspiration, to Leonora Carrington's real-life bouts with schizophrenia.[5] And pivotally, the women working among the surrealists often split their attentions—as did Zelda—between playing the (vehicular) model and "muse," and creating their own canvases or texts.[6] Using Carrington's dark and rowdy short story "The Debutante" (1937) as a kind of informative counterpoint, this chapter will explore the circumstances under which another debutante, Zelda's Alabama, might have been able, "with one great bound, [to] disappear through the window."[7] But this eventual resonance between Fitzgerald and the women of surrealism must be preceded by an (only seemingly contradictory) yoking of her language to the discourse and concerns of advertising.

For *Save Me the Waltz* concerns itself, above all, with the toll exacted by vehicular performance in a culture where commodification has shaped feminine identity. The novel provides an "anatomy" of the vehicle, a map of her world, and a catalog of the costs and benefits of her "work." It encourages us to look at the decorative, metaphoric, and purchasing functions of the female consumer as labor, which Alabama ultimately wrests out of the arena of the decorative and directs toward another end.

"The Art of Being an Object"

Alabama and her husband David Knight zero in on advertising's social impact in the final moments of the novel. Their lines, though far calmer and more content than the close of Zelda Fitzgerald's *life,* do reveal the ennui and vertigo suffered by the Fitzgeraldian protagonists, particularly the heroine.

> "We grew up founding our dreams on the infinite promise of American advertising. I *still* believe that one can learn to play the piano by mail and that mud will give you a perfect complexion."
> "Compared to the rest, you are happy."
> "I sit quietly eyeing the world, saying to myself, 'Oh the lucky people who can still use the word "irresistible." ' "
> "We couldn't go on indefinitely being swept off our feet," supplemented David. (195)

"Irresistible," the sort of word to which copywriters return like bar-pressing rats, conjures a heightened sense of desire by invoking the inciting inhibitions against which that desire labors mightily. Alabama's comment suggests that, having been seduced by advertising's "infinite promise" and having advertised, seduced, and promised herself, Alabama has desired and failed to resist too often. Her desiring muscle gone lax, she is wearied by a surfeit of both broken and fulfilled promises. The rather philosophical ennui she describes comes only after a long period of galloping excess:

> The post-war extravagance which had sent David and Alabama and some sixty thousand other Americans wandering over the face of Europe in a game of hare without hounds reached its apex. . . . Lespiaut couldn't make enough flowers for the trade. They made nasturtiums of leather and rubber and wax gardenias and ragged robins out of threads and wires. They manufactured hardy perennials to grow out of the meager soil of shoulder straps. The ladies went to the foundries and had themselves some hair cast and had themselves half-soled with the deep chrome fantasies of Helena Rubinstein. . . . They ordered the weather with a continental appetite, and listened to the centaur complain about the price of hoofs. (98–99)

The "post-war extravagance" seems decadent and excessive to the point of disorientation, mostly because it focuses on the production and exchange of simulacra of nature: flowers, summer, hair, soles/souls, weather, hoofs. "Hare[s] without hounds," these elegant commodity signifiers of the natural world seem to have no signified left from which to run, and yet they dash on, set loose in their own surrealistic chase. Reflections supersede the "original," which loses the status of reference point: "Girls with piquant profiles were mistaken for Gloria Swanson. New York was more full of reflections than of itself—the only concrete things in town were the abstractions" (49). We are in a Baudrillardian hyperreal: "It is no longer a question of imitation, or even reduplication, nor even of parody. It is rather a question of substituting signs of the real for the real itself; . . . a hyperreal henceforth sheltered from . . . any distinction between the real and the imaginary, leaving room only for the orbital recurrence of models and the simulated generation of difference."[8]

As if they had ever had control over their own duping, David says that the couple had finally finished with being "swept off [their] feet." In contrast, a 1928 industry manual by Carl Naether instructs that the advertiser "has it within his power [to] mold *permanently,* the thought and attitudes he wants his particular buying public to have . . . [because in time,] the cumulative suggestive influences of the advertising would . . . *sweep personal doubt and prejudice away.*"9

Despite David's "supplement," the novel doesn't tell us much about the protagonists' life *on* their feet; the dizzying prose sets Alabama aspin in a universe of freefall commodities and constructed, incited desire. In contradiction to David's interjection, Alabama declares that even what she knows, even her worldweariness and the relative calm associated with it, do not prevent her from believing that "mud will give you a perfect complexion." Although her remark is flippant, it implies an influence whose power extends beyond any rationale. Fitzgerald grants commodities, and indeed objects in general, an animism that disorients, that resists a realist perspective, that sometimes horrifies:

> Flushed with the heat of palpitant cheeks, the schoolroom swung from the big square windows and anchored itself to a dismal lithograph of the signing of the Declaration of Independence. Slow days of June added themselves in a lump of sunlight on the far blackboard. . . . Hair and winter serge and the crust in the inkwells stifled the soft early summer. (15)
>
> The New York rivers dangled lights along the banks like lanterns on a wire; the Long Island marshes stretched the twilight to a blue Campagna. Glimmering buildings hazed the sky in a luminous patchwork quilt. . . . Through the labyrinthine sentimentalities of jazz, they shook their heads from side to side and nodded across town at each other, streamlined bodies riding the prow of the country like metal figures on a fast-moving radiator cap. (57)

This is the voice of modernity, but its decentered tone and animated objects have as their referent less the detached, nostalgic lament of a T. S. Eliot, and more the language and aesthetics of advertising, with the two New York rivers set into motion only via their association with the high-status hood ornament. Consider, for instance, this 1926 *Vogue* ad, which evokes the same image of rich Americans unleashed on the Continent that Fitzgerald treats above (see figure 5): "The smartest women of America are off to the smartest playgrounds of Europe . . . big wardrobe trunks foaming with French gowns—special little shoe trunks with exquisite slippers . . . in big, bulging trunks." Note the sexual frenzy attributed to the suitcases: they "foam" and "bulge," as if it were the commodities and not the jet-setters that "lived" for pleasure. Or look at the verbal agency lovingly handed the commodities in this passage from an anony-

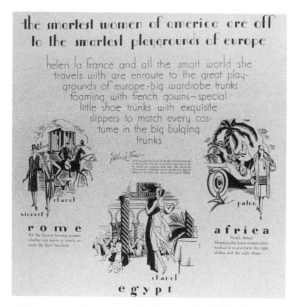

Figure 5   I. Miller Shoes ad, *Vogue*, 1 December 1926

mous advertiser's 1930 memoirs. In the final sentence, the writer feigns a modest step aside as the commodities themselves impersonate admen:

> Mingling with the customers, I would wander about until I had absorbed the spirit of the merchandise. The soft glow from hundreds of colored shades conveyed a message. . . . Romance clung to a simple pair of bellows and even fire tongs gripped me with their iron fingers. And I found that I could carry this imagination into every department. . . . [I]n the infants' wear section, the snowy fur caps suggested the little pink faces they framed, and the fur carriage robes wrote their own story of proud mothers.[10]

In *Waltz*, as in this department store, things, often quite lovely things, seem to perform an animated, disorienting dance around the characters, who are thereby set adrift or "swept off their feet." This commodity animism is interdependent with the "thingification" of the female figures, another component in the job description—or symptomology—of the vehicle. "Women love a pretty package. A girl in a pretty dress is a pretty package in herself," adwoman Dorothy Dignam comments, as if woman's posited exuberance for commodities were somehow proof of an affinity with them.[11] Similarly, Fitzgerald economically equates Alabama's physique with a piece of the clothing that could cover it:

> "I'm sure you can [become a dancer]—you certainly have the body!"
> Alabama went secretly over her body. . . . "It might do," she mumbled. . . .
> "Might?" echoed Dickie with conviction. "You could sell it to Cartier's for a gold mesh sweatshirt!" (108)

Along with the vehicle's disappearance into thing status, the obverse is true: increasingly, the things around the vehicle begin to take on agency. In *Waltz* (as in life) this induces both vertigo and fatigue. These "disturbances" in the book's depiction of its protagonist's selfhood have typically been understood as evidence of Fitzgerald's precarious psychology. For instance, the flap cover to James R. Mellow's biography of the Fitzgeralds sums up *Save Me the Waltz* as "kaleidoscopic images of [Zelda's] madness."[12] Although madness is a presence in the book, the corelessness, kinetic discontent, and object vivification in the novel predominantly exemplify not schizophrenia, but incisive social analysis on Fitzgerald's part. "Incisive" does not mean "objective": this exploration of *Save Me the Waltz* presumes an author whose own identity is fully implicated in commodity culture's constructions of the feminine self, and who writes restlessly from within those constructions.

Alabama experiences self-presentation as a high-stakes, highly gendered performance, and commodities become her props. As Fitzgerald describes it in a 1922 piece for *Metropolitan Magazine*, "Eulogy on the Flapper," such female social performers are "capitaliz[ing] on their natural resources . . . and applying business methods to being young" (Bruccoli 392–93). The cognitive dissonance begins when the vehicle confusedly discovers that *she* has also been cast as a prop, and that the commodities have a strange way of coming to life and mimicking characters, like an Alice in Wonderland plot twist. Such surrealism is par for the course in the posited world created by copywriters. To reintroduce a passage from Christine Frederick's *Selling Mrs. Consumer:* "I always think of advertising as a tremendous moving-picture device to keep ever and constantly changing before us, in film after film, reel after reel, all the good things that manufacturers make everywhere, set in a dramatic scenario which compels attention through the touch of advertising genius."[13] In the ads themselves, the industry's responsibility for the drama of goods it presents drops out of sight, as does a "moving-picture device," and we are left with animated commodities acting on their own. A typical 1928 advertisement for Pond's facial products engages in what Stuart Ewen has called the industry's "organization of objects and the dissolution of the subject," when it announces: "[These cosmetics] have taken wings and soared right to the hearts of . . . women everywhere."[14] Naether recommends that to exude class, copy be "written from the standpoint of the product": "the watch flees to the finger. . . . At night it becomes a piquant dinner ring" (44).

The commercial equation of the female body and commodities on display is made amply clear in a 1925 report on a talk given by J. Walter Thompson's (in)famous staff psychologist, Dr. John B. Watson, who suggests that if Florenz Ziegfeld "has a parade of bathing beauties in one scene, it is only fitting that he should show also, in his drug store scene, a counter display of Unguentine, so necessary to all bathers, beauties and otherwise. . . . If all [Norwich Pharmaceutical representatives] had their [store-owning] customers sold on display the way Mr. Ziegfeld is sold on it, Unguentine would be the first thing noticed in every drug store in the country."[15] The agency of the Ziegfeld girls drops entirely out of consideration here; their bodily presentation is entirely in the hands of the producer, just as product display is the responsibility of a drugstore owner.

The advertising context of display-cased women and energetic, mobile commodities is borne out in the "mountains of things" from *Waltz* that "represented something else, canapés like goldfish, and caviar in balls, butter bearing faces and frosted glasses sweating with the burden of reflecting such a lot of things to stimulate the appetite" (194). Beyond commodity animism—"faced" appetizers "sweating" and mimicking creatures—there is a commodity alliance with the heroine: the hors d'oeuvres and Alabama share the specific "burden" of overdetermined representation that is key to vehicular work. W. F. Haug, discussing Marx, provides an economic framework for the exchange that takes place in these narratives between eroticized things and commodified women. Both Haug and Marx extend verbal agency to commodities, while Haug emphasizes metaphoric borrowing:

> Marx says "commodities are in love with money" and that they ogle it with their price "casting wooing glances." . . . [C]ommodities borrow their aesthetic language from human courtship; but then the relationship is reversed and people borrow their aesthetic expression from the world of

the commodity. . . . Not only does this alter the possibilities of expressing the human instinctual structure, but the whole emphasis changes:
powerful aesthetic stimulation, exchange-value and libido cling to one
another.[16]

Haug does not theorize consumer resistance to the aestheticization and eroticization of commodities that he depicts. In *Save Me the Waltz*, though, Fitzgerald seems to thematize, rather than simply succumb to, this aesthetic "borrowing" and its impact on expressive possibility. She informs us about what it
means emotionally to negotiate interactions from within this borrowed—and
loaned—"language." In several instances, commodity description that sounds
remarkably like ad copy stands in for—and simultaneously *is*—eros. Instead of
merely replicating a commodifying aesthetics, Fitzgerald almost explicitly reveals an unexpected benefit that this proxying allows (and encourages?): privacy. We have seen how, in Larsen's *Quicksand*, protagonist Helga wears "an air
of remoteness" like an accessory, like one more "wisp of charm." Here, David
gets to hide "aloof," in the shelter of his own costume: "Dancing with David,
he smelled like new goods. Being close to him . . . was like being initiated into
the subterranean reserves of a fine fabric store exuding the delicacy of cambrics
and linen and luxury bound in bales. She was jealous of his pale aloofness" (39).

Desire, and especially effort, are most safely hid behind arrayed commodities. All depiction of the Knights' (relative) rags to (indisputable) riches story,
their climb to wealth and notoriety (often the subject matter in toto for the
American novel), Fitzgerald elides, or transforms, at any rate, into the blank
space between parts.[17] Part 1 ends by describing the newlyweds' straitened
circumstances, while part 2 begins with a fetishistic, plethoric, adlike portrayal
of the already achieved fruits of their unnarrated labor—a gigantic bed: "There
were shining black knobs and white enamel swoops like cradle rockers, and
specially made covers trailing in disarray off one side onto the floor. David
rolled over on his side; Alabama slid downhill into the warm spot over the mass
of the Sunday paper" (45). Are the amicable disorder and characters' physical
readjustments supposed to suggest that the Knights have just had sex? If so, the
glowing account of the bed becomes even more eroticized, as a surrogate of
their lovemaking, just as the "fine fabric store" fronts for Alabama's depiction of
being close to David for the first time. Again, the adlike narrative that appears
to pour from and enwrap commodities provides an entrancing, but especially a
discreet, veil for the protagonists' privacy.

The retreat behind elegant commodities at times approaches a failure of nerve, an emotional impotence: for instance, the rather hideously invulnerable Gabrielle Gibbs "withdr[aws] behind the fumes of Elizabeth Arden and the ripples of a pruned international giggle" (103). In this cultural context, however, self-disguise, commendable or not, is hardly an option. Here, we doubt there are recognizably unified selves who *could* "withdraw" to lurk coherently behind false fronts, particularly among the female characters. Much of canonical modernist literature bemoans this loss of (a semblance of) solidity. But in *Waltz's* "precession of simulacra,"[18] Alabama sometimes feels the creative thrill of a power of self-making that includes an endless flexibility (since there is no core self) and even the force to set things around her dancing that the aforementioned anonymous copywriter relishes so: "And I found that I could carry this imagination into every department." In his article "Cosmetics: Woman's Heritage through the Ages," Walter B. Neuberg, one-time advertising director for Coty, extends the sphere of influence of feminine self-making as far as it can possibly go. He explains that *cosmetics* comes "from the Greek *kosmeo,* to adorn; hence, the noun *kosmos,*—adornment, order, and by extension, the universe." The rather fantastic implication of this etymology is that "the cosmetic urge," instead of being set against the natural as artifice, becomes the creative force that propels—*everything.*[19] "I believe in the flapper as an artist in her particular field, the art of being—being young, being lovely, being an object," Fitzgerald (rather more modestly) proclaims in a 1925 article.[20] In *Save Me the Waltz,* she implies that "the art of being" is largely the art of being someone else.

> "I am a very self-sufficient person."
> "Oh, but are you? How narcissistic!"
> "Very. I am very pleased with the way I walk and talk and do almost everything. Shall I show you how nicely I can?"
> "Please."
> "Then treat me to a drink."
> "Come along to the bar."
> Alabama swung off in imitation of some walk she had once admired. "But I warn you," she said, "I am only really myself when I'm someone else whom I have endowed with these wonderful qualities from my imagination."
> . . . "You're as good as a book."
> "I am a book. Pure fiction." (69)

Alabama's flirtatious performance combines with her zestfully inconsistent persona to evoke a trend dominant in the period's perfume advertising. Ad copy of the twenties, especially for scents, banked on the notion of women's changeable nature, assuming and inciting the urge to apply "dabs" of "personality" as needed, much as Alabama samples and incorporates into her own performance attractive mannerisms and props from the women she observes around her.[21] "Four separate and distinct *odeurs* to express the four loveliest of feminine moods," declares a 1928 ad from Richard Hudnut, *parfumeur.*[22] This marketing strategy invoked a soft-focus psychological subtlety to push consumers toward brand diversification and multiple purchases.[23]

The approach suggests that women possess a natural tendency toward mutability, which they can enjoy and enhance, but which is far more inherent than it is the outcome of their creative manipulation. Packaged in many a perfume ad, this notion—that women's changing passions and allures derive from and are inextricably linked to an uncontrolled, contradictory inner essence—was essentially a pre-Victorian one, which Friedrich Nietzsche and others recirculated "daringly" during the early twentieth century. In *Beyond Good and Evil,* Nietzsche offers prose that would probably have worked well for Coty or Chanel:

> That which inspires respect in woman, and often enough fear also, is her *nature,* which is more "natural" than that of man, her genuine, carnivore-like cunning flexibility, her tiger-claws beneath the glove, her *naiveté* in egoism, her untrainableness and innate wildness, the incomprehensibleness, extent, and deviation of her desires and virtues. . . . That which, in spite of fear, excites one's sympathy for the dangerous and beautiful cat, "woman," is that she seems more afflicted, more vulnerable, more necessitous of love and more condemned to disillusionment than any other creature.[24]

The woman as cat, simultaneously dangerous and vulnerable, the ultimate artificer yet also more "natural" than man: many perfume ads are given their axis by exactly such an eroticization of these conflicting stereotypes—which predate even Milton's Eve, of course. The contradictory coupling has gone on to have commercial cachet as a feminizing hook, as Roland Barthes shows: "In Fashion, the individualization of the person depends on the number of elements in play . . . and on their apparent opposition (*demure and determined, tender and tough, casual and cunning*): these psychological paradoxes have a nostalgic value: they give evidence of a dream of wholeness according to which the human being would be everything at once, without having to choose."[25] Or, as model Christy Turlington intones in a recent Calvin Klein television campaign for the scent Contradictions, "I am a simple, complicated woman. I do what I want; that's all I *can* do."

Turlington's expression of obligatory caprice brings us back to the dilemma of agency. Advertiser Naether suggests that a woman does not entirely control her multiple moods: "Into [her correspondence, she] is wont to pour the colorful variety of the many little personalities which, during changing moods and under the nourishing stimulus of surging self-expression, she delights to let shine through . . . her words" (33). The rhetoric of an ungoverned female nature is belied somewhat by a perfume ad's address: selection, purchase, and employment of a slew of scents supposedly allows a woman to harness and exploit this "rainbow" psyche, all the way from tiger claws to tragic disillusionment. This version of personality is, as Barthes remarks, "a quantitative notion . . . an original combination of common elements . . . a *compound,* but it is not complex" (Barthes 1983, 255).

This active harnessing and performance of personality elements seems to be Alabama's modus. In the above conversation with the drunken Englishman, Alabama delights not in "changing moods" or "surges," but in the full possession of her (many) selves. She feels "self-sufficient" because, by performing, she gets what she wants (that is, a drink) and her imagination pulls the spectacle of her persona together. In his skeptical mode, even Naether, somewhat leery of his jargon's implications, contends that female consumers are engaging in alert acts of imitation rather than fluttering through kaleidoscopic mood swings: "While many a woman might not be desirous of obtaining . . . three different kinds of perfume just for the sake of expressing her 'rainbow moods' . . . she may . . . be persuaded to do so when she learns that the fashionable women of Paris . . . are using perfumes in this way" (201–2).[26]

"The Burdens of Reflecting"

The early section of *Waltz* detailing Alabama's training as a Southern woman shows her awareness of the fabrication and production of what she gauges "a damned good show" (32). Even when Alabama, the youngest of three girls, admires her big sister, what impresses her is Dixie's careful work on her own presentation.[27] To admit to vigorous artifice is typically to break down beauty,

Figure 6 Illustration
accompanying an article
by Margaret Weishaar,
titled " 'Psyching' Mrs.
Smith: Two Special
Feminine Urges Make
Her a Spender," in the
J. Walter Thompson
newsletter *People,*
October 1937

Figure 7 Djer Kiss ad (Kerkoff
Paris), *Vogue,* 1 July 1926

Figure 8 Djer Kiss ad (Kerkoff
Paris), *Vogue,* 1 December 1926

to reveal it as a hollow facade. Acknowledgment of Dixie's "work" on herself, though, does not preclude a sense of romance for Alabama; rather, the vehicular performance becomes the most apt and elegant approach to living well: "How did Dixie make herself so fluffy, so ready always for everything? Alabama thought that she herself would never have every single thing about her just right at once. . . . Dixie appeared to her sister to be the perfect instrument for life" (15). The process whereby Dixie "makes herself fluffy" is represented everywhere in the popular magazines of the day. In ad after ad, women sit alone in their boudoirs, heavy-lidded and only lightly smiling, holding a beauty product with lovely, elongated, almost phallically pointed fingers, gazing privately into mirrors at reflections the reader cannot see. The process of self-beautification becomes not a chore, not a shameful artifice to be hidden, but something alluring, exclusive, onanistic (see figures 6, 7, and 8).[28]

And Alabama chafes from the beginning at any obfuscation of the energetic gender performance that she and her sisters have undertaken. At one point, she has apparently succeeded in creating that undefinable, poignant atmosphere so exalted in advertisements, and (perhaps because she does not love the man present—indeed, wants him gone) she is all too happy to dispel the mist:

> "This porch is always the coolest, sweetest place," said Harlan.
> "That's the honeysuckle and star jasmine you smell," said Joan.
> "No," said Millie, "it's the cut hay across the way, and my aromatic geraniums."
> "Oh, Miss Millie, I hate to leave," [Harlan said]. . . .
> "Mamma, that smell is the pear trees," Joan said softly.
> "It's my perfume," said Alabama impatiently, "and it cost six dollars an ounce." (28)

Although this performative model for the female consumer's act of self-fashioning extends her more agency and savvy than does the "rainbow" approach, Fitzgerald's novel makes clear that a woman's cognizance of her own work as overseer can be burdensome. For one, it inspires guilt. "She knew her face glowed in the firelight like a confectioner's brewing, an advertisement of a pretty girl drinking a strawberry sundae in June. She wondered if David knew how conceited she was" (39). A confectioner "brews" with results in mind, not spontaneously. Similarly, while a "pretty girl" could theoretically be unself-aware, lost in the enjoyment of her ice cream, an "advertisement of a pretty girl" is indisputably at work, striving for effect. In fact, the posited advertising model here does classically vehicular work, heightening the appeal of the sundae with the allures of her lovely face.

The often-agonized and only sometimes zesty self-scrutiny that Alabama condemns as "conceited" seems, in the world of the book, far too requisite a stance to deserve such moral opprobrium. Trained as a society belle, Alabama needs to stay sensitized to the impact of her self-presentation, to maintain control over her experience. As John Berger puts it in his seminal *Ways of Seeing:* "She comes to consider the *surveyor* and the *surveyed* within her as the two constituent yet always distinct elements of her identity as a woman. . . . Men survey women before treating them. Consequently how a woman appears to a man can determine how she will be treated. To acquire some control over this process, women must contain it and interiorize it."[29] Berger describes a divided feminine self, with an "I" alertly split between "surveyor" and "surveyed." Mary Ann Doane (in her comments on masquerade) has labeled such "divisiveness of self" as *"constitutive* of self in psychoanalysis."[30] The self-critique that Alabama invokes in her use of the term *conceited* above, however, indicates that the very process of "containing the surveyor" limned by Berger, which should perhaps be understood as one culturally valenced version of consciousness itself, comes thanklessly weighted with moral censure.

The enforcing flip side to such censure is popular culture's pervasive eulogy to unselfconsciousness, often revealed as hollow on closer inspection. The Clara Bow vehicle *IT* (1927), devotes significant screen time to queries about the meaning of that "magnetic," elusive quality, "IT" (always capitalized in the titles).[31] The only aspect of IT that the movie articulates is "indifference as to whether you are pleasing or not." "The possessor of IT must be absolutely unselfconscious." Not surprisingly, only the film's unattractive characters care about the phenomenon. Hearing about IT is almost synonymous with wondering whether you have it, and to wonder this is to fail the first and only test of unselfconsciousness. Thus, the audience member, forced into cognition of IT, is cast in a league with the film's ungainly strivers. Ironically, Betty Lou (Clara Bow), the IT girl, is by no means indifferent about her ability to please. She tries constantly and shamelessly to please and perform for her employer love-interest. In fact, IT is more a matter of eager, uninhibited enjoyment of both self-scrutiny and performance than of unselfconsciousness, at least as Bow plays it.[32] In her "anti-sentimental, irreverent" engagement with this act, she functions, Lori Landay has argued, as a "trickster" rather than a disingenuous naïf.[33] Unselfconsciousness seems to be a state from which no one actually operates; tributes to its virtue appear designed, ultimately, only to shame those who are—unavoidably—conscious of self.[34]

So, guilt about artifice accompanies the performance that calls for such alert self-scrutiny. Nonetheless, because she wants to perform effectively, Alabama often imitates "bits" from the other *female* female impersonators around her.[35] Gabrielle Gibbs, a celebrity dancer in the Knights' social set, cannot be imitated, however, because there is no point of entry; inviolate, slick, and entrancing to David, she can only be experienced from without. Fitzgerald's hostile description of Gabrielle at a party where the dancer ends up "borrowing" David for the night is a violent, seductive portrait of a woman completely given over to the alluring performance. Here, the normally internalized loathing and condemnation of the performing woman commingles with Alabama's jealousy over Gabrielle's success.

> She was as dainty and rounded as a porcelain figure; she sat up and begged; she played dead dog, burlesquing her own ostentation attentively as if each gesture were a configuration in some comic dance she composed as she went along and meant to perfect late. . . . Miss Gibbs withdrew behind the fumes of Elizabeth Arden and the ripples of a pruned international giggle. . . . [H]er personality was alive like a restless pile of pink chiffon in a breeze. (103)

The passage critiques Gabrielle not simply for triviality, but for the excessive consciousness that "attentively" siphons her performance toward the artificial, the decorative, the undignified, the unliving. Descriptions of Gabrielle emphasize the artificiality of her self-commodification, comparing her to marble, porcelain, something just "delivered from the taxidermist," "bought in sets," the "background of an allegorical painting," and, of course, "pink chiffon" (102–3).[36] In disguise as a commodity, Gabrielle is "playing dead dog"; she is an animate creature borrowing the properties—and safety—of the inanimate plane. Alabama is drawn by the success of this performance, while the tropes used to figure its triumphs bespeak the terrifying homeostasis that such a performance apparently entails.

Artifice, itself shameful, also implies some original deficiency that must be hid. A second bane of the gender spectacle is lack of self-acceptance, a self-loathing that the act of imitation seems to prove. In a cultural milieu that encourages women to tend watchfully to social performance, self-loathing emerges as the bitter motivation for such careful disguise. Ironically, the act of disguise may retroactively generate this motivation. Covering her face with pancake daily, a woman may conclude that it needs to be hidden, that its qualities and even presence are problems. "Comparing herself with Miss Axton's elegance, [Alabama] hated the reticent solidity . . . of her body. . . . Compared with Miss Douglas' elimination, her Patou dress felt too big along the seams" (101). Invisibility—in fact, annihilation—seem to be the anorexic unspoken ideals: Alabama finds her "solidity" hateful, her dress "too big," and contrasts the indisputable *presence* of her dress and body with the heightened-because-insubstantial allures of "elegance" and "elimination." Her body, irrefutable and dense, prevents her from attaining the "pale aloofness" that she initially envied in David as he lurked behind his fragrant linens. This process of eradication returns us to the terrain of hidden labors marked out by Frances Maule, the adwoman whose success manual urged hopeful businesswomen to control their bodies, approximating the impossible ephemerality of "motionlessness" and "noiselessness." Remember that Maule seemed to be trying to protect women against the contaminating force of their own "intrusion" into the workplace. In *Waltz,* Alabama finds most vile the indicators that her body is capable of and, indeed, engaged in *work.* It takes work to mount Alabama's "damned good show," and the traces of that labor remain. Since the key task handed to the woman of "leisure" is to betoken the class status that enables her inactivity, any signs that this "show" also requires effort are dangerously unsettling.

At times, the "damned good show," though tinged with and partially fueled by self-censure and self-loathing, is an exuberant triumph over exactly these assaults on the self. Fitzgerald portrays the obstacles to artistic endeavor for women in Alabama's position and attempts to celebrate their gendered showmanship as the form of creative expression most readily open to them. The celebration has its limits: a burlesque of "femininity" is the third and rather global shortcoming of "the [vehicular] art of being." This snatch of dialogue suggests both Alabama's limitlessly combinatory creativity and her sense of its circumscription, when she playfully declares to her daughter, " 'I'll be an Agamemnon fish . . . ' 'But how can you be two things at once?' 'Because, my daughter, I am so outrageously clever that I believe I could be a whole world to myself if I didn't like living in Daddy's better' " (80). Transforming what elsewhere seems a necessity into a matter of choice, Alabama has elected to rein herself in, to "live in Daddy's world." Much earlier, Fitzgerald presents David's "world" as an engulfing, threatening environment for Alabama. In an astonishing passage that we can almost denote as her literary "signature" speech, Fitzgerald depicts romantic intimacy as the "finespun" doorway to psychotic surrealism: Alabama's first kiss with David leads her into an (anatomically correct) journey within his brain. Her "fantastic voyage" reveals the amorphousness of her identity, at least as self-perceived, and manifests the joy and fear of this plastic mutability. The "trench war" landscape grows increasingly harrowing, and the nightmare of being subsumed within the male ego is given material form.[37]

> So much she loved the man, so close . . . [that] she felt herself that he became distorted in her vision, like pressing her nose upon a mirror and gazing into her own eyes. She felt the essence of herself pulled finer . . . , very small and ecstatic. Alabama was in love.
>
> She crawled into the friendly cave of his ear. The area inside was grey and ghostly classic as she stared about the deep trenches of his cerebellum. There was not a growth . . . to break those smooth convolutions. . . . "I've got to see the front lines." . . . The lumpy mounds rose wet above her head. . . . Before long she was lost. . . . She stumbled on and finally reached the medulla oblongata. Vast torturous indentations led her round and round. Hysterically, she began to run. David, distracted by a tickling sensation at the head of his spine, lifted his lips from hers. (40)

The medulla oblongata—whirling, black heart of Alabama's panic, her First World War—directs involuntary bodily functions like respiration and circulation. When Fitzgerald places her French-kissing protagonist in this almost mechanical "control center," naturalism's accuracy of detail and horrible fixation on determining forces beyond our volition meet with the "distorted" dream perspective and emphasis on "mad love" that most characterize surrealism. Her linking of naturalistic and surrealistic forms and content results in both a heightened horror and the glimmering possibility of escape. Tragic determinism is an audible strain in F. Scott Fitzgerald's work as well, but his variation seems to focus on the involuntary trajectory of characters' lives across a societal landscape. Zelda's determinism, as painted in this passage, drags the social into the realm of the psychic; the gendered social of marriage is rendered claustrophobic, internal, and unsettled by its interaction with the unconscious.

With just this claustrophobia as a founding principle in the Knights' relationship, Fitzgerald presents "modern" womanhood as the only avenue for creative expression open to a woman residing in "Daddy's world." In the first days of their courtship, David had carved into a tree, "David david david Knight knight knight and Miss Alabama Nobody" (39), thus setting the tenor for their respective professional trajectories. After their engagement, David's letters reiterate, " 'You are my princess and I'd like to keep you shut forever in an ivory tower for my private delectation.' The third time he wrote that about the princess, Alabama [foreshadowing her discontent] asked him not to mention the tower again" (42).[38]

As the quirky, brilliant, but unsurprisingly leisured wife of a vigorously productive painter, Alabama faces a situation also treated by Kate Chopin, Henry James, Charlotte Perkins Gilman, Edith Wharton, and others.[39] Infantilized, Alabama is nonetheless chastised for acting like "a child." Luxury is her substantial yet inadequate booby prize. Her indolent efforts to raise her head and consider options for her own work are aborted early on:

> "It's a man's world," Alabama sighed, measuring herself on a sunbeam. "This air has the most lascivious feel—". . . . David worked on his frescoes; Alabama was much alone.
> "What'll we *do*, David," she asked, "with ourselves?" David said she couldn't always be a child and have things provided for her to do. (78–79)

> "I don't see why," expostulated David, "when you complain of having nothing to do, you can't run this house satisfactorily." (83)

> Alabama read Henry James in the long afternoon. She read Robert Hugh Benson and Edith Wharton and Dickens while David worked. . . . "What can I do with myself?" she thought restlessly. . . . "Can't you at least not interfere, Alabama? . . . Peace is absolutely essential to my work." (87)

> [And when she finally jumped into dance training, David said,] "Are you under the illusion that you'll ever be any good at that stuff?" (119)

When David is done with his work, they debauch excessively, of course, this being the world of the Fitzgeralds. Alabama toys with an affair, she travels, and she drinks. Throughout, it becomes increasingly obvious that she is supposed to represent and augment David's persona. In other words, Alabama *is* at work, and her work is vehicular. So, stymied in other artistic efforts, she pours her creativity into her "job": the "art of being."

In "What Became of the Flappers?" Fitzgerald appears deeply divided about the "revolutionary" societal work of the young women she discusses. Clearly, the modern scene captivates Fitzgerald's creative and aesthetic sense, but she seems resentfully ironic about the flapper's obedience to men and the status quo.

> I believe in the flapper as an artist in her particular field, the art of being— being young, being lovely, being an object.
>
> For almost the first time we are developing a class of pretty yet respectable young women, whose sole functions are to amuse and to make growing old a more enjoyable process for some men and staying young an easier one for others.
>
> The flapper! She is growing old. She forgets her flapper creed [earlier defined: "to give and get amusement"] and is conscious only of her flapper self. . . . [She] has gone at last, where all good flappers go—into the young married set, into boredom and gathering conventions and the pleasure of having children, having lent for a while a splendor and courageousness and brightness to life, as all good flappers should.[40]

This last phrase hints at Fitzgerald's bitterness about the ultimate compliance of this ostensibly liberated figure. The flapper obeys by pleasing the men around her. She obeys by playing the rebel for a time, "as all good flappers should," and at the appropriate moment, by disappearing into convention. What, then, is her "courage," and to what end is her "work"?

In the first two parts of the book, the psychic cost of Zelda's own "burdens of reflecting" can be felt, perhaps, in some of her dialogue, which is sometimes preposterously stilted:

> "Consciousness is the goal, I think."
>
> "Then the direction of education should be to teach us to dramatize ourselves, to realize to the fullest extent the human equipment?"
>
> "That's what I think."
>
> "Well, it's hooey." (66)

In exchanges like this, the effortful compression of ideas makes it look as if Fitzgerald were trying to conduct her characters' intellectual life—and her own—crammed within the confines of arch repartee, to the detriment of both intellect and wit. When her heroine later flings herself into the dance studio, the expulsive force of mental and physical energy reined in for too long seems the catapult. Fitzgerald's protagonist finally hits her breaking point: " 'I can't stand this any longer,' she screamed at the dozing David. 'I don't want to sleep with the men or imitate the women, and I can't stand it!' " (111).

Driving the Devils

Alabama's turn to dance takes up almost half of the book. Plunging into this new world, she fights to "drive the devils that had driven her" (118), to take "the art of being young and lovely" and turn it into an art indeed, committing everything she has to the ephemera of gesture. She will discipline that objectified body, control its effect, choreograph with a trained eye the dance that she has been brought up to perform. This odyssey, in part, is one of empowering reappropriation of the only tools she had been trained to wield. It also participates in the more masculinized paradigm of redemption or transcendence through art. Above all, however, Fitzgerald's description of Alabama's dancing is more about tasks than either tools or transcendence. It is about work—grueling, repetitive, physical effort—a discovery of labor formerly either untapped or devoted to producing the spectacle of gender. "[Madame] pulled and twisted the long legs along the bar. Alabama's face grew red with effort. The woman was literally stripping the muscles off her thighs. . . . There were blue bruises inside above the knee. . . . Arienne wrung out her tights in pools of sweat" (116–18). When it comes time for Alabama's first professional solo, the narrative ignores what we gather was a successful performance, cataloging only the physical tokens of her exertion.[41] "She worked so hard that she felt like an old woman. . . . [Her] feet were bleeding as she fell into bed. When at last her first performance was over . . . , her eyes throbbed with the beat of her pulse, her hair clung like Plasticine about her head" (159).

Instead of "soaring" accomplishment or a Mae Westian mimetic subversion of traditional gender roles, it is the dancers' fantastic industry and open hunger that mark this final phase as contrastingly and transformatively real, to the extent that it is. And, pivotally, Alabama bucks David. She does not leave the marriage, but she certainly does "quit her job" as his accessorizing muse and show-wife. Pushing against David's disbelief in her autonomy and ability, Alabama slowly learns to dance.

A wholehearted embrace of the model of redemption through art would portray Alabama as an insistent applicant to the rarified, transcendent, masculine world of "Art with a capital A," a world hitherto inaccessible because of her sex. By traversing this essentially Romantic terrain (championed uncritically by many modernists), by acting as if she were a male artist, she would be able to transcend the tedium and superficiality that had been her lot as an accessorized wife and objectified female.[42] A passage from James Joyce's *A Portrait of the Artist as a Young Man* is echoed in *Waltz:*

> He was alone. He was unheeded, happy and near to the wild heart of life. He was alone and young and willful and wildhearted, alone amid a waste of wild air and brackish waters and the seaharvest of shells.[43]

> Alabama stood alone with her body in impersonal regions, alone with herself and her tangible thoughts, like a widow surrounded by many objects belonging to the past. Her long legs broke the white tutu like a statuette riding the moon. (140)

These segments, however, differ as much as they resonate. Alabama the artist is depicted not as a "young man" poised in "wild air," but as a "widow" dancing anyway amid the clutter of her "past," a woman who has passed forever what one 1928 Pond's Cold Cream ad termed "the long twenty-nine."[44] Throughout the book's last half, the gendering of this artistic portrait affects its content, positively and negatively, to such a degree that the narrative finally undercuts the very tradition of artistic homage in which it engages.

When Alabama leaves behind the life of a decadent, high society expat, the main, constitutive elements of this previous "job" become the fundamental building blocks of her new obsession; this makes it impossible to read *Save Me the Waltz* as a text about feminine entry into the male echelons of high art. The project of the dance (especially in the virtually all-female world shown here) is far too caught up with visible effect and presentation of the female body to be completely delineated from Alabama's earlier, vehicular "work."[45] The very aspects of her previous life as an "object" that seemed most to be liabilities she dives into, claims control over, and exploits *in their most extreme form.* This is a deep reinvestment in and investigation of a subjectivity rooted in object-status, especially in the competition with other women and the self-abnegation that most characterized that status. Fitzgerald's depictions of the physical tortures of the dancers, their excruciations and frenzies, are so strikingly immoderate that they sabotage any easy notion of an "unsullied" artistic plane. This is the arena of the taboo, so relished by Bataille and the other "rebel" surrealists whose work perhaps most resonates with Zelda's text: advertising during this period lingered obsessively on the need to avoid exactly the effluvia (blood, sweat, and tears) that flow in such quantities at the studio.[46] Fitzgerald creates a female community so engaged and laced with both desire and competition that *Waltz* could never be mistaken for the bildungsroman of an insulated, monadic soul.[47] The "transcendence" possible, never highlighted as her goal anyway, is qualified: Alabama sweats far more than she soars. That same body that she struggles so hard to master succumbs ultimately to a blood disease, and she must stop dancing. The novel also acknowledges the vastly negative impact that her dancing has on her parenting, a problem that a paean to art in the romantic register with a male protagonist is unlikely to consider.

In its focus on travail, Alabama's arduous, painful experience at the studio contrasts utterly with the "dainty" ease of Gabrielle Gibbs's "burlesque" and her showy personality like a "restless pile of pink chiffon." Ironically, Alabama's initial dive into the dance world is presented as a competitive reaction against the adored Gabrielle. Part 3 begins Alabama's era as an aspiring dancer; part 2 has just concluded with Alabama's declaration, "I am going to be as famous a dancer as there are blue veins over the white marble of Miss Gibbs" (112). Alabama refers to the far-reaching reputation of Gabrielle's translucent flesh; the language equates her with a statue, in keeping with Gabrielle's triumphant self-objectification, and in stark opposition to the aching limbs that Alabama hauls about, fighting gravity throughout the book's last section. All the descriptions of Gabrielle focus on the external results of her dance training: beauty, poise, sex appeal, and effortlessness. When Alabama approaches dance, Fitzgerald gives us the opportunity to peer inward at the process behind those alluring results, to apprehend the sheer exertion required to bear the "burden of reflecting."

But Alabama forges a complex contract with that very exertion, hungrily seeking out its exhaustions and excesses. She uses dancing not as an advanced form of seduction/reflection, but as an escape from her old social scene, again in marked contrast to Gabrielle's life as a dancer, which apparently revolves around pleasing others with her affect. Eager to retreat from public scrutiny, Alabama replaces the dizzying confinement of marriage, illustrated by her voyage through David's brain, with the equally stifling Madame's studio. Rather than freeing herself from immurement, she chooses to circumscribe herself to a tiny, insular "cave," short on ventilation and the site of blinding, all-consuming labor. When investigating Alabama's reasons for barring her society friends from the studio, her dance mate asks, " 'But why? It is for the appreciation of your friends that you will dance.' 'No, no!' Alabama protested. 'I cannot do two things at once'" (128). Now, Alabama used to be wonderfully able to juggle two things. (Recall, for example, the "Agamemnon fish.") In fact, as a social performer monitoring her own performance, she usually was; the focus and frank sweat mark this project as her effort to push forcibly into another realm. In rejecting a bifurcated, directing/performing self, in fanatically striving after a unified perspective, she rejects most completely the vehicular work that had preceded her dancing, and thus, comes closest to participating in the myth of the whole-selfed romantic artist.

Emphatically, this psychic refocusing does not require discarding the former "tools of her trade." Although her economic and consuming practices change dramatically, Alabama's "*Verkleidungstreib*" (the drive to dress) is undiminished.[48] If anything, she gets far more enjoyment and significance from the mirror and dressing than she had previously. The descriptions of clothes feel different, plethoric, more sheerly aesthetic, more linked to lived experience and self-expression:

> There was a red and white check for weather like Normandy, a chartreuse for decadent days, pink for her lessons at midday, and sky blue for late afternoon. . . . For the waist she bought cotton bicycle shirts and faded them in the sun to pastel shades, burnt orange to wear over the pink, green for the pale chartreuse. . . . The habitual flamboyance expressed in her street dress flowered in this less restricted medium. (136)

To some extent, this echoes almost embarrassingly the ad industry's insistence that women's adornment should reflect their "rainbow moods." Yet Alabama already owns these clothes and is merely savoring them for the first time, so her "many moods" do not require an act of conspicuous consumption. Furthermore, she finds the private, all-female studio a "less restricted medium" than "the street," where she has been trained to publicly present herself. In *Waltz*'s first half, characters seem to "duck behind" their possessions, anxious for the privacy provided by their veneer. The studio, however, offers a microcosmic retreat from the male gaze, and Alabama's dressing, once a facade, becomes free, expressive. Alabama observes in counterpoint, during now-rare dinners out with David, "jeweled women glittering like bright scaled fish in an aquarium" (122), encased for display.

Similarly, contrasting the artificial flowers in the Lespiaut passage (quoted earlier in this chapter), Fitzgerald describes the abundance of real flowers that Alabama buys for Madame. This is only part of a remarkably lengthy catalog:

> She had abandoned so many of the occasions of exercising personal
> choice [through consumption] that she spent the hundred-franc notes in
> her purse on flowers, endowing them with all the qualities of the things
> she might have bought under other circumstances, the thrill of a new hat,
> the assurance of a new dress. Yellow roses she bought with her money like
> Empire satin brocade, and . . . pink tulips like molded confectioner's
> frosting, and deep-red roses like a Villon poem, black and velvety as an
> insect wing, . . . a bowl of nasturtiums like beaten brass, . . . malignant
> parrot tulips scratching the air with their jagged barbs, and the volup-
> tuous scrambled convolutions of Parma violets. (130)

The flowers become fabric, food, a poem, a metal; not only lyrical, the bouquet
includes the rather savage parrot tulips and the chaos of the Parma violets that
Fitzgerald articulates with the sheerly evocative strokes of an abstract painter.
In the Lespiaut passage, tabulating the production and consumption of artificial flowers among the Continental wealthy, despite the flowers' omnipresence,
Fitzgerald struck an impoverished tone: "Rubber and wax gardenias and
ragged robins out of threads and wires" grow from "the meager soil of shoulder
straps" (98). Here, in a context of reduced consumption and financial restraint,
it is the authenticity of the flowers that makes them so fecund metaphorically,
so ready to be "endowed" with extrinsic qualities.

Beginning to separate financially from David, Alabama ceases to consume
"professionally." She conserves her resources, buys far less than she had, and
savors and preserves what she does own, because she is getting something from
financial independence. "Spending money had played a big part in Alabama's
life before she had lost, in her work, the necessity for material possessions"
(131). This understated comment invokes its opposite in F. Scott Fitzgerald's
Tender Is the Night (1934), which covers roughly the same period in the Fitzgeralds' marriage in a similarly semiautobiographical way.[49] Fitzgerald's description of the shopping habits of female protagonist Nicole Diver lurks
behind the rather modest statement about the "big part" once played by
"spending money" in Alabama's life. Nicole Diver's consumerism, retroactive
and omnivalent, causes industry. What adwoman Frederick termed an "en-
tente cordiale" between consumer and capital,[50] Fitzgerald portrays as something giant and sprawling, pitched toward a certain "doom."

> Nicole . . . bought colored beads, folding beach cushions, artificial flow-
> ers, honey, a guest bed, bags, scarfs, love birds, . . . [etc.] She . . . bought

all these things not a bit like a high-class courtesan buying underwear and jewels, which were after all professional equipment and insurance, but with an entirely different point of view. Nicole was the product of much ingenuity and toil. For her sake trains began their run at Chicago and traversed the round belly of the continent . . . men mixed toothpaste in vats . . . girls worked rudely at the Five-and-Tens on Christmas Eve; half-breed Indians toiled . . . and dreamers were muscled out of patent rights in new tractors—these were some of the people who gave a tithe to Nicole, and as the whole system swayed and thundered onward it lent a feverish bloom to such processes of hers as wholesale buying, like the flush on a fireman's face holding his post before a spreading blaze. . . . She illustrated very simple principles, containing in herself her own doom. (54)

Nicole's "point of view" and the "very simple principles" that she illustrates go mysteriously unmentioned. F. Scott Fitzgerald shows industry as a vast, seething organism, "sway[ing] and thundering onward" like Frank Norris's octopus, and set into motion by Nicole's unspecified and unappeasable desire for things. But this desire—indeed, Nicole herself as conflated with the principle of desire—is "the product of much ingenuity and toil." Fitzgerald's catalog emphasizes the "toil" of working-class laborers; the unportrayed "ingenuity" that "produces" Nicole (while she simultaneously inspires industry) is the savvy of the advertiser, who knows how to incite and then channel her yearnings toward the act of purchase. Despite her "grace," the impending "doom" latent in Nicole stems from the top-heavy quality of this paradigm: all those running trains, fuming factories, and toiling workers "give tithe," in Fitzgerald's formulation, not to a powerful cohort of corporate employers, but to the thin-shouldered Nicole.

When the protagonist of *Waltz* stops her "wholesale buying," and industry's reflected "flush" fades from her cheeks, it is replaced by the flush of her own effort. We discover the link between the producers and consumers of commodities: *labor*. This association was hinted at with F. Scott's invocation of the courtesan, but then suppressed through the passage's emphasis on the consumer as galvanizer. In *Waltz*, the "toil" of feminine self-production is as inescapable a theme as are purchases. This potential correspondence between production and consumption is developed only insofar as it does not override the class positioning of the dancers at Madame's studio.

Save Me the Waltz connects the effort of dance, depicted so viscerally, with economic deprivation and a pared-down consumption. In particular, the lengthy portrait of the poor, unmarried, would-be dancer Stella plays up her impoverishment in all its demoralizing, sensory specificity; through Stella's dogged, pathetic perseverance, poverty mingles in the narrative with the physical travail of dance. Coming close to romanticization, Alabama, who "thought she could work better when she felt poor" (130), claims Stella's destitution somehow as her own, not that it is, nor that it's fun. In fact, Alabama's mere presence at the studio at her advanced age marks her as a leisure-class individual. Though Fitzgerald hovers on the brink of joining her protagonist in aestheticizing the destitute artist, ultimately she does not depict Alabama's dancing as lifting her beyond the reach of class dynamics. Her affluent husband, and indeed, the economic status of each student at Madame's, clearly influence the interactions there. For example, Arienne tells Alabama, " 'I want to give a party, but Madame will not come. She goes out to dine with you—she will not go out with [me]. I ask her why—she says, "But it is different—you have no money." I will have money someday' " (147).

Class tensions intertwine with professional rivalry. The women are often petty, jealous, power mad, pathetic—fistfighting in the dressing room and vying for prominence on the studio floor. The bonds between Fitzgerald's dancers, by no means utopian, exaggerate Alabama's prior relations with other women, the competitors whose performances and allures she has charted so closely in the book's first half. At the studio, the jealousy and desire between women are made utterly material, hyperbolized into the slapstick eros of the catfight:

> Arienne shoved Alabama into the group of naked girls. Somebody pushed her hurriedly back into Arienne's gyrating body. The eau de cologne spilled over the floor and gagged them. A swat of the towel end landed over Alabama's eyes. Groping about she collided with Arienne's hot, slippery body.
>
> "Now!" shrieked Arienne. "See what you have done! . . . You have hit me in the breast from a bad spirit! . . . You will pay!"
>
> . . . Out in the fresh air [Alabama's] knees trembled as she waited for a taxi. . . . Her upper lip felt cold and peppery with drying sweat. . . . What was it all about, she said to herself—fighting like two kitchen maids and just barely getting along on the ends of their physical resources, all of them?

"My God," she thought. "How sordid! How utterly, unmitigatedly, sordid!" (150)

In Alabama's earlier competition with Misses Axton, Douglas, and Gibbs, the women's focus on their adornment and the male attention for which they vied deflected somewhat their avid attention for one another. By contrast, when Arienne and Alabama fight naked and unadorned in the dressing room, both passion and competition are made absolutely palpable, and thereby transmogrified. It is not a dissipation of the rivalry, but an overt enactment of both the "sordid" power struggle and the sheer engagement between women that allows them to befriend one another as they pursue a common goal; indeed, Arienne and Alabama, the studio's top dancers, share many moments of impassioned and philosophical friendship. This view of friendship, not explicitly coded as lesbian, is laced with the kind of identificatory desire that marked Larsen's sketching of the association between Helga Crane and Audrey Denny (also played out on a dance floor), and similarly opens itself for queer reading pleasure.

Alabama sees these women as her dance rivals, as opposed to competitors in a gender spectacle, which spells a change in her expression and implementation of class-specific practices. Earlier, self-loathing and competition had intertwined in Alabama's life to induce a focus on consumption. Now, rather than buying a designer gown and then anxiously "comparing herself [to] Miss Axton's elegance" (130), Alabama buys flowers for Madame with Adele. Both the size of the outlay and the motivation for purchase have changed. The friendship among these dancers is characterized most tellingly by a shared, courageous acknowledgment that "life is sad" (120), a declaration repeated verbatim three times during this half of the book, and borne out repeatedly as the dancers struggle with one another and against the limits set by their own bodies. This fact is exactly what the advertising industry does not want to make explicit, since the anxiety that consumers feel as they try to push this "sadness" from their consciousness compels them to shop.

Self-loathing, like competition, winds up not evaporating but combusting, when Alabama "turns over a new leaf." In brief moments, her attitude as a dancer contravenes her earlier self-abnegation: Alabama had once "hated" the "reticent solidity" of her body, which so resisted the insubstantiality of "elegance" (101). But "by springtime, she was gladly, savagely proud of the strength of her Negroid hips, convex as boats in a wood carving" (127). Her transition could easily be cataloged among the familiar narratives of female "healing," whereby a fashion-induced self-disgust simply fades away in the face of an all-powerful "self-acceptance." Such a model does not work for *Waltz*, though. The dichotomy between the expensive ephemerality of elegance and curvaceous energy of the "primitive" is both class- and race-inflected. The two terms seem semiotically interdependent through their opposition, making Alabama's jubilation about her claim to "Negroid hips" more a case of imperialism of the body than a true transformation of values. These moments of "savage" celebration are rare. It was self-loathing that made Alabama "hate" the "reticent solidity" of her body, its refusal to dissolve, and that led simply to an act of consumption—the purchase of the Patou frock. This imploding condemnation of her own materiality alchemizes into the driving force behind her dancing.

> The human body was very insistent. Alabama passionately hated her inability to discipline her own. Learning how to manage it was like playing a desperate game with herself. She said to herself, "My body and I," and took herself for an awful beating: that was how it was done. (118)

> Alabama's work grew more difficult. In the mazes of the masterful fouetté her legs felt like dangling hams; in the swift elevation of the entrechat cinq she thought her breasts hung like old English dugs. It did not show in the mirror. She was nothing but sinew. To succeed had become an obsession. She worked till she felt like a gored horse in the bullring, dragging its entrails. (144)

The term *masochistic* is in common parlance severed from its sexual connotations and used as an unproblematic synonym for *self-defeating*. But when Alabama disengages self-loathing from the realm of consumption and exaggerates it through work until it ascends to the plane of the masochistic, she effects an evolution from nagging self-critique to rite of passage.[51] Consumer culture both incites and assumes self-loathing as a motivator, but also buffers and sedates it through the short-term relief of each new purchase. Alabama has transformed from shopper to dancer, though. Taking herself "for an awful beating," she attempts to find out how much "my body and I" can bear, and only passage through these trials opens up the possibility of transmutation. Gilles Deleuze calls the submissions and tortures undergone by the masochist "so many steps in their climb toward the Ideal. . . . The ascent from the human body to the work of art and from the work of art to the Idea must take place under the shadow of the whip."[52] In "The Death Instinct," Deleuze discusses the role of repetition in the masochistic experience, how the rhythmic interchange between sensation and suspension is a play between "Eros and Thanatos" (111–21): in a related spirit, *Waltz's* depictions of the rigors of dance accentuate the ritualistic zeal for repetition. In her meditation on a body-builder's "reps," which require exertion to the point of failure to instigate muscle growth, Kathy Acker remarks that "the physical or material, that which is, is constantly and unpredictably changing: it is chaotic. This chaos twines around death. For it is death that rejects all of our paths, all of our meanings. Whenever anyone bodybuilds, he or she is always trying to understand and control the physical in the face of his death. No wonder bodybuilding is centered around failure."[53]

Behind Fitzgerald's listing of physical excruciation stands like a sentinel the inevitability of decay and death. Like Eros and Thanatos, work—or produc-tion—and death—or disintegration—form a dialectical matrix the implosion of which structures the dancers' "struggle for plastic beauty" (140). The repre-sentational acts in which they engage, using and abusing their bodies as me-dium, exemplify what Georges Bataille called "*altération*"—whereby "the for-mation of an image is . . . the deformation of its model," to quote Hal Foster, scholar of surrealism.[54] "Art," says Bataille, "proceeds by successive destruc-tions," signifying both "a partial decomposition analogous to that of cadavers" and a "passage toward a perfectly heterogeneous state" (in Foster 113). In a marriage of masochism and mysticism that Deleuze charts as typical, Alabama strives "under the shadow of the whip," executing 400 battements every night.

This ballet exercise is performed on the order of Alabama's instructor. The parallel between the masochist and the Fitzgeraldian dancer extends with her depiction of Madame. The masochist seeking discipline needs to procure the assistance of a dominatrix. Madame functions much as does the mistress of a "slave," insisting on careful repetition of undoable, agonizing tasks and smartly reprimanding whomsoever disobeys. To achieve perfect turnout, Alabama is instructed to sleep with her feet twisted through the bars of her iron bed frame. The friendship between Madame's dancers revolves primarily around a shared abject admiration for their instructor, the aging Russian beauty with "malice" in her face and sad eyes, she who metes out their torture. The women compete bitterly for her approval, but they also comfort one another when Madame absents herself from the studio, shop together for flowers for Madame, and build a camaraderie based on a common commitment to Madame.

The spectacle of female self-presentation has been transmuted indeed, but to what end remains unclear.

> At her last lesson, Alabama searched behind the dismantled segments of the mirror for . . . the ends of a thousand arabesques.
> There was nothing but thick dust, and the traces of hairpins. . . . "I thought I might find something," she explained shyly. . . .
> "And you see there is nothing!" said the Russian, opening her hands. "But in my new studio you may have a tutu. . . . [I]n its folds, who knows what you may find." . . .
> [They] helped Madame to move her piles of old abandoned skirts, worn toe shoes. . . . As [they] sorted . . . these things redolent of the struggle for plastic beauty, Alabama watched the Russian.
> "Well?" said Madame. "Yes, it is very sad," she said implacably. (140)

Alabama's furtive search behind the mirror (which so typifies self-presentation) for something of substance, yields nothing. The Lacanian mirage of a solid self is rendered absurd by the sad discovery of "dust to dust." In a discussion about self-representation and female surrealists that resonates with this one, Whitney Chadwick quotes Trinh T. Minh-ha:

> Rare are the moments when we accept leaving our mirrors empty. . . . [S]till, we persist in trying to fix a fleeting image and spend our lifetime searching after that which does not exist. This object we love so, let us just turn away and it will disappear.[55]

Although there is only dust behind the mirror in *Save Me the Waltz*—and by extension, only "dust" in front of it—there is an unnamed mystery in the folds of Madame's tutu: Fitzgerald treats Alabama's striving with a purposefully ambiguous pair of images. The mirror holds nothing, yet the tutu—a quintessentially vehicular display piece, a skirt that does not cover at all but adorns and extends the influence of a woman's hips—symbolizes both the attainment of skill, as does a black belt in karate, and an enigmatic, fecund vaginicism.

"Les Femmes Enfants": Zelda and the Surrealists

What does Alabama find in the tutu's folds? Not much, perhaps: the novel ends in qualification and contemplative resignation rather than triumph. But Alabama's hopes for dance are not expressed in terms of popular success. One day, her socialite friends barge into the studio, only to exclaim,

> "She'll never be able to get up in a drawing room and do *that!* What's the good of it?"
> Alabama had never felt so close to a purpose as she did at that moment. "Cabriole, failli"—"Why" was something [Madame] understood and Alabama almost understood. She felt she could know when she could listen with her arms and see with her feet. (134)

These goals are surrealistic, pushing the envelope of the possible as they do: Fitzgerald's supra-anatomical challenge for Alabama combines "adorable improbabilities" (the phrase is André Breton's) and sheer desire so as to shock the impossible into being. Breton wrote of the surrealist predilection for startling juxtapositions in his first *Manifeste:* "Surrealism is based on the belief in the superior reality of certain forms of associations hitherto neglected, in the omnipotence of dreams. . . . This summer roses are blue; wood is glass."[56] Philippe Soupault's nonconformist sentiments, from the first number of *La Révolution Surréaliste,* also align themselves with Alabama's mission: "I mistrust public opinion, that old skull full of bugs and desiccated clippings. . . . Desires, such are the sole witnesses, the sole faithful spokesmen."[57] Behind the mirror and in the gauzy folds of the tutu hide the surrealists—especially the surrealist women—who worked just a stone's throw away from Zelda Fitzgerald.

Initially, the link appears strained between this personality so popular in mass culture, who published often in national magazines catering to the American middle class, and the oft-ridiculed yet well-established, sometimes revered, self-referential and self-marginalizing, mostly European surrealists. Yet Fitzgerald's rendering of modernity's effects on the psyche and her daringly unconventional approach to narrative were both misunderstood in the cultural mix in which she moved. On closer scrutiny, profound connections can be drawn between Fitzgerald and the surrealists in the areas of form, content, and biography. To begin with, stylistic ties abound. To see a surrealistically tinged formal project in Fitzgerald's work, look at her strange twisting of perspective in the dream voyage Alabama takes through her lover's brain, or this astonishing nightmare of a sickbed hallucination:

> Sometimes her foot hurt her so much that she closed her eyes and floated off. . . . Invariably she went to the same delirious place. There was a lake

there so clear she could not tell the bottom from the top. . . . Phallic
poplars . . . whose foliage flowed out of the sky covered the land. Nebu-
lous weeds swung on the current: purple stems with fat animal leaves. . . .
Crows cawed from one deep mist to another. The word "sick" effaced
itself against the poisonous air and jittered lamely about. . . . "Sick"
turned and twisted about . . . like a roasting pig on a spit, and woke
Alabama gouging at her eyeballs with the prongs of its letters. (180)

Here, she emphasizes the materiality of the eyeball, origin of the gaze, and
subjects it to penetration by the word *sick*, and thus by language, site of
abstraction. Fitzgerald participates in the surrealistic project also undertaken
by Bataille with his novella *Story of the Eye* and Salvador Dalí and Luis Buñuel
in their film *Andalusian Dog*, each of which feature sutured eyeballs. Consider,
too, Fitzgerald's fairy tale and *Alice in Wonderland* paintings, with their dizzying perspective, hallucinatory nod to the unconscious, and use of animal
imagery.[58] Both Fitzgerald and the surrealists reeled at their own immersion in
commodity culture and responded in the same way, taking up as central
themes commodification and the image of woman—think of Man Ray's photographs, Hans Bellmer's violent "Dolls," Meret Oppenheim's fur-covered teacup, and the rows of eerily attired mannequins at the 1938 International Surrealist Exhibition.[59] As mentioned earlier, another topic for Zelda and the
surrealists was madness. Look at the movement's fiftieth anniversary celebration of hysteria as a supreme form of creative expression (*La Révolution Surréaliste*, 1928) or at Breton's *Najda*—a strangely unfeeling "paean" to a woman
who winds up institutionalized, and thereby serves as sacrificial muse to the
bubbly male narrator.[60]

Like Zelda, the women in surrealism resisted certain conventionally feminine choices, the domestic, the demure. Much of their work focused on the
problem of self-representation as contextualized by a ubiquitous "male" gaze,
just as did Zelda's.[61] Most of them shared the vehicular concerns of Zelda and
her protagonists: Surrealist men often used these women as models for their
own work, and had made it a founding principle of their movement that the
young, beautiful, slightly at risk "*femme enfant*" was their Calliope and raison
d'être.[62] Man Ray, for instance, took nude photos of Lee Miller, Meret Oppenheim, Dora Maar, and other female artists in his social set.[63] Playing the
muse to surrealism was a classically vehicular task, representing and augmenting the appeal of artistic production to the men around one, being creative

oneself, but more in one's persona and "spontaneous" expressions than in one's ability to shape and formalize an artistic movement. How is the femme enfant engaging in anything different than "the art of being, being young, being lovely, being an object"?

In examining how female surrealist artists responded to the role of muse, Whitney Chadwick argues that in many individual cases, these women gave somewhat spottier attention to their work than did the men.[64] Patronized and treated as enfants, no matter how desirable, rather than fellow artists, these women could easily invest more in their performance as personas and lovers than in their texts and canvases. Zelda, too, both in her lifetime and since, has been seen as trendsetting flapper extraordinaire, muse to Scott, and mad-woman, rather than an artist in her own right. And indeed, Zelda's attention to writing prior to her short-lived immersion in dance, was spotty, and her work probably did mature less fully than it might have due to this.

This does not mean that less formalized, more ephemeral self-expression— as in dress, speech acts, and style—should be seen as the invalid booby prize for women restricted from the sphere of "real," lasting "art." The more obvious rewards must often have seemed to be elsewhere, for Dorothea Tanning to party in a leopard-skin dress covered with breasts, for Lee Miller to sport green fingernails and golden handcuffs, for Eileen Agar to turn a fish basket upside down and wear it as a hat, and for Zelda and Alabama to be "artists of being" in a similarly modern (though less exhaustively unconventional) way.[65] Although ballet, despite its demimonde beginnings, has now been canonized as "high" art, it remains true that when Zelda and her heroine Alabama become dancers, they channel all their insight and stamina into the production not of concrete, lasting artifacts, but of transient kinesis, the "art of being."[66]

Social and cultural divergences notwithstanding, important parallels can be drawn between Zelda and the female surrealists, particularly the British-born painter and writer Leonora Carrington. Like Fitzgerald, Carrington was born into class privilege and "society"; struggled with madness; was possessed of daring, unconventional wit and a surrealist response to the twentieth century. Like Fitzgerald, she experienced the double-edged sword of working alongside a strongly egoed, successful male artist (Max Ernst, in Carrington's case).[67] Fitzgerald, though, was more isolated than Carrington, more at risk psycholog-ically, and probably hindered by her greater investment in the dominant cul-ture. To follow Susan Rubin Suleiman's line of reasoning, perhaps the avant-garde, "for all its [considerable] participation in the patriarchy," allowed

Carrington greater access to artistic and personal survival than Zelda enjoyed. Ernst and the surrealists certainly supported her initial "liberation from
middle-class propriety and . . . attainment of an identity as an artist."[68] Moreover, accustomed to rebellion from just this commitment to surrealism's unor-
thodoxy, Carrington was more primed to rebel, too, against the avant-garde's
patriarchal restrictions on her development. Indeed, Whitney Chadwick describes a number of the more productive female artists shrugging off affiliation
with the movement proper: Leonora Fini, Frida Kahlo, Dora Maar, and to a
lesser degree, Carrington all resisted too strong an identification with the
movement and insisted on the autonomy—and often the personal specificity—
of their work. The women who cleaved most closely to the movement also
asserted the androgyny of art, vehemently suppressing the belittling connotations of the femme enfant label.[69] It is also possible that surrealism itself, in its
avid pursuit of the unconscious, offered Carrington an artistic structure that
featured—unlike David's brain—exit doors, chances for egress, for emergence.

While Zelda wound up dying in a 1948 fire during yet another institutionaliza-
tion, Carrington's serious breakdown became just one episode in an altogether
unconventional life. Her community of friends, far less perturbed by the borders of sanity than F. Scott Fitzgerald's letters depict him, helped her survive
the illness.[70] For example, when she was committed to a mental hospital, in
contrast with Zelda, Carrington had a friend help her escape.[71] Carrington had
long been immersed in a subculture that applauded experimental writing and
efforts to express alternate modes of consciousness; surrealist friends André
Breton, Pierre Mabille, and Jeanne Megnen encouraged Carrington in her
cathartic *Down Below,* a hair-raising narrative of her breakdown.[72] Fitzgerald's
doctors, on the other hand, wrote worried letters to Scott about the discontinu-
ity in Zelda's drafts of *Waltz,* and critics of the popular press called her prose
style a "desperate attempt to be contrary and enigmatic" that only made her
resemble "an insane child."[73] Furthermore, Zelda's own attempts to make
madness a subject in *Save Me the Waltz* were soundly suppressed by Scott, who
felt that he had dibs on the material for his own novel, *Tender Is the Night.*[74]

   After she relocated to Mexico, Carrington found herself in a community of
artists, and her friendship with painter Remedios Varo, in particular, provided
the kind of female support and inspiration that protagonist Alabama experiences at Madame's studio, but that Zelda essentially did without, after collapse
drove her from dance. In Mexico as well, Carrington triumphed by happily

raising two children (with Hungarian photographer Chiqui Weisz), fashioning for herself a rewarding relationship to maternity—something that eluded not only Zelda but most of the women surrealists, who faced eerily similar conflicts about the female persona, art, and conventional feminine roles.[75] Susan Rubin Suleiman's beautiful *Subversive Intent,* which couples examinations of surrealist and feminist texts, has at its heart the disruptive, provocative picture of a laughing, playful mother. This figure, Suleiman contends, is suppressed—even unthinkable—in most theories of the avant-garde, while her reinstatement has the power to revitalize and repoliticize the artistic encounter.[76] Carrington in Mexico, raising two boys and painting pictures of women aloft thanks to impossible flying machines, is the kind of mother figure Suleiman describes.

She brings us back to *Save Me the Waltz,* where there is no playing mother: when Alabama attempts this sort of maternity, throwing an unorthodox children's party during her daughter Bonnie's visit, dismal failure results (166). Luxury and mass culture consistently win Bonnie's attention—as does more constant care than an increasingly disengaged Alabama can offer. Fitzgerald brutally catalogs Alabama's shortcomings as a mother and the shifts in Bonnie's affections and loyalties. In a particularly cruel fillip, Fitzgerald has Bonnie gush about the glamorous Gabrielle to Alabama, now holed up alone in an Italian garret (165). After a truly agonizing description of Bonnie's unsatisfactory visit to Alabama's run-down lodging in Naples, where Alabama is fulfilling her first professional engagement as a dancer, Fitzgerald shows the ease and gratitude with which the young girl, returned to her wealthy, luxury-loving father, sinks into the pleasures of protected femininity and conspicuous consumption. Fitzgerald uses the automobile, so rich a metaphor during its early years, as a figure for these joys.

> The children, wrapped in the bright armor of Bonnie's father's car, dozed against the felt cushions. Safe in the glittering car, they rode: the car-at-your-disposal, the mystery-car, the Rajah's-car, the death-car, the first prize, puffing the power of money out on the summer air like a seigneur distributing largesse. (173)

That night, Bonnie explains to David that Alabama " 'said her piece of advice that she had to give me was not to be a backseat driver about life.' 'Did you understand?' 'Oh, no,' sighed Bonnie gratefully" (176). While Alabama herself has taken on the task, at least for a time, of learning to "drive the devils that have driven her" (118), her daughter seems hungry, instead, to *be driven* . . . in "élégance" (168). Having just depicted the deliciousness of lounging in a (literal and metaphorical) backseat, Fitzgerald purposefully undercuts the efficacy of Alabama's counsel to her daughter. In so doing, she leaves vexed, aching, and unresolved the issue of the artist's maternity, and instructs us, too, in how a certain form of feminine identity construction lives on through commodity culture's seductions. Indeed, the laughing mothers circulating in this period were often the women in ads, laughing because their purchasing power had liberated them from work entirely, thereby alchemizing maternity into another proof of (Veblenian) leisure.

"Plastic Beauty"

The conclusion of *Save Me the Waltz* emphasizes not transcendence but qualifiers. A troubled maternity limits the novel's celebration of artistic endeavor: this is a sociohistorically determined qualifier. The body sets the other limits requiring submission: Fitzgerald depicts these as existential, but these physical limits, too, can be read as socially defined. Despite many appreciative portraits of dancers, Fitzgerald repeatedly sketches them as almost ugly in the mortality of their overworked bodies. In the dressing room, Alabama averts her gaze, because "[s]he knew her eyes would see the sagging breasts like dried August gourds and wound themselves on the pneumatic buttocks like lurid fruits in the pictures of Georgia O'Keeffe" (160). One doesn't need to turn to O'Keeffe for visual parallels. In Fitzgerald's own painting *Costumes for a Children's Theater,* the grotesque troupe look like marionettes designed by Francis Bacon, and the figures in her 1941 *Ballerinas Dressing* are most notable for their gnarly, massive feet and hands: earthbound and huge, the lower extremities and drooping arms pour, drip, and crowd to the bottom of the canvas as if down a drain (see figure 9).[77] Their small heads are mostly turned away; the one directed toward the viewer is faceless. Gravity predominates, especially because of the picture's misaligned perspective, as if the room itself, with walls the color of dried blood, were tipping the already weighted dancers toward the picture's bottom right hand corner. In *Waltz,* the limits of Alabama's body, constantly shackling her, eventually assert themselves: blood poisoning—from bleeding feet and a dirty toe shoe—sends Alabama to the hospital and ends her dancing days. The "struggle for plastic beauty" (140) she has engaged in so wholeheartedly bears fruit only when Alabama looks at her father's corpse. "Death is the only real elegance," Alabama says. "There was nothing to be

Figure 9   Zelda Fitzgerald, *Ballerinas Undressing,* circa 1941, oil on canvas, 42 × 30 in. Courtesy of Kristina Kalman Fares.

afraid of, only plastic beauty and immobility" (188). All the movement and effort, all the formerly masked desire, point toward the stillness of Thanatos— death, as beyond the reach of those still living as it is inevitable.

In the final tally, the novel leaves us with the "plastic beauty" that Alabama's father achieves in the coffin, and the late-night, filled-ashtray, cozy yet hollow ennui of the last scene: "We could not go on indefinitely being swept off our feet" (195), David pronounces, rigidly wry. The united front presented by David and Alabama as the novel ends appears inexplicable after the estrangement of their pursuits; the defeat and ostensible survival that are supposed to explain their togetherness instead make it utterly implausible. Abandoning without a whimper the desire that Alabama had poured into her dancing, this conclusion touts the soothingly familiar cynicism of the long-term sophisticate as its resting place. It is with this conclusion that the novel's "flawed" status rings most true, rather than with Fitzgerald's "psychotic" imagery earlier in *Waltz,* which I have tried to revalue here as writerly experimentation and social analysis. The ending in the published version of *Waltz,* however, is apparently not the one originally intended by Fitzgerald—Zelda, that is. She excised all mention of her protagonist's mental illness, as we saw earlier, after Scott insisted on reserving this bit of (auto?)biography for his *Tender Is the Night.* Had she developed and retained the material on Alabama's madness, her text might have continued to participate in the kind of hungry Bataillean merger between life force and death drive, the "assenting of life up to the point of death,"[78] that characterized her narrative treatment of Madame's studio.

The revised ending abandons this urge to shuck off the constraints of identity. Its blasé stasis indicates more of a surrender to psychic deterioration than does the vertiginous surrealism of Fitzgerald's most fanciful passages. When she makes a nod to the elegance of her father's corpse, it is a return to the arch, brittle compressions and homeostasis of the book's first half, rather than a continuation of the push to move past both objectification and subjecthood that drove her dancing. In fact, though the book's "happy" conclusion diverges from autobiography more blatantly than anything that precedes it, Zelda's real-life unhappy ending, her madness, was most tragic in its stasis, as reflected in her immobilizing, armor-like eczema, her extended periods of inactivity, and her increasingly rigid and judgmental Christianity.

The enforced immobility that seems the most horrific aspect of Zelda's decline—more death grip than death drive—can be detected in a pose that first appears in her paintings as recurrent, then almost compulsory, and finally ubiquitous: the heads of her figures are flung back. The effect is hard to read. In her earlier paintings, the exposed throat and closed eyes appear insouciant, pertly self-satisfied and disengaged (see figure 10). In the final paintings, all deeply religious biblical scenes, the heads of the many figures are upturned, and one senses that they are supposed to look beatific, devout, in communion with a higher force (see figure 11). To throw the head back, close the eyes, and expose the throat is a pose that typifies the moment of orgasm, too—and that erotic interiorization is visible, though distorted, in Fitzgerald's raised faces. In *Erotism: Death and Sensuality,* Bataille groups images of such figures as emblems of sacrifice, dissolution, and desire—from St. Thérèse, to a voodoo practitioner in a trance, to an illustration of a hanged woman for an edition of Sade's *Justine.*[79] All Fitzgerald's heads, however, in both the earlier and the later canvases, seem held back and held still *by force*—and sometimes the exposed throat appears almost as if an oval plate were planted there, holding the head back and at an angle, making it impossible for the figure to see or return the gaze of the viewer.[80] The rigid lack of languor in her figures can be read as a commentary on the cost of the "burden of reflecting," a gendered concern that a writer like Bataille did not address. An eerily similar (and equally phallic) effect is visible in a 1926 ad for Fioret perfumes (see figure 12). The stylized

Figure 10 Zelda Fitzgerald, *Old Mother Hubbard,* circa 1943–1947, gouache on paper, 12 × 19 in. Courtesy of Cecilia L. Ross.

Figure 11 Zelda Fitzgerald, *Marriage at Cana,* late 1940s, gouache on paper, 17¼ × 22⅝ in. Courtesy of Cecilia L. Ross.

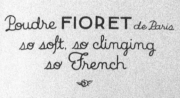

Poudre **FIORET** *de Paris*
so soft, so clinging
so French
~❧~

SOME powders cling but are sticky and coarse. Others are
light and quickly blow away under the slightest breeze.

But Fioret Powder, the creation of a French perfumer, is as
fine as the down on a butterfly's wing and clings as if it
adhered by magic to the cheek and to the nose!

Never has there been a powder that clings so tenaciously—
a powder so ethereal—never before a powder that gave to the
complexion of the smart women who wear it an effect so lovely
and so smooth.

And it has another charm unsuspected 'til you use it as
your own. For it is scented with the incomparable odeur of
Jouir—a fragrance subtle and discreet.

Figure 12   Les Parfums Fioret ad, *Vogue,* 1 December 1926

female figure in this ad features a neck that extends at least three times longer
than any human throat, fingers as long and thin as bulrushes, and a jutting,
upturned head that apparently forgoes the capacity for interaction with or
apprehension of anything but the sky. The eros and self-absorption of the pose
are poor compensation for the loss of flexibility they certainly require. No
escape is forged by women's performative labor.

Carrington's oeuvre includes the short story "The Debutante," written in
1937–1938 and included first in *La Dame Ovale.*[81] As the title suggests, Carrington and Fitzgerald share another biographical trait: as young women, both
"came out" (not in the contemporary sense) in society. The narrator's coming-
out ball in "The Debutante" is to be held in 1934, as was Carrington's. The
ingenue-protagonist spirits her dear friend the hyena out of the zoo to impersonate her so that she will not have to attend the ball. The hyena, perpetually
ravenous, is eager for party food. Back in the narrator's bedroom, the disguise
they devise includes the narrator's ball gown, gloves, and high heels, which the
hyena learns to master parading around in front of a mirror. The furry face is
the nagging problem; the hyena's solution is to eat the maid and use the
corpse's face as a "mask," which indeed fits perfectly. This act of violence
damns not the hyena, but the upper-class world that the animal has entered,
making unavoidably manifest both the violent indifference of the rich toward

the humanity of the serving class and the anonymous exchangeability of the gender masquerade. Though the hyena's stench is overpowering, she heads for the ball, leaving a happy narrator to spend the evening reading *Gulliver's Travels.* Unfortunately, she is interrupted by her furious mother, who bursts in exclaiming, "That thing sitting in your place . . . shouted, 'So I smell a bit strong, what? Well, I don't eat cakes!' Whereupon it tore off its face and ate it. And with one great bound, disappeared through the window."[82]

A review of the visual and textual work of women surrealists reveals a shared use of certain animal figures as totems for female resistance, sexuality, and the unconscious. Both the hyena and lemur serve this symbolic function in numerous canvases. In Carrington's most well-known image, a 1936–1937 self-portrait titled *The Inn of the Dawn Horse,* she sits next to a hyena; they each present the viewer with a level gaze, one hand or paw extended.[83] In "The Debutante," the hyena's fantastically unladylike hunger, her fur, loud voice, and pervasive animal stench, make her a forceful symbol of female desire, presence, irrefutability, rebellion, and sexuality. The last two qualities are precisely what is suppressed in *Waltz,* but the dancing part of Fitzgerald's novel is full of almost violently unfeminine, visceral effects, as the women sweat, bleed, curse, and fight, as hungry as hyenas to push themselves behind the mirror, or out the window.

In a remarkable coincidence of vision, Fitzgerald also put a furry carnivore in an evening gown. Throughout her life, she created astonishing paper dolls with matching costumes. When they weren't explicit images of Zelda, Scott, and Scottie, these dolls were developed in series based on popular fairy tales or adventures: *The Three Musketeers, Goldilocks and the Three Bears,* and so on (as the number three should suggest, these dolls provided Zelda with opportunities for family portraiture). The later dolls are often fascinating, sexy, and highly androgynous—all are broad-shouldered, narrow-hipped, and muscular, and the male characters are as likely as the females to be given flouncy, skirted costumes.[84] A later series depicting *Little Red Riding Hood* serves as an example (see figures 13 and 14).[85] The wolf looks sexy and dangerous in grandma's revealing red undies, his (her?) mouth a red gash, hands folded over or pointed at the crotch, a big bushy tail extended phallically next to the leg. But the wolf "also owns a party dress," and there s/he stands in a bridelike gown replete with flowers, veil, and even angel wings (an early paper doll depicts Scott with angel wings). As if the masked aggression and ravenous hunger of the gowned wolf were not sufficient, Fitzgerald also depicted "the bigger and badder of wolves."

Figure 13   Zelda Fitzgerald, "Wolff, Wolff," from *Little Red Riding Hood* series, gouache on poster board and paper. Courtesy of Cecilia L. Ross.

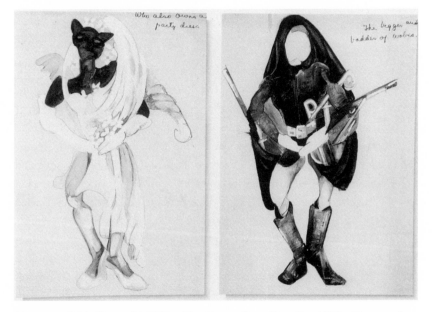

Figure 14   Zelda Fitzgerald, "Who Also Owns a Party Dress" and "The Bigger and Badder of Wolves," from *Little Red Riding Hood* series, gouache on poster board and paper. Courtesy of Cecilia L. Ross.

This final image really does look female, with a breast line implied beneath the snug superhero costume. This wolf has an executioner's hood and a hilarious excess of weaponry in a spray around her hips.

Madame promises Alabama not an arsenal but a tutu, with a treasure in its folds. In *Waltz,* Fitzgerald uses the verblike kinesis of dance to militate against the "nouning" of the female protagonist in a commodity culture that understands women as (static) objects. In the end, *Save Me the Waltz* fails to maintain the kinetic energy, desire, or bodily fury of the dancers' effort. Instead of the tutu's treasure, Fitzgerald gives us the "plastic beauty" of death (with a ploddingly stately commentary on its inevitability) and the hollow, chic resolution of wearily sophisticated ennui. Censored, she was unable to write herself a hyena. David and Alabama's stance in the final scene bespeaks neither contentment nor escape, but angst and critical acumen that have been appropriated, managed, and restructured by the economics and aesthetics of commodity culture, leaving the protagonists themselves wry, idle, and quietly at home. Meanwhile, Carrington's hyena is gone in the night, its mask off, hopefully carousing with Zelda's "wolff." And Carrington herself, debutante-manqué and soul sister to Zelda, still lives and works in Oak Park, Illinois, and Mexico City.

Epilogue

Contradictory impulses have fueled this project. Anyone writing about mass culture must hammer out some locatable relationship with the highbrow/lowbrow divide. A thoroughly constructed dichotomy well deserving the destabilization to which it has now been subjected, the highbrow/lowbrow paradigm has, nonetheless, governed the way that cultural producers and audiences have experienced popular culture for more than a century.[1] In my case, a strong personal identification with the "lowbrow" has sat rather uneasily with a growing concern about the impact of advertising, and this acutely divided sensibility has driven my entire investigation. Assumed throughout is that the advertising industry has had enough social force to modify the way people approach the very concept of selfhood. But how cognizant were twenties' advertisers of their "perpetration" of some large-scale agenda? Did they see themselves as acting on a passive populace, as inducing social change, as wielding powers sufficient to transform the experience of subjectivity and gender?

Advertisers of the 1920s may have helped to launch a cultural era devoted to the fetishization of commodities and the commodification of experience, but in the process, they were typically focused on micromanaging their own arena. These affairs were those delineated in their minds by what Marx rather subtly cataloged as "old memories, personal enmities, fears and hopes, prejudices and illusions, sympathies and antipathies, convictions, articles of faith and principles."[2] A twenties' advertiser would have been trying, say, to get a promotion, to find a way for the women in her agency to exert more influence, or to push through her own idea for a campaign. During the early decades of its ascendance, the industry vacillated between softsell—atmospheric, "mood" advertisements—and hard sell—fact-driven "reason why" ads; these were, by and large, the "revolutions" and struggles that gripped advertisers, caught up (as we all usually are) in the furious drama of their own lives.[3]

Still, as we have seen, some advertisers did come close to personifying the most paranoid fantasies of removed, Machiavellian social manipulators. A portion of these self-fashioned puppeteers may have been deluding themselves about their own capacity to transcend societal conditioning and ideology, yet they were right about one thing: they were not synchronous with the "man or woman on the street"—not on the level of class identification, education, or agenda. And they helped to create a professional culture generally permissive of manipulation and deceit, as licensed by a showy display of self-regulation and "self-policing" at its borders, via the Associated Advertising clubs of America.[4] To declare too readily that critiques of national advertising and popular culture are inherently elitist and antipopulist is to ignore the reality of the snobbism of many of those producers who "catered" to the "mob." The discussion of William Day and William Esty in the first chapter, for instance, makes it clear that disrespect for the "common man" was not limited to Ezra Pound–like proponents of the highbrow.

Although there were some misanthropes among advertisers of the twenties, eager to profit from an audience they viewed with contempt, one doesn't need an objective, triumphantly willed villain in order to critique the overall effect of the industry. Celebration of the popular audience (or even the ambivalent creativity that infuses much advertising) should not extend outward to support unreservedly the entire, complex apparatus that makes the generation of commodity culture possible. For in this arena so driven by market forces, something sinister *is* afoot, perhaps, even though it is not at the hands of purposive "evil perpetrators."

Working, shopping, staring at ads, and longing for change, most of us hope to make not a killing but a living. We struggle to make an impression as well. Consuming and performing in the societies that we have inherited without choice, we both sustain and modify them daily with our wildly various, intimate decisions and actions. In part because of this ongoing, urgently personal, localized investment, commodity culture careers forward.

Many 1920s' advertisers, sophisticated and alert, wished to see themselves as unswayed by the commercial messages they deployed. For example, Esty made sense of his work by envisioning himself as "strong" enough not to be influenced by the cultural forces he was wielding. But the kind of power imagined here—both the existentialist interior freedom that ensured Esty's place above the fray and Day's *übermenschlich* leadership—is ultimately driven, restless, and vulnerable. The real cultural strength comes from the will to use what's available to make one's life "go." We see this in Ruth Waldo's female advertising team, perched before their desks in smart, ladylike hats (and in their secretaries, who soon donned their own chapeaux). In their novels, Lewis, Fitzgerald, and Larsen also illustrate the vigor and imagination that animate what Michel de Certeau calls "the practice of everyday life": George Babbitt's son biting his pencil eraser as he answers the ad for a night school in mechanics, or Helga Crane and Alabama Knight pouring creativity and love into the fabulous ensembles they wear. Some of the "work" that I've discussed in this book is anxious and compelled, and some brings furtive pleasure, but all of it betokens human drives and energies. The last two chapters show consumer-vehicles trying to use their performative, representative social positioning—since that is what's available to them—trying to "tweak" it, to allow for greater social force, but also to allow for escape through transmutation.

Does the creative realm offer superior tools for these impulses toward survival and metamorphosis? Literary characters certainly take center stage here, but what is their social force? No one would argue that the authors responsible for creating these characters operated from beyond the marketplace. The Fitzgeralds, Larsen, and Lewis all invoked the commercial address in their narratives, and all wrote with a market in mind. Emerging from the swirling center of bourgeois experience as they do, don't these books simply become commodities themselves? The literary critique, even a (semi)scathing one, has a place within mainstream culture, and the jeremiad or bemoaning of certain social ills can be said to form one component in hegemonic cultural practice.[5] To a significant degree, this "bourgeois self-loathing as a literary force" works in odd tandem with bourgeois self-congratulation, and functions to channel, manage, and diffuse societal doubts and contradictions.[6]

Nonetheless, though the authors explored here were eager to sell books and hardly free from the constraints of social conditioning (any more than were Esty, Christine Frederick, Claude Hopkins, or Waldo), their writing contains revelations that are not merely "folded back in" or dispersed in the process of commodification. For their fiction vividly illustrates the psychic economy of the "poor fit." The models for selfhood generated within the context of a market-driven commodity culture and available to characters like George, Alabama, or Helga are shaping or constitutive of the personalities and choices they display—but only to an extent, since there is excess.

Poor fits: we tend, like dough with too much yeast, to ooze out from beneath the commercial cookie cutter. If subjecthood does not transcend or predate the society that invents and imagines the self as a category, and if ideology is "a practice producing subjects," then one needs to ask, What sort of industrial kitchen is warehousing that production, and how does it work? Chantal Mouffe, following Louis Althusser, insists that "the subject is not the originating source of consciousness, the expression of the irruption of a subjective principle into objective historical processes, but the product of a specific practice operating through the mechanism of interpolation."[7] While the Althusserian model for social subject formation is useful and has obviously proved a powerful corrective, the "hailing" so energetically and unceasingly underway in a commodity culture is a messy, hit-or-miss affair. The interpolation is not exact, as if Jane were called and Joan (or John) answered, always feeling a little abashed that the name didn't quite fit, but thinking, disconcerted, "Jane *must* be my name. I keep getting called that!" Neither the rubric of the individual will nor that of socially constructed identities is sufficient to the task of describing subjectivity in commodity culture or any other. Different nodes and loci of agency and power intertwine, different subcultural practices weave together with mass cultural messages, as do different interpretive models for understanding the self.

And because so much of the work of subject formation resides in and produces meaning via language, creative writing can intensely exhibit these "dialogic" multiplicities, or poor fits, that resonate throughout our culture.[8] Drives and doubts on the part of the author, as well as the characters emerging from his or her pen, do not align neatly with categorizable identity choices like these "offered" to women in a 1929 J. Walter Thompson advertising campaign: the "debutante, sportswoman, wife, co-ed, mother, woman in the arts, woman in the professions, sub-deb, bride, grandmother, and business girl."[9] Neither individuals nor the social formations of which they comprise a tiny part are this static. The work of approximating these persona categories convincingly and according to commercial definition is often experienced as compulsory, though sometimes the source of keen pleasure, too. This field of labor, typically unmarked, has been the site for the present study.

Large impersonal forces, social biases, and the permutations of fate determine the array of roles open to us at any given point; so do our own predilections. We move from role to role depending on the accidents of our social placement; our negotiations with gender, class, regional, and racial norms; our time in life and the time of day. We very often have complicated, idiosyncratic attitudes about each of the "hats" we wear. From consumer to producer, shopper to vehicle, subdeb to grandmother, and no matter how many additional categories are generated for us in the interim by market surveys, we insist on forging unpredictable relationships to the roles we inhabit for a time. It is this indeterminacy, flux, multiplicity, and excess after which capital chases, in the form of endless commercial address. "Hailed" and even rapt with attention, yet inexhaustively stranger than the marketer's greetings, we remain hard to catch.

Notes

Introduction

1 See for instance, Kevin Goldman, "Study Finds Ads Induce Few People to Buy," *Wall Street Journal*, 17 October 1995, B10. See also Michael Schudson, *Advertising, the Uneasy Persuasion: Its Dubious Impact on American Society* (New York: Basic Books, 1984).

2 Jean Baudrillard argues: "Even though we may be getting better and better at resisting advertising in the *imperative* . . . we do indeed 'believe' in advertising: what we consume in this way is the luxury of a society that projects itself as an agency for dispensing goods" (*The System of Objects*, trans. James Benedict [New York: Verso, 1996], 166).

3 Christine Frederick *Selling Mrs. Consumer* (New York: Business Bourse, 1929), 337.

4 Jackson Lears, "The Ad Man and the Grand Inquisitor: Intimacy, Publicity, and the Administrative State in America, 1880–1940" (paper presented at the Davis Center Seminar, Princeton University, 30 March 1990), 5.

5 See Bruce Barton, *The Man Nobody Knows* (1925; reprint, Indianapolis, Ind.: Bobbs-Merrill, 1980).

6 As a case in point, George Faulkner contended in a presentation on radio advertising that "The word showman carries an undignified, cheap connotation. It has a vaguely semitic, Barnumish, Broadway air to it. . . . This impression of cheapness is due to a misunderstanding . . . we confuse showmanship with one of its branches . . . exploitation" (Staff Meeting Minutes, 12 August 1930, J. Walter Thompson Archives, Duke University; hereafter cited as JWT Archives).

7 On "rainbow moods," see Carl Naether, *Advertising to Women* (New York: Prentice Hall, 1928), 204.

8 See my discussion of Paul K. Edwards's *The Southern Urban Negro as a Consumer* in chapter 4.

9 *Chicago Tribune*, 8 February 1920. Still listed as appearing in 1923 in a compilation of *Ladies Home Journal* headlines (Cutex Accounts, JWT Archives).

10 Judith Butler, *Excitable Speech: A Politics of the Performative* (New York: Routledge, 1997), 134; emphasis added.

11 Michael Uebel, "Men in Color," in *Race and the Subject of Masculinities*, ed. Harry Stecopoulus and Michael Uebel (Durham, N.C.: Duke University Press, 1997), 3.

12 Frank Presbrey, *The History and Development of Advertising* (Garden City, N.Y.: Doubleday and Doran, 1929), 613.

13 The phrase is from Stuart Ewen, *All Consuming Images: The Politics of Style in Contemporary Culture* (New York: Basic Books, 1988).

14 On capitalism's impact on the formation and experience of the leisure sphere, which is obviously heavily mediated by commerce, see, for instance, Eva Illouz, *Consuming the Romantic Utopia: Love and the Cultural Contradictions of Capitalism* (Berkeley: University of California Press, 1997). Public leisure practices throw into question the artificial divide between public and private life.

15 See T. J. Jackson Lears, "From Salvation to Self-Realization: Advertising and the Therapeutic Roots of the Consumer Culture, 1880–1930," in *The Culture of Consumption: Critical Essays in American History, 1880–1980,* ed. Richard Wightman Fox and T. J. Jackson Lears (New York: Pantheon, 1983), 3–38; and Frederick Winslow Taylor, *The Principles of Scientific Management* (1911; reprint, New York: W. W. Norton, 1967). See Max Ernst, "C'est le chapeau qui fait l'homme," 1920 collage, in Werner Spies, *Max Ernst Collages: The Invention of the Surrealist Universe* (New York: Abrams, 1991).

16 On commodity fetishism, see Karl Marx, *Capital: A Critique of Political Economy,* vol. 1, ed. Friedrich Engels, trans. Samuel Moore and Edward Aveling (New York: International Publishers, 1977), 71–83. In *Fables of Abundance: A Cultural History of Advertising in America,* Jackson Lears argues that commodity fetishism, in part, both exemplifies and circumscribes an animistic hunger for the symbolic powers latent in "the things themselves" (New York: Basic Books, 1994).

17 See, for instance, Gary Lindberg, *The Confidence Man in American Literature* (New York: Oxford University Press, 1982); and Glenna Matthews, *"Just a Housewife": The Rise and Fall of Domesticity in America* (New York: Oxford University Press, 1987).

18 See Max Weber, "Protestant Asceticism and the Spirit of Capitalism" (an excerpt from *The Protestant Ethic and the Spirit of Capitalism,* 1905), in *Max Weber: Selections in Translation,* ed. W. G. Runciman, trans. Eric Matthews (Cambridge: Cambridge University Press, 1978), 138–73. I also refer to Talcott Parsons's translation of *The Protestant Ethic and the Spirit of Capitalism* (1958; New York: Scribner's, 1976).

19 Werner Sombart, *The Jews and Modern Capitalism,* trans. M. Epstein (New Brunswick, N.J.: Transaction Books, 1981).

20 See also Natalie Zemon Davis, "Religion and Capitalism Once Again? Jewish Merchant Culture in the Seventeenth Century," *Representations* 57 (summer 1997): 56–84.

21 Essentially taking Weber's model and revaluing it, Michel Foucault provides an example of the same mythologized split appraised in a different way. The supposed liberation that Foucault deems such a misguided model in his *The History of Sexuality, Volume 1: An Introduction* is, in large part, an injunction not just to confess, but to consume. Toward the book's end, Foucault posits a future people who will wonder "how we came to congratulate ourselves for finally . . . having broken free of a long period of harsh repression, a protracted Christian asceticism, greedily and fastidiously adapted to the imperatives of bourgeois economy" (158).

22 Here, I use the Althusserian notion of an ideology that interpolates or "hails": "The individual is interpolated as a (free) subject in order that he shall (freely) accept his

subjection . . . [and] make the gestures and actions of his subjection 'all by himself' " (Louis Althusser, "Ideological State Apparatuses," in *Lenin and Philosophy and Other Essays*, trans. Ben Brewster [London: New Left Books, 1971]).

23 Paul Cherington, quoted in Stephen Fox, *The Mirror-Makers: A History of American Advertising and Its Creators* (New York: William Morrow and Co., 1984).

24 Thorstein Veblen, *Theory of the Leisure Class: An Economic Study of Institutions* (1899; reprint, New York: Modern Library, 1934), 25.

25 Frances Maule, "The Snob Appeal," News Bulletin, March 1923, 11, JWT Archives.

26 See Roland Marchand, *Advertising the American Dream: Making Way for Modernity, 1920–1940* (Berkeley: University of California Press, 1985), 208–17.

27 Stuart Ewen, *Captains of Consciousness: Advertising and the Social Roots of Consumer Culture* (New York: McGraw-Hill, 1976), 36.

28 Odorono ad, *Ladies Home Journal*, October 1928, 155.

29 *New York American*, 12 December 1920; *Cleveland Plain Dealer*, 17 October 1920; and *Chicago Tribune*, 8 February 1920. All in Accounts Files: Chesebrough-Pond's, JWT Archives; Marchand 211.

30 Karl Marx, "Wage Labor and Capital," excerpted in *Marx-Engels Reader*, ed. Robert C. Tucker (New York: W. W. Norton, 1972), 186.

31 Robert J. Heilbroner, *The Nature and Logic of Capitalism* (New York: Norton, 1985), 57.

32 For a brilliant instance of such a correlation, see Walter Benn Michaels on *Sister Carrie*, in *The Gold Standard and the Logic of Naturalism: American Literature at the Turn of the Century* (Berkeley: University of California Press, 1987), 31–58.

33 Jennifer Wicke makes an elitist delineation between advertising and literature impossible in *Advertising Fictions: Literature, Advertisement, and Social Reading* (New York: Columbia University Press, 1988).

34 See Ellen Gruber Garvey, "Reframing the Bicycle: Advertising-Supported Magazines and Scorching Women," *American Quarterly* 47, no. 1 (March 1995): 66–101. See also "The Hungry Husband and the Chiffon Frock," *Ladies Home Journal*, May 1924, 167, for an example of the story-ad, reprinted and considered in a fascinating discussion by Jennifer Scanlon, *Inarticulate Longings: "The Ladies Home Journal," Gender, and the Promises of Consumer Culture* (New York: Routledge, 1995), 75.

35 Along with John Barrymore and Cornelius Vanderbilt Jr., Fitzgerald had to select the "loveliest debutante, sportswoman, wife, co-ed, mother, woman in the arts, woman in the professions, subdeb, bride, grandmother, and business girl" (*Newsletter*, 31 March 1929, JWT Archives). In the ad, he is shown sifting through photographs with an extremely strained, lecherous grin on his face. (Mysteriously, the campaign was a flop.)

36 See, for instance, much of Luigi Manca and Alessandra Manca, eds., *Gender and Utopia in Advertising: A Critical Reader* (Lisle, Ill.: Procopian Press, 1994). See also Doris-Louise Haineault and Jean-Yves Roy, *Unconscious for Sale: Advertising, Psychoanalysis, and the Public*, trans. Kimball Lockhart with Barbara Kerslake, vol. 86

of *Theory and History of Literature* (Minneapolis: University of Minnesota Press, 1993).

37 Rachel Bowlby, *Shopping with Freud* (New York: Routledge, 1993).

38 On the politics and construction of the highbrow/lowbrow divide and its artificiality, see for instance, Lawrence Levine, *Highbrow/Lowbrow: The Emergence of Cultural Hierarchy in America* (Cambridge, Mass.: Harvard University Press, 1988).

39 Bowlby argues convincingly for the interpenetration between the fields of psychology and advertising, something that my own research bears out. The growth of market capitalism was the determining context for the coterminous emergence of psychology and advertising.

40 A thank you to Rachel Bowlby for discussing her argument with me.

41 Sinclair Lewis, quoted in William Holtz and Speer Morgan, eds., "Fragments from a Marriage: Letters from Sinclair Lewis to Grace Hegger Lewis," *Missouri Review* 11, no. 1 (1988): 83.

42 See Cynthia H. Enloe, *Bananas, Beaches, and Bases: Making Feminist Sense of International Politics* (Berkeley: University of California Press, 1990); Nancy L. Green, *Ready-to-Wear, Ready-to-Work: A Century of Industry and Immigrants in Paris and New York* (Durham, N.C.: Duke University Press, 1997); and Andrew Ross, ed., *No Sweat: Fashion, Free Trade, and the Rights of Garment Workers* (New York: Verso, 1997).

43 See Warren I. Susman, "'Personality' and the Making of a Twentieth-Century Culture," in *Culture as History: The Transformation of American Society in the Twentieth Century* (New York: Pantheon, 1984), 271–86; Karen Halttunen, *Confidence Men and Painted Women: A Study of Middle-Class Culture in America, 1830–1870* (New Haven, Conn.: Yale University Press, 1982), 198–210; and Gail Bederman, *Manliness and Civilization: A Cultural History of Gender and Race in the United States, 1880–1917* (Chicago: University of Chicago Press, 1995). Lori Merish times the shift that Susman describes as beginning far earlier in the nineteenth century (see "'The Hand of Refined Taste' in the Frontier Landscape: Caroline Kirkland's *A New Home, Who'll Follow?* and the Feminization of American Consumerism," *American Quarterly* 45, no. 4 [December 1993]: 485–523).

44 Sinclair Lewis, *Babbitt* (1922; reprint, New York: Penguin, 1980).

45 John D'Emilio and Estelle B. Freedman, *Intimate Matters: A History of Sexuality in America* (New York: Harper and Row, 1988), 189.

46 As Jean Baudrillard contends: "Consumption is primarily organized as a discourse to oneself. . . . [T]he object of consumption creates distinctions as a stratification of statuses: if it no longer isolates, it differentiates; it *collectively assigns* the consumers a place in relation to a code, without so much as giving rise to any *collective solidarity* (but quite the opposite)" ("Consumer Society," in *Selected Writings*, ed. Mark Poster [Cambridge: Polity Press, 1988], 54–55).

47 See Peter Laipson, "I Have No Genius for Marriage: Bachelorhood in Urban America, 1870–1930 (Ph.D. diss., University of Michigan, 1996); Katherine Snyder, *Bachelor Narrative: Gender and Representation in Anglo-American Fiction, 1850–*

1914 (Cambridge, Mass.: Yale University Press, 1991); and Andrew Wernick, "From Voyeur to Narcissist: Imaging Men in Contemporary Advertising," in *Beyond Patriarchy: Essays by Men on Pleasure, Power, and Change,* ed. Michael Kaufman (New York: Oxford University Press, 1987).

Chapter 1

1 Stephen Fox, *The Mirror-Makers: A History of American Advertising and Its Creators* (New York: William Morrow and Co., 1984), 13–20.

2 For general histories of the American advertising industry ranging from the critical to the celebratory, see Stuart Ewen, *Captains of Consciousness: Advertising and the Social Roots of the Consumer Culture* (New York: McGraw-Hill, 1976); Fox, *The Mirror-Makers;* Jackson Lears, *Fables of Abundance: A Cultural History of Advertising in America* (New York: Basic Books, 1994); and Roland Marchand, *Advertising the American Dream: Making Way for Modernity, 1920–1940* (Berkeley: University of California Press, 1985). See also Daniel Pope, *The Making of Modern Advertising* (New York: Basic Books, 1983).

3 See Marchand, *Advertising the American Dream,* 8; and Steven Vaughn, *Holding Fast the Inner Lines: Democracy, Nationalism, and the Committee on Public Information* (Chapel Hill, N.C.: University of North Carolina Press, 1980).

4 Though the process should be read more as an interpenetration than a monolithic suppression of "pure" cultural forms, these nationwide endeavors can be seen as having helped to squelch or modify other, more grassroots or localized practices. For example, one campaign waged by the National War Advisory during World War II attempted to "link [women] up with war sentiment" by selling them on the patriotic value of buying ready-made bread rather than baking it at home. Memos from the planning stages of this campaign are explicit about the benefits of this shift to the manufacturers. They assert that the development and aggressive pro-motion of a "standardized War Loaf" or "Liberty Loaf" will get women used to buying baked bread in the name of civic duty, thereby "increas[ing] the baking industry, not only temporarily, but permanently" ("Advertising Plan for the War Emergency Council of the Baking Industry," Microfilm Reel #195, 16 mm. series, 1–14, J. Walter Thompson Archives, Duke University; hereafter cited as JWT Archives). Stuart Ewen points out another instance: the diversity of multiple for-eign language papers for immigrant populations did not imply that they were unshaped by the forces of national advertising. He describes the American Associa-tion of Foreign Language Newspapers as an influential advertising agency that provided space for corporate advertising (and editorials) in foreign language news-papers all over the United States, guaranteeing, as its 1920s' director remarked, that "the American point of view will prevail" (Ewen 1976, 63–64). Finally, Kathy Peiss describes the interplay between African American entrepreneurial beauty culture and white corporations that ultimately sought to tap the African American market. It would clearly be wrong to claim that entrepreneurs like Madame C. J. Walker

and Annie Turnbo Malone were uninfluenced by capitalist principles or dominant cultural values. Nonetheless, African American beauty culture was a mode of commerce, business networking, and aesthetic practice that was perceived by many as being good for the Black community, and it was seriously transformed and restricted by the incursions later made into the cosmetic arena by national corporate advertising. See Kathy Peiss, *Hope in a Jar: The Making of America's Beauty Culture* (New York: Henry Holt, 1998).

5 See Jackson Lears, "The Ad Man and the Grand Inquisitor: Intimacy, Publicity, and the Administrative State in America, 1880–1940" (paper presented at the Davis Center Seminar, Princeton University, 30 March 1990).

6 Marjorie Beale, "Metaphors of Management in French Advertising and Film in the 1920s" (paper presented at the Managing the Visuals of Desire conference, Doreen B. Townsend Center for the Humanities, University of California at Berkeley, September 1993).

7 P. T. Barnum, *Struggles and Triumphs, or Forty Years' Recollections of P. T. Barnum* (Buffalo: Courier Co., 1875). Let me acknowledge the helpful discussion on this point in Donald McQuade's graduate seminar on advertising and literature, University of California at Berkeley, fall 1991.

8 Neil Harris, *Humbug: The Art of P. T. Barnum* (Boston: Little, Brown, 1973); Jennifer Wicke, *Advertising Fictions: Literature, Advertisement, and Social Reading* (New York: Columbia University Press, 1988), 54–86; and Jackson Lears, "From Salvation to Self-Realization: Advertising and the Therapeutic Roots of the Consumer Culture, 1880–1930," in *The Culture of Consumption: Critical Essays in American History, 1880–1980*, ed. Richard Wightman Fox and T. J. Jackson Lears (New York: Pantheon, 1983), 3–38.

9 Michael Schudson invokes both Northrop Frye and Leo Spitzer, who have each argued that the ironic detachment expected from audiences actually allows ads greater impact; we know we're not being "fooled" by the ads, so we relax and let our guard down. See Michael Schudson, *Advertising, the Uneasy Persuasion: Its Dubious Impact on American Society* (New York: Basic Books, 1986); Northrop Frye, *The Modern Century* (Toronto: Oxford University Press, 1967); and Leo Spitzer, "American Advertising Explained as Popular Art," in *Leo Spitzer: Representative Essays*, ed. Alban K. Forcione et al. (Stanford, Calif.: Stanford University Press, 1988).

10 For example, National Public Radio's *Morning Edition* runs stories on the "Cola Wars," tracking the point lead in market shares and analyzing advertising strategies as Diet and Pepsi Cola "square off" (Josh Buloz, 20 May 1997; or Brian Milner, "Seagram's Sells Tropicana to PepsiCo $3.3 Billion (U.S.) Deal for Juice Unit Opens New Front in War with Coca Cola," *The Globe and Mail*, July 21, 1998, B1). See also Roger Enrico and Jesse Kornbluth, *The Other Guy Blinked: How Pepsi Won the Cola Wars* (New York: Bantam, 1986).

11 Anne McClintock, *Imperial Leather: Race, Gender, and Sexuality in the Colonial Contest* (New York: Routledge, 1995), 63–64.

12 Indicative of this phenomenon, the visuals for the highly effective antiadvertising video, *The Ad and the Ego,* come almost entirely from ads themselves; one realizes how much advertisers are engaged in an ongoing commentary on advertising and its effects in the ads themselves. Many of the critics' most subtle points were also being made in the ads they presented (often rather brilliantly), and yet somehow, the self-reflexive nature of these ads does not make them less compelling as sales incentives (see *The Ad and the Ego,* directed by Harold Boihem, California Newsreel, San Francisco, 1996).

13 See Susan Curtis, *A Consuming Faith: The Social Gospel and Modern American Culture* (Baltimore, Md.: Johns Hopkins University Press, 1991).

14 Susan Curtis quotes Bishop Charles D. Williams: "Selfishness, the direct effort to *save* your life, is paganism. Spend your life, your soul, your self—that is the very fundamental of Christian experience" (*A Consuming Faith,* 239).

15 Jennifer Scanlon treats this utopic urge carefully; see her *Inarticulate Longings: "The Ladies Home Journal," Gender, and the Promises of Consumer Culture* (New York: Routledge, 1995). See also George H. Rowell, *Forty Years an Advertising Agent, 1865–1905* (New York: Printers Ink, 1906); Christine Frederick, *Selling Mrs. Consumer* (New York: Business Bourse, 1929); Frank Presbrey, *The History and Development of Advertising* (Garden City, N.Y.: Doubleday and Doran, 1929); Claude Hopkins, *My Life in Advertising* (New York: Harper, 1927); Earnest Elmo Calkins, *Business the Civilizer* (Boston: Little, Brown and Co., 1928); and Bruce Barton, *The Man Nobody Knows* (1922; reprint, Indianapolis, Ind.: Bobbs-Merrill, 1980).

16 Catherine Beecher, with Harriet Beecher Stowe, *American Woman's Home* (New York: J. B. Ford and Co., 1869).

17 See Dolores Hayden, *The Grand Domestic Revolution: A History of Feminist Designs for American Homes, Neighborhoods, and Cities* (Cambridge, Mass.: MIT Press, 1981), for a helpful study of the late-nineteenth-century materialist feminists' struggle to dissolve the borders between the public and private spheres. She reaches the conclusion that, finally, Catherine Beecher was "the ultimate domestic feminist" (55).

18 Warren I. Susman, *Culture as History: The Transformation of American Society in the Twentieth Century* (New York: Pantheon, 1984), 129.

19 See Helen Woodward, *Through Many Windows* (New York: Harper and Bros., 1926), 160–61.

20 Robert J. Heilbroner, *The Nature and Logic of Capitalism* (New York: W. W. Norton, 1985), 36–37.

21 Max Weber, *The Protestant Ethic and the Spirit of Capitalism,* trans. Talcott Parsons (New York: Scribner's, 1958), 54.

22 "Fear of Publicity Hid a Great Invention," *Newsletter,* no. 142, 22 July 1926, 173, JWT Archives.

23 In a relevant parallel, the seventeenth and eighteenth centuries' condemnation of avarice, just like the early twentieth century's condemnation of advertising, re-

quired an anti-Semitic branding as Hebraic of those professions (lender, merchant, advertiser, entertainment producer) and qualities that were actually crucial to social and economic functioning in an incipient capitalist society, since capitalism was not easily aligned with extant "Christian" virtues.

24 Quoted in *Newsletter*, no. 76, 16 April 1925, 5, JWT Archives.

25 Merle Higley, *Women in Advertising in New York Agencies* (New York: Young Women's Christian Association, 1924).

26 In an undated J. Walter Thompson *Newsletter* from the twenties, staff member Jim Young poked extended fun at Claude Hopkins, writing "Fraud Hopkins's" *Life in Advertising*. The main targets of his satire are Hopkins's self-contradictions and ostensible populism. Young's ribbing is energetic enough that it reminds us of how alert and cynical advertisers often were, how detached they could be from the hyperbole generated within their own profession.

27 Presbrey's obsession with hygiene here and elsewhere in his work evokes Jackson Lears's discussion of the link between advertising's hard sell of "high sanitary standards," and national concerns about immigration and integration and their impact on racial "purity" (1990, 33).

28 William L. Day, Staff Meeting Minutes, 26 July 1927, 7, JWT Archives.

29 "In Government at the present time, in spite of all the efforts at organization that are characteristic of a Democracy, we see greater governmental efficiency being achieved in two countries, Italy and Russia, under a dictatorship. That is something for the people in this country to think about. The result of guidance by one man, of dictation by one man, is more efficient than the result of mass cooperation in this country. Mussolini said the other day that Italy could not financially afford a Republic. He meant that he as dictator had been able to stamp out the graft that is characteristic of all republics, and to run the country on more economical lines" (William L. Day, "The Modern Fetish: Organization," Staff Meeting Minutes, 19 January 1932, 7, JWT Archives). There were interesting links between American advertisers and Mussolini's government. To cite one: in 1925, Mussolini's government sold advertising space on Italian postage stamps to American companies (*Newsletter*, no. 76, 16 April 1925, 2). See also Karen Pinkus, *Bodily Regimes: Italian Advertising under Fascism* (Minneapolis: University of Minnesota Press, 1995).

30 William L. Day, Staff Meeting Minutes, 17 February 1931, 2, JWT Archives.

31 Lary May, *Screening out the Past: The Birth of Mass Culture and the Motion Picture Industry* (New York: Oxford University Press, 1980), xii.

32 For more on specific interpenetrations between the two worlds, including product placement, see Charles Eckert, "The Carole Lombard in Macy's Window," in *Fabrications: Costume and The Female Body*, ed. Jane Gaines and Charlotte Herzog (New York: Routledge, 1990), 100–21.

33 "Rising Value of Emotional Appeal Seen in Advertising Copy Trends," William Esty, quoted in *News*, November 1930, 5, JWT Archives.

34 Mildred Holmes, *Newsletter*, 15 October 1928, JWT Archives (punctuation in original).

35 "Talk Given by Mr. James Quirk, Editor of *Photoplay Magazine* in the Assembly Hall on March 24th, 1930," Staff Meeting Minutes, JWT Archives.

36 On movie palace ushers, the luxury around them, and the negotiations with class, racial, and ethnic heterogeneity that the movement from nickelodeon to cinematic "cathedral" indicated, see "You Are the Star: The Evolution of the Theater Palace, 1908–1929," in May, *Screening out the Past*, 147–66.

37 Jim Young, "My Life in Advertising, by Fraud Hopkins," *Newsletter*, n.d., 90, JWT Archives.

38 Mr. Crampton, Staff Meeting Minutes, 7 December 1932, 15, JWT Archives.

39 On the "vehicle," see the introduction and chapters 4 and 5 of this book. See Philip Fisher, "Appearing and Disappearing in Public: Social Space in Late-Nineteenth-Century Literature and Culture," in *Reconstructing American Literary History*, ed. Sacvan Bercovitch, *Harvard English Studies* 13 (1986): 159–60.

Chapter 2

1 Glen A. Love, *"Babbitt": An American Life* (New York: Twayne, 1993), 12; and Stephen Fox, *The Mirror-Makers: A History of American Advertising and Its Creators* (New York: William Morrow and Co., 1984), 107.

2 Sinclair Lewis, *Babbitt* (1922; reprint, New York: Penguin, 1980), 82.

3 See, for instance, James M. Hutchisson, *The Rise of Sinclair Lewis, 1920–1930* (University Park: Pennsylvania State University Press, 1996); and chapter 3 of this book.

4 Bruce Barton, *The Man Nobody Knows* (1922; reprint, Indianapolis, Ind.: Bobbs-Merrill, 1980), 12.

5 See also Ralph Waldo Trine, *The Power that Wins: Henry Ford and Ralph Waldo Trine in an Intimate Talk on Life—the Inner Thing—the Things of the Mind and Spirit—and the Inner Powers and Forces that Make for Achievement* (Indianapolis, Ind.: Bobbs-Merrill, 1929). Note that this text by the prolific "inspirational" writer Trine was a Bobbs-Merrill production just like Barton's book.

6 Michel Foucault, *The History of Sexuality, Volume I: An Introduction*, trans. Robert Hurley (New York: Random House, 1990), 124.

7 John D'Emilio and Estelle B. Freedman, *Intimate Matters: A History of Sexuality in America* (New York: Harper and Row, 1988), 234. See also Nathan G. Hale Jr., *Freud and the Americans: The Beginnings of Psychoanalysis in the United States, 1876–1917* (New York: Oxford University Press, 1971).

8 See Hazel V. Carby, " 'On the Threshold of the Woman's Era': Lynching, Empire, and Sexuality in Black Feminist Theory," in *"Race," Writing, and Difference*, ed. Henry Louis Gates Jr. (Chicago: University of Chicago Press, 1986), 301–16; Kathy Peiss, *Cheap Amusements: Working-Women and Leisure in Turn-of-the-Century New York* (Philadelphia: Temple University Press, 1986); D'Emilio and Freedman, *Intimate Matters;* Timothy Gilfoyle, *City of Eros: New York City, Prostitution, and the Commercialization of Sex, 1790–1920* (New York: W. W. Norton, 1992); Edward J.

Bristow, *Prostitution and Prejudice: The Jewish Fight against White Slavery, 1870–1939* (New York: Schocken, 1983); and Richard Fung, "Burdens of Representation, Burdens of Responsibility," in *Constructing Masculinity,* ed. Brian Wallis and Simon Watson (New York: Routledge, 1995).

9 Gail Bederman, *Manliness and Civilization: A Cultural History of Gender and Race in the United States, 1880–1917* (Chicago: University of Chicago Press, 1995), 21.

10 Richard Dyer, "The White Man's Muscles," in Stecopoulus and Uebel, *Race and the Subject of Masculinities,* 289.

11 For a reading of the corporatization of American culture, see Oliver Zunz, *Making America Corporate, 1870–1920* (Chicago: University of Chicago Press, 1990).

12 Elizabeth Lunbeck, *The Psychiatric Persuasion: Knowledge, Gender, and Power in Modern America* (Princeton, N.J.: Princeton University Press, 1994), 240–44.

13 See Bill Boisvert, "Apostles of the New Entrepreneur: Business Theory and the Management Crisis," *Baffler,* no. 6: 69–81.

14 Bob Briner, *The Management Methods of Jesus* (Nashville, Tenn.: Thomas Nelson Inc., 1996); reviewed by Gustav Niebuhr, "New Book on Jesus, Corporate Manager Nonpareil," *New York Times,* 16 March 1996, 9.

15 T. J. Jackson Lears, "From Salvation to Self-Realization: Advertising and the Therapeutic Roots of the Consumer Culture, 1880–1930," in *The Culture of Consumption: Critical Essays in American History, 1880–1980,* ed. Richard Wightman Fox and T. J. Jackson Lears (New York: Pantheon, 1983), 30.

16 See Claude Hopkins, *My Life in Advertising* (New York: Harper, 1927), 88, 98.

17 Its way paved for it by her earlier book about the nineteenth century, *The Feminization of American Culture,* Ann Douglas's *Terrible Honesty: Mongrel Manhattan in the 1920s* seems to replicate Barton's model for the drama of the twentieth century: his gendering of the supposed struggle between a feminized, overly sanctimonious, outmoded Victorianism and a testosterone-based, refreshingly virile modernity is re-created at close to face value in *Terrible Honesty* (Ann Douglas, *The Feminization of American Culture* [New York: Doubleday, 1988], and Ann Douglas, *Terrible Honesty: Mongrel Manhattan in the 1920s* [New York: Farrar, Straus and Giroux, 1995]).

18 For instance: "Every American . . . lives in an atmosphere of action. . . . It is different in Europe. There the social and economic life of the people has crystallized into rigid forms. Advertising is revolutionary . . . [since] it induce[s] people to do something that they never did before. It is a form of progress and it interests only progressive people. Stupid people are not much impressed with advertising. They move in a rut of tradition" (J. Walter Thompson, *The J. W. T. Book: A Series of Talks on Advertising,* 1909, 5–9, J. Walter Thompson Archives, Duke University; hereafter cited as JWT Archives).

19 See "From Salvation to Self-Realization." For a brilliant discussion of G. Stanley Hall's work, see Bederman, *Manliness and Civilization,* 77–120.

20 "Wrigley on Advertising," *Newsletter,* 5 November 1922, 7, JWT Archives.

21 See Theodore Menten, *Advertising Art in the Art Deco Style* (New York: Dover, 1975).

22 "Get the Warier Game Too," *Newsletter,* no. 146, 19 August 1926, 193, JWT Archives.

23 Letter from William Groom to Stanley Resor, 9 June 1924, 67, Account Files: Woodbury, "The Story of Woodbury's Facial Soap," JWT Archives.

24 Earnest Elmo Calkins, *Business the Civilizer* (Boston: Little, Brown and Co., 1928), vi. "No such tales of woe"? Calkins seems to ignore, for instance, the 1911 fire at the Triangle Shirtwaist Company in Manhattan, where 146 pieceworkers died because their employers had locked them in to ensure high productivity (see Nancy L. Green, *Ready-to-Wear, Ready-to-Work: A Century of Industry and Immigrants in Paris and New York* (Durham, N.C.: Duke University Press, 1997), 56.

25 Hardly a bit player in his day, Calkins cofounded an advertising agency with Ralph Holden, and was responsible for the ubiquitous "Sunny Jim" and "Phoebe Snow" jingle campaigns. The advertising industry's main trade paper, *Printer's Ink,* described Sunny Jim as being "as well known as President Roosevelt or Pierpont Morgan" (Fox, *The Mirror-Makers,* 47).

26 For instance, Lydia Hunt Sigourney wrote at length about the function of tedium in women's lives. For her, the capacity to endure it proved a woman's worth, though the irony lay in her own refusal to relegate herself to the "trifles" of the domestic arena, as the prodigious outpourings from her study made evident. "Household occupations, to men . . . seem a tissue of trifles. Yet . . . 'trifles make the sum of human things.' " "A habit . . . of complaining of the inconveniences of our lot . . . destroys innocent cheerfulness, and marks even the countenance with malevolence. The satisfaction which it brings is morbid, and betokens internal disease" (Lydia Hunt Sigourney, *Letters to Young Ladies* [New York: Harper and Bros., 1836], 216, 168).

27 Elizabeth Lunbeck describes a contemporaneous move that follows a similar progression. Psychiatrists in the teens and twenties, as eager as were advertisers to legitimate their field and hoping to gain predominance over the female social workers who shared their professional turf, "represented science as male." They used "language shot through with muscular masculinism," in part to deflect attention from the fact that domestic problems, emotions, love relations, and child rearing—"the stuff of psychiatrists' ambitious reach" and often the primary topics addressed by advertisers as well—"fell within women's traditional purview; all were culturally 'feminine' " (Lunbeck, *The Psychiatric Persuasion,* 34).

28 Oliver Zunz (*Making America Corporate*) argues forcefully against the notion that the period's "true" story was that of the ruling class, the company presidents, and the wheelings and dealings of financial capitalists. He insists that the "salesmen of prosperity" were by no means simply errand boys to the top rung of the business world, but active agents in their own right. *Babbitt,* while participating in the progressive critical tradition that Zunz thinks we must question, does provide a corrective by making a midlevel manager and his world its entire focus.

29 In a piece written for the *Post* in 1921, Lewis lambasted an American mythologization of pioneer machismo, complaining both that it was used to excuse a stultifying

anti-intellectualism and was unearned. Though he does not explicitly mention the gendering of this myth, his satiric prose is redolent with it, as in *Babbitt*. Frustratingly, his coupling of American and European pioneering ignores the imperialistic violence done to indigenous populations in these global conquests of the inhabited "wilds." See "The Pioneer Myth," in Hutchisson, *The Rise of Sinclair Lewis*, 217–21.

30   For example, see Paula Fass ("Making and Remaking an Event: The Leopold and Loeb Case in American Culture," *Journal of American History* 80, no. 3 [December 1993], 919–51) on the press coverage of the sensational 1920s' Leopold and Loeb murder case. Fass explains that Nathan Leopold's precocious brilliance and his "over" education were the focus of much anxious speculation, and played a central part in the depiction of Leopold as "abnormal" (925). Here, too, intellectual accomplishments were linked to a matrix of other "abnormal" social traits: Leopold and Loeb were Jewish, wealthy, and apparently involved in a homosexual union. Of course, "abnormalities" tend to be scapegoated and judged in conceptual clusters. Bookishness, for instance, has often been labeled effeminate; Jewish men have frequently had their heterosexuality challenged by anti-Semites, and mistrust of Jewish scholasticism has generally been a component of anti-Semitism (see Sander Gilman, *Smart Jews: The Construction of the Image of Superior Jewish Intelligence* [Lincoln: University of Nebraska Press, 1996]).

31   See, for one, Nancy Armstrong, *Desire and Domestic Fiction: A Political History of the Novel* (New York: Oxford University Press, 1987).

32   Jennifer Wicke, *Advertising Fictions: Literature, Advertisement, and Social Reading* (New York: Columbia University Press, 1988), 172–75.

33   See personnel files for Helen Brown Becket and Frances Maule (JWT Archives), both of whom went on to become longtime J. Walter Thompson employees. In part, recommenders rush to assure employers of the practicality of their candidates exactly because of the advertising industry's long-term appeal to artistic individuals. Industry wide, ambivalence reigned about the professional value of "creativity."

34   See Stephen Fox (*The Mirror-Makers*, 108–11) with regard to Barton's doubts and ambivalences about his craft. And see the ambivalent advertiser modeled after Barton, Barnham Dunn, in Harford Powel Jr.'s novel *The Virgin Queene* (Boston: Little, Brown and Co., 1928).

35   At the 1900 Paris Exposition, Henry Adams ("The Dynamo and the Virgin," in *The Harper American Literature*, ed. Donald McQuade et al. [New York: Harper and Row, 1987]) felt the "forty-foot dynamos as a moral force, much as the early Christians felt the Cross" (449). Barton also figures the moral force of Christ as a dynamo—hardly a surprising inversion during an era that saw commerce transformed by the practical applications of this energy converter, when the workings of individuals and social formations were increasingly figured as systems of energy distribution and transformation, operating with varying degrees of efficiency. See also Frederick Winslow Taylor, *The Principles of Scientific Management* (1911; re-

print, New York: W. W. Norton, 1967), for the classic example of the mechanistic management model.

36 On "personal magnetism" and corporate America, see Karen Halttunen, *Confidence Men and Painted Women: A Study of Middle-Class Culture in America, 1830–1870* (New Haven, Conn.: Yale University Press, 1982), 206–9.

37 See Ralph Waldo Emerson, "The Over-Soul" (1841), in *Selected Essays*, ed. Larzer Ziff (New York: Penguin, 1982), 205–24. See also Jackson Lears, "The Things Themselves," in *Fables of Abundance: A Cultural History of Advertising in America* (New York: Basic Books, 1994), 379–414. The chapter title invokes Emerson: "The soul answers never by words, but by the thing itself that is inquired after" (215).

38 This emphasis on public perception remains a crucial component in the philosophy that drives industry oversight of truth in advertising. Self-regulation was an early and indispensable ensurer of industry legitimization, urged and overseen from early in this century by the American Association of Advertising Agencies (see T. J. Jackson Lears, "The Ad Man and the Grand Inquisitor: Intimacy, Publicity, and the Administrative State in America, 1880–1940" [paper presented at the Davis Center Seminar, Princeton University, 30 March 1990]; and Stuart Ewen, *Captains of Consciousness: Advertising and the Social Roots of the Consumer Culture* [New York: McGraw-Hill, 1976]). In its current form, the International Code of Advertising Practice of the International Chamber of Commerce begins: "All advertising should be legal, decent, honest and truthful. Every advertisement should be prepared with a due sense of social responsibility, and should conform to the principles of fair competition as generally accepted in business. No advertisement should be such as to impair public confidence in advertising" (quoted in J. J. Boddewyn, *Advertising Self-Regulation and Outside Participation: A Multinational Companion* [New York: Quorom Books, 1988], 3).

39 Warren I. Susman, *Culture as History: The Transformation of American Society in the Twentieth Century* (New York: Pantheon, 1984), 129.

40 Max Weber, *The Protestant Ethic and the Spirit of Capitalism*, trans. Talcott Parsons (New York: Scribner's, 1976), 52.

41 Mr. Kimball, Staff Meeting Minutes, 25 November 1930, JWT Archives.

42 Anne McClintock, *Imperial Leather: Race, Gender, and Sexuality in the Colonial Contest* (New York: Routledge, 1995), 124.

43 Lears, "The Ad Man and the Grand Inquisitor," 23. See also Lears, *Fables of Abundance*, 212.

44 On P. T. Barnum, see Wicke, *Advertising Fictions*, 54–86.

45 Jackson Lears quotes a 1908 *Printers' Ink* report about a manufacturer who exclaimed, "Every time I get mixed up with my advertising problems, I feel the ground sink away from me, and I am floated away into the imponderable ether!" (Lears 1994, 215). This engagement with the intangible, with "ether," was both a mortification to and an opportunity for advertisers.

46 "Rising Value of Emotional Appeal Seen in Advertising Copy Trends," *News*, November 1930, 5, JWT Archives.

47 H. G. Wells, *Tono-Bungay* (1908; reprint, New York: Duffield and Co., 1927), 177.

48 Staff Meeting Minutes, 9 January 1929, 2, JWT Archives.

49 "A Little-Understood By-Product of Advertising," *Newsletter*, no. 176, 17 March 1927, 257, JWT Archives.

50 Powel gives Dunn an office decorated precisely like Barton's, with which Powel was quite familiar (Fox, *The Mirror-Makers*, 109).

51 See Stephen Fox (*The Mirror-Makers*, 109–11) regarding Barton's own ambivalence about advertising.

52 On copywriters' cross-gender impersonations, see chapter 3 of this book.

53 See Sheldon Norman Grebstein, "*Babbitt*: Synonym for a State of Mind," in *The Merrill Studies in "Babbitt,"* ed. Martin Light (Columbus, Ohio: Merrill, 1971), 32–44; Love, *An American Life*, 77.

54 Eve Kosofsky Sedgwick, *Epistemology of the Closet* (Berkeley: University of California Press, 1990).

55 See Ellen Gruber Garvey, *The Adman in the Parlor: Magazines and the Gendering of Consumer Culture, 1880s to 1910s* (New York: Oxford University Press, 1996), 80–105, for a discussion of advertising brand names' entry into fictional texts.

56 Do we have here a hidden Jew? Tanis's odd last name sounds like a melding of "Jewish" and "unique," two highly dangerous qualities for the characters in Babbitt's world. Thanks to Natalie Zemon Davis, in conversation, for this insight. To keep this footnote collaborative, let me also mention the astute remark made by Rachel Bowlby (in a letter) that the surname Judique also has a French ring, which "reinforc[es] the . . . cliché of the bohemian / cosmopolitan 'set.' "

57 H. L. Mencken and George Jean Nathan, *The American Credo* (New York: Knopf, 1920), 37. See Grebstein, "State of Mind."

58 Lunbeck, *The Psychiatric Persuasion*, 240–42. Lunbeck quotes Earnest Elmo Southard, "The Mental Hygiene of Industry: A Movement that Particularly Concerns Employment Managers," *Industrial Management* 59 (1920): 100–106.

59 David Riesman, *The Lonely Crowd: A Study of the Changing American Character* (New Haven, Conn.: Yale University Press, 1950). Grebstein ("State of Mind," 36) links *Babbitt* to Bourne's 1920 *History of a Literary Radical: And Other Essays*, ed. Van Wyck Brooks (New York: B. W. Huebsch, 1920).

60 Thomas Frank, "Babbitt Rex: Boob and Boho in the Businessman's Republic," *Baffler* 10: 7–9.

61 Martin Light, "Editor's Preface," to a special issue on Sinclair Lewis, *Modern Fiction Studies* 31, no. 3 (fall 1985): 482–83.

62 Christopher P. Wilson, "Sinclair Lewis and the Passing of Capitalism," *American Studies* 34, no. 2 (fall 1983): 95–108.

63 Letters from Sinclair Lewis, quoted in Grace Hegger Lewis, *With Love from Gracie: Sinclair Lewis, 1912–1925* (New York: Harcourt Brace and Co., 1955), 210–12.

64 Of course, one of these avenues is Babbitt's affair with Judique. In a fascinating recent discussion of adultery, Laura Kipnis considers the piercing hungers for happiness and transformation that fuel most decisions to embark on an affair. In so

doing, however, she downplays the many social conventions and presumptions that have led adultery to become, most often, a way to channel, manage, and dispense with these otherwise potentially anarchic drives (Laura Kipnis, "Adultery," *Intimacy,* a special issue of *Critical Inquiry* 24, no. 2 [winter 1998]: 289–327).

65 Personnel Files, Application file, Helen Brown Beckett, 1924, JWT Archives.

66 Thomas Frank considers this emphasis in *Babbitt* not merely as the protagonist's shrinking from rebellion, but as Lewis's retreat from political involvement: "For the left politics in which Lewis ached to participate, *Babbitt* substituted a politics of authenticity, an aestheticized struggle still fought today through TV commercials" (Frank, "Babbitt Rex," 9).

67 On the concept of cultural safety valves, see anthropologist Victor Turner, *The Ritual Process: Structure and Anti-Structure* (Chicago: Aldine Pub. Co., 1969).

68 Stuart and Elizabeth Ewen, *Channels of Desire: Mass Images and the Shaping of American Consciousness* (New York: McGraw-Hill, 1982), 266.

Chapter 3

1 Robert Carey, address to the League of Women Advertisers, 18 September 1923, quoted in Dorothy Dignam, "Record of Annual Dinners and Dinner Dances from 1913," Dignam Papers, Schlesinger Library, Radcliffe College; hereafter cited as Schlesinger Library.

2 Helen Rowland, 20 March 1917, quoted in Dorothy Dignam, "Record of Annual Dinners and Dinner Dances from 1913," Dignam Papers, Schlesinger Library.

3 Two books published since I developed this work, both excellent contributions to the field, discuss the women at J. Walter Thompson Company Women's Editorial Department. See Jennifer Scanlon, *Inarticulate Longings: "The Ladies Home Journal," Gender, and the Promises of Consumer Culture* (New York: Routledge, 1995), 169–227; and Kathy Peiss, *Hope in a Jar: The Making of America's Beauty Culture* (New York: Henry Holt, 1998), 97–166.

4 Waldo spent her entire advertising career with the J. Walter Thompson Company, becoming its first female vice president in 1944. In the 1960s, she was interviewed by a company archivist. See the Sidney Bernstein Papers, J. Walter Thompson Archives, Duke University; hereafter cited as JWT Archives.

5 Carl Naether, *Advertising to Women* (New York: Prentice Hall, 1928), xii.

6 Claude Hopkins, *My Life in Advertising* (New York: Harper, 1927). Indeed, a "Rural and Small Town Investigation," conducted by the Research Department of the JWT agency in 1923, interviewed 326 women versus only 23 men in Putnam County, New York, and 787 women versus 93 men in Randolph County, Indiana (JWT Research Department Records, JWT Archives).

7 *News Bulletin* 123, July 1926, 7, JWT Archives.

8 See, for an instance of such theorizing, Walter Dill Scott, *The Psychology of Advertising* (Boston: Small, Maynard, 1903), which was revised many times after its initial publication. See also Edward K. Strong, *The Psychology of Selling and Advertising*

(New York: McGraw-Hill, 1925). Or consider the career of John B. Watson, who in 1924 left behind a position of some prestige as a behavioral psychologist at Johns Hopkins University to become resident psychology expert at the JWT agency. T. J. Jackson Lears has argued that the crystallization and codification—the scientification—of advertising's art of influence was a key development in an industry-wide effort to become one of American society's "managerial" professions. (Jackson Lears, "The Ad Man and the Grand Inquisitor: Intimacy, Publicity, and the Administrative State in America 1880–1940" [paper presented at the Davis Center Seminar, Princeton University, 30 March 1990]).

9   Oft cited, Christine Frederick's *Selling Mrs. Consumer* (New York: Business Bourse, 1929) was also sometimes parroted, as a fascinating article by Margaret Weishaar, entitled " 'Psyching' Mrs. Smith: Two Special Feminine Urges Make Her a Spender," makes clear (*People* [JWT newsletter], October 1937, 4–7, JWT Archives).

10 Christine Frederick, "Advertising and the So-Called 'Average Woman,' " chapter 14 of an undisclosed book, Christine Isobel MacGaffey Frederick Papers, Schlesinger Library, 229.

11 On Hoover's philosophy of abundance, see William Leach, "Herbert Hoover's Emerald City and Managerial Government," in *Land of Desire: Merchants, Power, and the Rise of a New American Culture* (New York: Pantheon, 1993), 49–378.

12 In a similar vein, an earlier inspirational writer, Orison Swett Marden, declared that while "proper economy" has its place, "this gloomy fear . . . this postponing," is a "disease of narrow, untrustful souls" enervated by what he terms "fear-germs" (*Every Man a King, or Might in Mind-Mastery* [New York: T. Y. Crowell, 1906]). Presciently, he brings together advertising's injunction to spend and its awestruck invocation of the germ.

13 Jackson Lears discusses related themes in *Fables of Abundance: A Cultural History of Advertising in America* (New York: Basic Books, 1994).

14 Margaret King Eddy, interview by Sidney Bernstein, 19 November 1963, 7, Sidney Bernstein Papers, JWT Archives.

15 See anonymous, "Notes on the Woodbury Investigation in Boston, Part Two," Department of Records, Microfilm Reel, no. 45, 16 mm. series, 22 May 1923, JWT Archives.

16 "Toilet Soap Survey," Microfilm Reel, no. 47, 16 mm. series, JWT Archives.

17 Edith Lewis and Aminta Casseres, Staff Meeting Minutes, 5 January 1932, 15, JWT Archives.

18 The work of the adwoman "unveils the fact that, if women are such good mimics, it is because they are not simply resorbed in this function. They also remain elsewhere" (Luce Irigaray, "This Sex Which Is Not One," trans. Claudia Reeder, in *New French Feminisms*, ed. Elaine Marks and Isabelle de Courtivron [Brighton, U.K.: Harvester, 1980], 76).

19 May Heery, quoted in Dorothy Dignam, "Trends in Advertising," 1928, 5, Dignam Papers, Schlesinger Library.

20 Ruth Waldo, quoted in Doris E. Fleischman (a.k.a. Mrs. Edward Bernays), ed., *An Outline of Careers for Women: A Practical Guide to Achievement* (Garden City, N.Y.: Doubleday, Doran, 1931), 13.

21 See also Peiss, *Hope in a Jar*, 120.

22 Dorothy Dignam, "It's Different When You Get Acquainted," 1937, A–114, box 3, folder 18, Dignam Papers, Schlesinger Library.

23 See Jennifer Scanlon (*Inarticulate Longings*, 169–227) and Roland Marchand (*Advertising the American Dream: Making Way for Modernity, 1920–1940* [Berkeley: University of California Press, 1985], 35–38) for more demographically accurate profiles of the women in advertising, who were middle to upper middle class, often single, urban, secular, and highly educated.

24 On advertising's efforts to sell itself as reputable, see, for instance, Lears, "The Ad Man and the Grand Inquisitor."

25 Helen Brown Beckett, Personnel Files, 1924, JWT Archives.

26 Jennifer Scanlon's work suggests that despite such invocations of the consumer role, women applying for work at JWT were careful to distance themselves from stereotypically "feminine" menial office work (Scanlon, *Inarticulate Longings*, 182).

27 See Jennifer Scanlon (ibid., 173) for statistics about the exclusion of women from these spheres that validate Waldo's stance.

28 A JWT newsletter editorial (coyly anonymous) noted that in a display of completely subversive solidarity, the secretaries in Waldo's department had also struck up the practice of wearing their hats in the office—probably eager themselves to claim professional dignity. "By the time the stenographers begin wearing their hats, there may be nobody left to give executive directions to except us men. Shall we keep our derbies on, in self-defense?" ("Shall We Join the Hatties?" *Newsletter*, vol. 10, no. 20, 15 October 1928, JWT Archives). Waldo became vice president of JWT in 1944, after twenty-nine (be-hatted) years with the agency. She served in this capacity until 1960.

29 As Catherine Oglesby made clear in a 1930 article, however, this agency was not a maverick so much as an exemplar of the industry's increasing openness to women ("Women in Advertising," *Ladies Home Journal*, October 1930, 22–23, 61). Nonetheless, even at JWT, staff meetings were almost invariably 70 to 90 percent male, and even top female ad executives just about never earned more than $15,000 a year.

30 "Women in Advertising," House Ad, *Advertising Club News*, 6 May 1918, JWT Archives.

31 See "Edith Lewis," in "Important Women (Early Days)," Sidney Bernstein Papers, JWT Archives; and Personnel Files, JWT Archives.

32 Thanks to Ellen Gartrell at the JWT Archives for helping with this information.

33 Agnes Court, quoted in Nancy Stephenson, "Helen Resor Was a Militant Suffragist," Sidney Bernstein Papers, JWT Archives. Dorothy Dignam details the gradual about-face of the League of Advertising Women of New York regarding the suffrag-

ists; in 1913, two league members were "willing women should vote if they want to" but disapproving of suffragette militancy. In 1917, the club quietly decided to enter a contingent in the suffragist parade, and by December of that year, the league's membership chair was campaigning vigorously for the New York State Suffrage Party (Dorothy Dignam, "Causes," 1–2, Dignam Papers, Schlesinger Library).

34 See Scanlon, *Inarticulate Longings*, 187–89, for elaboration.

35 Sam Meek, quoted in "Mr. Resor—Nepotism," typescript in Resor biographical file, 16 March 1964, Sidney Bernstein Papers, JWT Archives.

36 Oglesby, "Women in Advertising," *Ladies Home Journal*, October 1930, 61.

37 "Re: Mrs. Resor and Separation of Women's from Men's Editorial Group," Ruth Waldo, quoted in Sidney Bernstein Papers, JWT Archives. In a 1963 interview, adwoman Margaret King Eddy remarked that, by contrast, " 'Now we appear to be sliding into a supervisory system. . . . ' 'Who are the supervisors? Not men, are they?' 'Oh yes. [laughs] Oh yes. That's the point, of course. I'm talking really quite off the record, because that's not the sort of thing they would want published' " (interview by Sidney Bernstein, 16 November 1963, 4, Sidney Bernstein Papers, JWT Archives).

38 *Newsletter,* September 1975, 3, Sidney Bernstein Files, JWT Archives.

39 Aminta Casseres, Staff Meeting Minutes, 21 October 1930, JWT Archives. In keeping with Casseres's stance, Christine Frederick asserts often that though "women are admirers of female beauty," "the American woman . . . resents the mere idea of so promiscuously using woman as bait. She sees the all too obvious machinery of the advertising puppet show behind the flaunting of woman in advertising" ("Women as Bait in Advertising Copy," a speech before the League of Advertising Women, 19 October 1920, 17, Frederick Papers, Schlesinger Library).

40 Dorothy Dignam, "Club Achievements," 3, Dignam Papers, Schlesinger Library.

41 Staff Meeting Minutes, 25 May 1932, 7, JWT Archives.

42 *Newsletter,* May 1930, 5, JWT Archives.

43 Pond's Cold Cream ad, *Good Housekeeping,* November 1923, 87.

44 Helen Woodward, *Through Many Windows* (New York: Harper and Bros., 1926), 160–61.

45 "Our Navy" was apparently a niche market magazine, possibly governmentally funded, designed for sailors and one of the placement organs for Lux advertising. See a Mr. Laverty's commentary, Staff Meeting Minutes, 16 April 1932, 5–8, JWT Archives.

46 Ibid.

47 See also Kathy Peiss (*Hope in a Jar,* 116) on the promotional leaflets penned by Carl Weeks in the 1930s.

48 See Emily Apter on masculine fetishization of "feminine" accessories: *Feminizing the Fetish: Psychoanalysis and Narrative Obsession in Turn-of-the-Century France* (Ithaca, N.Y.: Cornell University Press, 1991).

49 Ibid., 106. The full quote, on female fetishism as empowerment, is: "A current rereading of historical femininity dislocates essentialism through the instantiation

of perversion. . . . A woman's search for *jouissance* in the socially sanctioned rituals of object veneration would be seen no longer as a manifestation of a tame, essential femininity but, rather, as the semiosis of a subversively erotic practice, thoroughly 'perverse' in its own terms." See also Jennifer Wicke, "Lingerie and (Literary) History: Joyce's *Ulysses* and Fashionability," *Critical Quarterly* 36, no. 2 (summer 1994): 25–41.

50 The phrase is Homi Bhabha's; see "Difference, Discrimination, and the Discourse of Colonialism," in *The Politics of Theory*, ed. Francis Parker et al. (Colchester, U.K.: University of Essex Press, 1983), 205.

51 Frances Maule, *She Strives to Conquer: Business Behavior, Opportunities, and Job Requirements for Women* (New York: Funk and Wagnall's, 1934), 2.

52 See Roland Marchand (*Advertising the American Dream*, 208–17) for examples of some of these ads.

53 Mary Douglas, *Purity and Danger: An Analysis of the Concepts of Pollution and Taboo* (London: Ark, 1984).

54 "She Likes Prize Fights," *News*, May 1930, 5, JWT Archives.

55 Marianne Keating, 1964, Sidney Bernstein Papers, JWT Archives.

56 See Roland Marchand (*Advertising the American Dream*, 34) with regard to the disparity between male and female salaries in advertising during this era.

57 Dorothy Dignam, "Section on Relations with Men's Clubs," Dignam Papers, Schlesinger Library.

Chapter 4

1 I. A. Richards, *The Philosophy of Rhetoric* (New York: Oxford University Press, 1936), 96.

2 Carl Naether, *Advertising to Women* (New York: Prentice Hall, 1928), 258–59.

3 Stuart Culver, "What Manikins Want: *The Wonderful Wizard of Oz* and *The Art of Decorating Dry Goods Windows*," *Representations* 21 (winter 1988): 107.

4 Rachel Bowlby, *Just Looking: Consumer Culture in Dreiser, Gissing, and Zola* (New York: Methuen, 1985). See also Stuart Culver ("What Manikins Want") on the displayed commodity and the identity constructed around desire.

5 Laura Mulvey, "Visual Pleasure and Narrative Cinema," in *The Sexual Subject: A Screen Reader in Sexuality*, ed. John Caughie, Annette Kuhn, and Mandy Merck (New York: Routledge, 1992).

6 Sara K. Schneider, *Vital Mummies: Performance Design for the Show-Window Mannequin* (New Haven, Conn.: Yale University Press, 1995), 52.

7 For a related discussion of women's comparative surveillance of other women, see Charlotte Herzog, " 'Powder Puff' Promotion: The Fashion Show-in-the-Film," in *Fabrications: Costume and the Female Body*, ed. Jane Gaines and Charlotte Herzog (New York: Routledge, 1990), 134–59.

8 Richards, *Philosophy of Rhetoric*, 100–101.

9 No "mere embellishment," the vehicle can reasonably be considered in the com-

pany of the fetish. I theorize the woman as vehicle here; in a related vein, Emily Apter (*Feminizing the Fetish: Psychoanalysis and Narrative Obsession in Turn-of-the-Century France* [Ithaca, N.Y.: Cornell University Press, 1991]) theorizes the woman as fetish object, not by conflating her "deficient" self with the objects that compensatorily wrap and enveil her, but by "empowering the female collectible" (43). She reads the fetish (Marx's commodity fetish, Freud's libidinal fetish, and those of the fictional "perverts" she examines) as a fluid and unrepresentable force that—like Richards's vehicle—has more transmutational power than initially expected. And because it prompts desire, Apter's fetish—again like Richards's vehicle—has the capacity to become a driving power, able to unsettle the dominant paradigm.

10 Like the vehicular woman, the metaphoric vehicle in language can also work in a variety of ways, sometimes simultaneously: "A very broad division can thus be made between metaphors which work through some direct resemblance between the two things, the tenor and vehicle, and those which work through some common attitude which we may (often through accidental and extraneous reasons) take up towards them both. The division is not final or irreducible, of course. . . . So much misinterpretation comes from supposing that if a word works one way it cannot simultaneously work in another and have simultaneously another meaning" (Richards 118–19).

11 In a study of the spousal duties of diplomatic and military wives that considers such gendered labor along with domestic work, prostitution, and sweatshop workers, Cynthia Enloe has detailed this sort of wifely work in its most extreme modality: when representation of the spouse and the state are conflated, and when the "private, informal," and unpaid work of entertaining most explicitly enables the husband's professional endeavor (Cynthia Enloe, *Bananas, Beaches, and Bases: Making Feminist Sense of International Politics* [Berkeley: University of California Press, 1990]).

12 Thorstein Veblen, *The Theory of the Leisure Class: An Economic Study of Institutions* (1899; reprint, New York: Modern Library, 1934), 60.

13 Frank Presbrey, *The History and Development of Advertising* (Garden City, N.Y.: Doubleday and Doran, 1929), 616.

14 *Our Modern Maidens* was directed by Harry Beaumont; its screenplay was written by Josephine Lovett. To some extent, movies such as these substantiate Paula Fass's claim that the "wild" youth of the twenties actually maintained and self-regulated their own, nonthreatening moral code, despite the apparent blurring of the limits of acceptability. In part, however, the two films show Hollywood grasping to contain a cultural movement that must have allowed at least some women a truly liberating exploration of their own sexual and social enthusiasms (Paula Fass, *The Damned and the Beautiful: American Youth in the 1920s* [New York: Oxford University Press, 1977], 260–90).

15 Frances McFadden, "Skyscraper Clothes," *Ladies Home Journal,* October 1928, 49; clothes designed by H. M. K. Smith and his students. See also fashion designer Manolo's mid-nineties' line of clothes that "pays tribute" to the Brooklyn Bridge,

incorporating wire, magnets, and steel wool (Amy M. Spindler, "Manolo's Ode to Brooklyn Bridge," *New York Times*, 14 April 1994, B4).

16 "The Long Twenty-Nine," Pond's Cold Cream ad, in *Punch, or the London Charivari*, 13 June 1928, *Accounts*, xvii, J. Walter Thompson Archives, Duke University; hereafter cited as JWT Archives.

17 Dorothy Dignam, "Cosmetics, Woman's Heritage through the Ages," 14–15, Dignam Papers, Schlesinger Library, Radcliffe College. Kathy Peiss takes up the topic of cosmetics and wartime morale in *Hope in a Jar: The Making of America's Beauty Culture* (New York: Henry Holt, 1998), 238–345.

18 Susan Porter Benson, *Counter Cultures: Saleswomen, Managers, and Customers in American Department Stores, 1890–1940* (Urbana: University of Illinois Press, 1986), 137. Here, she quotes "Train the Salespeople," *Dry Goods Economist* 65 (3 December 1910), 45.

19 Edward Steichen, Staff Meeting Minutes, 31 January 1928, JWT Archives.

20 Kenneth M. Goode and Harford Powell Jr., *What about Advertising?* (1927), excerpted in *The Plastic Age, 1917–1930*, ed. Robert Sklar (New York: George Braziller, 1970).

21 Margaret Weishaar, " 'Psyching' Mrs. Smith: Two Special Feminine Urges Make Her a Spender," *People* (JWT Newsletter), October 1937, 6, JWT Archives.

22 On the performativity of gender identity, see Judith Butler, *Gender Trouble: Feminism and the Subversion of Identity* (New York: Routledge, 1990).

23 Mary Ann Doane, "Masquerade Reconsidered: Further Thoughts on the Female Spectator," *Discourse* 11, no. 1 (fall/winter 1988–1989): 47.

24 See Joan Riviere, "Womanliness as a Masquerade" (1929), in *Formations of Fantasy*, ed. Victor Burgin, James Donald, and Cora Kaplan (New York: Methuen, 1986), 35–44.

25 Jacqueline Rose, introduction to *Feminine Sexuality*, by Jacques Lacan, ed. Juliet Mitchell and Jacqueline Rose, trans. Jacqueline Rose (New York: Pantheon, 1982), 48. Teresa Brennan has argued that Lacan's claims are at their least effective when read as transhistorical. Rather like the prolific Slavoj Žižek, she reads him instead as a theorist of bourgeois consciousness and the formation of the bourgeois subject. This would explain the utility of his work in the present context (Teresa Brennan, *History after Lacan* [New York: Routledge, 1993]).

26 See Elaine Scarry on labor being that which "resists representation" in *Resisting Representation* (New York: Oxford University Press, 1994), 49–90.

27 Pond's Cold Cream, *American Weekly*, 22 November 1925.

28 See Lauren Berlant, "National Brands/National Body: *Imitation of Life*," in *Comparative American Identities*, ed. Hortense Spillers (New York: Routledge, 1991). For a consideration of Freud's role in theorizing women's cathexis to their own material presence, see Doane, "Masquerade Reconsidered."

29 For the notion of woman as trademark, see Berlant, "National Brands," 110–40. In the 1890s, advertisers first developed the conviction that brand names, slogans, jingles, and trademarks were crucial mnemonic aids for barbing the short attention

of busy American consumers (see Presbrey, *The History and Development of Advertising*). Some once-ubiquitous trademark figures are Sunny Jim, Phoebe Snow, and Spotless Town.

30 In addition to chapter 2 in this book, see Roland Marchand, *Advertising the American Dream: Making Way for Modernity, 1920–1940* (Berkeley: University of California Press, 1985); and Jackson Lears, *Fables of Abundance: A Cultural History of Advertising in America* (New York: Basic Books, 1994).

31 F. Scott Fitzgerald, "The Freshest Boy," in *The Stories of F. Scott Fitzgerald*, ed. Malcolm Cowley (New York: Macmillan, 1951), 326–45; and F. Scott Fitzgerald, "Jacob's Ladder," in *The Short Stories of F. Scott Fitzgerald*, ed. Matthew Bruccoli (New York: Scribner's, 1989), 350–71.

32 Roland Marchand (*Advertising the American Dream*) offers examples of the "Fisher Body Girl" (104), "one of the most prominent advertising characters of the late 1920's" (178–79), whose elegant female body advertised Fisher car bodies. Sometimes she would "moonlight" to advertise other products, and once she escaped the commodity altogether to grace the cover of the *Saturday Evening Post*. She may or may not be Fitzgerald's reference here: her creator's name was not Harrison Fisher, but McClelland Barclay.

33 "Art" as a category is often defined and constituted by its antithetical relations with advertising, and yet, the lived lives of practicing artists throughout this century show how permeable the borders between the commercial and artistic really are. For interesting treatments of this issue, see Rachel Bowlby, *Shopping with Freud* (New York: Routledge, 1993); Jackson Lears, "The Courtship of Art and Advertising" (paper presented at the Conference on Popular Culture East and West, Indiana University, 1986); and Stuart Ewen, *Captains of Consciousness: Advertising and the Social Roots of the Consumer Culture* (New York: McGraw-Hill, 1976), 61–67. Fitzgerald perceived his own career in terms of the tension between artistic and commercial output. See Robert A. Martin, "Hollywood in Fitzgerald: After Paradise," in *The Short Stories of F. Scott Fitzgerald: New Approaches in Criticism*, ed. Jackson R. Bryer (Madison: University of Wisconsin Press, 1982).

34 Fitzgerald wrote two Hollywood stories in 1927, "Jacob's Ladder" and "Magnetism." Both feature an affair between a man in his thirties and a girl of seventeen. This mirrors an actual romance that Fitzgerald had with Lois Moran. See Martin, "Hollywood in Fitzgerald," 139–40.

35 Trade ad, *Dry Goods Economist*, Toilet Goods Section, 24 March 1928; and "Parfum Cappi," touted as a successful campaign piece having "pulled over 4500 inquiries" from readers in *News Bulletin*, May 1922, 4, JWT Archives.

36 F. Scott Fitzgerald, *The Great Gatsby* (1920; reprint, New York: Collier, 1987), 120. On perfume as a cultural currency, see also Jennifer Craik, *The Face of Fashion: Cultural Studies in Fashion* (New York: Routledge, 1994), 164–72; M. De Long and E. Bye, "Apparel for the Sense: The Use and Meaning of Fragrances," *Journal of Popular Culture* 24, no. 3 (winter): 81–88; Doris-Louise Haineault and Jean-Yves Roy, *Unconscious for Sale: Advertising, Psychoanalysis, and the Public*, trans. Kimball

Lockhart with Barbara Kerslake, vol. 8 of *Theory and History of Literature* (Minneapolis: University of Minnesota Press, 1993), 99; and Veleda J. Boyd and Marilyn M. Robitaille, "Scent and Femininity: Strategies of Contemporary Perfume Ads," in *Gender and Utopia in Advertising: A Critical Reader,* ed. Luigi Manca and Alessandra Manca (Lisle, Ill.: Procopian Press, 1994), 49–54.

37 Steichen, Staff Meeting Minutes.

38 Countess Ceccaldi quoted in Kathy Peiss, *Hope in a Jar: The Making of America's Beauty Culture* (New York: Henry Holt, 1998), 145. See also Peiss (ibid., 136–40) in regard to the society testimonials for Pond's, a campaign devised by the adwomen at J. Walter Thompson. These paid testimonials were the source of some controversy. Earnest Elmo Calkins critiqued them roundly before the American Association of Advertising Agencies in 1925, and an overly optimistic Roy Durstine remarked in 1928 that "it seems fairly evident, thank goodness, that the life of these testimonials is pretty definitely limited" (*This Advertising Business* [New York: Scribner's, 1928], 48).

39 Angela Partington, "Popular Fashion and Working-Class Affluence," in *Chic Thrills: A Fashion Reader,* ed. Juliet Ash and Elizabeth Wilson (Berkeley: University of California Press, 1992), 145–61.

40 Matthew J. Bruccoli, introduction to *Zelda Fitzgerald: The Collected Writings,* by Zelda Fitzgerald, ed. Matthew J. Bruccoli (New York: Macmillan, 1991), 273.

41 Though not the focus of this reading, one of the story's central effects is its almost Sinclair Lewis–like satire of regional provincialism.

42 Zelda Fitzgerald, "Our Own Movie Queen," in *The Collected Writings,* ed. Matthew J. Bruccoli (New York: Macmillan, 1991), 273.

43 Michel de Certeau, *The Practice of Everyday Life* (Berkeley: University of California Press, 1984), xii–xiv.

44 See P. T. Barnum, *Struggles and Triumphs, or Forty Years' Recollections of P. T. Barnum* (Buffalo: Warren and Johnson, 1872), for unending descriptions of Barnum's publicity ploys, including his public relations use of his own Orientalist mansion, "Iranistan."

45 This is exactly Betty Lou Spence's move in the film *IT.* Betty Lou (played by Clara Bow) is a shopgirl at Waltham's Department Store. She is joined by all the other girls in Lingerie when she pines after the young tycoon-to-be, Cyrus Waltham. Since she has "IT," she does wind up marrying her boss. On the saleswoman's hopes for glamour and romance on the shop floor, see Benson, *Counter Cultures,* 215. On Hollywood's portrayal of a female working population that increased dramatically between 1910 and 1930, see Sumiko Higashi, *Virgins, Vamps, and Flappers: The American Silent Movie Heroine* (Montreal: Eden Press Women's Publications, 1978).

46 See de Certeau, *Everyday Life,* xii–xv.

47 For a fascinating discussion of the shopgirl's tactics of resistance to management control, see Benson, *Counter Cultures,* 227–82.

48 The term is Daniel J. Boorstin's, *The Image: A Guide to Pseudo-Events in America* (New York: Harper, 1961).

49 For more on the Fleischmann's testimonial campaign, see Marchand, *Advertising the American Dream,* 16–18.

50 "All This for $50!" *Newsletter,* 25 March 1922, JWT Archives.

51 As vigorously documented by Fass, *The Damned and the Beautiful.*

52 See Marchand, *Advertising the American Dream,* 314.

53 See Martin, "Hollywood in Fitzgerald," 134.

54 See de Certeau, *Everyday Life,* xii.

55 Hazel V. Carby, *Reconstructing Womanhood: The Emergence of the Afro-American Woman Novelist* (New York: Oxford University Press, 1987), 170. See also Deborah E. McDowell, introduction to *"Quicksand" and "Passing,"* by Nella Larsen (New Brunswick, N.J.: Rutgers University Press, 1989); and Lillie P. Howard, " 'A Lack Somewhere': Nella Larsen's *Quicksand* and the Harlem Renaissance," in *The Harlem Renaissance Re-examined,* ed. Victor A. Kramer (New York: AMS Press, 1987).

56 "Critics . . . have consistently criticized the endings of [Larsen's] novels *Quicksand* (1928) and *Passing* (1929), which reveal her difficulty with rounding off stories convincingly" (McDowell, introduction, xi). Ann duCille also charts—and challenges—the common critiques of Larsen for being too far removed from the vernacular, "authentic" Black tradition, and too materialistically middle class in her concerns (Ann duCille, "Blues Notes on Black Sexuality: The Texts of Jessie Fauset and Nella Larsen," in *American Sexual Politics: Sex, Gender, and Race since the Civil War,* ed. John C. Fout and Maura Shaw Tantillo [Chicago: University of Chicago Press, 1993], 193–219).

57 On Fitzgerald, see Mary Gordon, introduction to *Zelda Fitzgerald: The Collected Writings,* ed. Matthew J. Bruccoli (New York: Macmillan, 1991), xvi. On Larsen, see McDowell, introduction, x.

58 DuCille, "Blues Notes on Black Sexuality," 204.

59 On "things" in *Quicksand,* see, for instance, 6, 67, 116, 133. For the "nameless" "something" in the same novel, see, for example, 11, 21, 47, 81, 83, 91, 95, 108.

60 McDowell, introduction, xvi–xxii.

61 Ewen, *Captains of Consciousness,* 45.

62 Nella Larsen, *"Quicksand" and "Passing"* (1928; reprint, New Brunswick, N.J.: Rutgers University Press, 1989), 1–2.

63 Quoted in Weishaar, " 'Psyching' Mrs. Smith." The twenties' notion of the home as an indicator of the essence of its presiding hostess differed somewhat from the nineteenth century's cult of the homemaker. In urban America's mid–nineteenth century, the parlor was popularly envisioned as the set for social scrutiny and performance, according to Karen Halttunen. The rest of the house, however, was imagined as a more private space for "renewal." As Roland Marchand sums up, the entire home was presented by twenties' advertisers less as a private realm contrasting and preparing for the marketplace, than as a perpetual "opening night" in a performance before critical eyes that would never close. See Karen Halttunen, *Con-*

fidence Men and Painted Women: A Study of Middle-Class Culture in America, 1830–1870 (New Haven, Conn.: Yale University Press, 1982); and Roland Marchand, "The Parable of the First Impression," in Marchand, *Advertising the American Dream*, 208–17. See also T. J. Jackson Lears, "From Salvation to Self-Realization: Advertising and the Therapeutic Roots of the Consumer Culture, 1880–1930," in *The Culture of Consumption: Critical Essays in American History, 1880–1980,* ed. Richard Wightman Fox and T. J. Jackson Lears (New York: Pantheon, 1983), 25; and Gillian Brown, *Domestic Individualism: Imagining the Self in Nineteenth-Century America* (Berkeley: University of California Press, 1990).

64 Once, I looked through a *Vogue* magazine with my then four-year-old daughter. She dizzied us both, calling out, "I'm her! No, I'm her!" in response to more and more of the models' pictures. Finally, she remarked, "This is a lovely magazine. I'm going to be changing all day."

65 Gina Lombroso, an Italian psychologist cited warmly by both Christine Frederick and Stanley Resor (as a reminder, leading advertisers of the twenties), explains that "woman's expansiveness [leads to] a most peculiar form of illusionism, the vivification of inanimate things. . . . When a woman speaks of her furniture . . . as her 'friends,' and says she 'could not live without them,' she is not pronouncing empty words. . . . She loves them like human beings. . . . [T]his ingenuous love . . . is a great social bulwark, for it forms the basis of woman's eagerness to care for everything around her" (Gina Lombroso, *The Soul of Woman: Reflections on Life* [New York: Dutton, 1923]).

66 Pond's ad, *Harper's Bazaar,* December 1928, 117.

67 Marchand, *Advertising the American Dream,* 64.

68 Peiss, *Hope in a Jar,* esp. chapters 3, 4, and 7.

69 Paul K. Edwards, *The Southern Urban Negro as a Consumer* (New York: Prentice Hall, 1932). Many thanks to Kathy Peiss for this reference in conversation.

70 For example, in Edwards, *Negro as a Consumer,* a male "common laborer" is quoted in response to a Rinso Soap Powder ad: "Colored woman painted as though she loved to work for white people"; and a skilled laborer remarks, "Why not a white laundress?" (236). A female "common laborer" explains that she has "never bought Aunt Jemina flour, because it pertains to [a] slavery type of Negro" (243).

71 In his discussion of *Quicksand,* Walter Benn Michaels seems to accept at face value the assumption that life in Denmark could provide Helga with an escape from the issue of race. This acceptance of what the novel proves to be a faulty premise "colors" his reading of her return to America, and of the book generally (Walter Benn Michaels, *Our America: Nativism, Modernism, and Pluralism* [Durham, N.C.: Duke University Press, 1995], 115–16).

72 Of course, advertising's oft-made claim that a commodity can express some subtle idiosyncrasy in the individual psyche—the "psychological" pitch—runs parallel with the contradictory social pitch, with which the commodity is sold as a readily discernible indicator of class belonging.

73 On this phenomenon, see W. F. Haug (*Critique of Commodity Aesthetics: Appearance, Sexuality, and Advertising in Capitalist Society* [Minneapolis: University of Minnesota Press, 1986]), who describes one Rosemarie Heinecke as "well known for her bust size, which is her trademark" (29), and which became so associated with her professional name, Rosy-Rosy, that she and a lingerie company engaged in a protracted legal suit over it. Haug describes also the hostesses used in a promotional campaign as "living packaging" (37).

74 Howard, "A Lack Somewhere," 232.

75 On stereotyping of black female sexuality, see Patricia Hill Collins, *Black Feminist Thought: Knowledge, Consciousness, and the Politics of Empowerment* (New York: Routledge, 1991); Laura Doyle, *Bordering on the Body: The Racial Matrix of Modern Fiction and Culture* (New York: Oxford University Press, 1994); bell hooks, "Selling Hot Pussy: Representation of Black Female Sexuality in the Cultural Marketplace," in *Writing on the Body: Female Embodiment and Feminist Theory*, ed. Katie Conboy, Nadia Medina, and Sarah Stanbury (New York: Columbia University Press, 1997). Mariana Torgovnick discusses the conflation of black female sexuality and primitivism as a presence in modernism in *Gone Primitive: Savage Intellects, Modern Lives* (Chicago: University of Chicago Press, 1990).

76 See Ann Douglas, *Terrible Honesty: Mongrel Manhattan in the 1920s* (New York: Farrar, Straus and Giroux, 1995): "For black minstrels to succeed, they had to meet the expectations of their white audiences. . . . The Negro minstrel performer donned blackface himself and perforce imitated, with variations, the white performers playing, and distorting, blacks" (75). On minstrelsy and dance, see Jacqueline Shea Murphy, "Unrest and Uncle Tom: Bill T. Jones/Arnie Zane Dance Company's *Last Supper at Uncle Tom's Cabin/The Promised Land*," in *Bodies of the Text: Dance as Theory, Literature as Dance*, ed. Jacqueline Shea Murphy and Ellen W. Goellner (New Brunswick, N.J.: Rutgers University Press, 1995), 81–105. See also Eric Lott, "White Like Me: Racial Cross-Dressing and the Construction of American Whiteness," in *Cultures of United States Imperialism*, ed. Amy Kaplan and Donald E. Pease (Durham, N.C.: Duke University Press, 1993), 474–95.

77 Levine's "Jazz and American Culture" offers a fascinating exploration of the dialectic between jazz and "high" culture in the teens and twenties, two terms that he describes as semiotically interdependent in the American imagination through their opposition. Along the way, Levine details both the equation of jazz with savagery and the elision of race from discussions of jazz (Lawrence Levine, "Jazz and American Culture," in *The Unpredictable Past: Explorations in American Cultural History* [New York: Oxford University Press, 1993], 160–75). See also Lewis A. Erenberg, *Steppin' Out: New York Nightlife and the Transformation of American Culture, 1890–1930* (Westport, Conn.: Greenwood Press, 1981).

78 Lynn Montross, "Bass Drums," in *Town and Gown*, ed. Lynn Montross (1923; reprint, Freeport, N.Y.: Books for Libraries Press/Doubleday, 1970).

79 This conflation probably grew out of—and definitely facilitated—the rape of Black female slaves by white slaveholders. See Carby, *Reconstructing Womanhood*, 30. See

also Angela Y. Davis, *Women, Race, and Class* (New York: Vintage/Random House, 1983), 182.

80 For a forceful description of this danger and the strategies employed by African American women writers to combat it, see Hazel V. Carby, " 'On the Threshold of the Woman's Era': Lynching, Empire, and Sexuality in Black Feminist Theory," in *"Race," Writing, and Difference*, ed. Henry Louis Gates Jr. (Chicago: University of Chicago Press, 1986), 301–16. Carby has also written about the extremely different cultural expression of African American female blues singers, who during the same period were using the license associated with their marginal position to explore the erotics and challenges of their social/sexual perspective. Perhaps they were less reined in than their literary counterparts because economic success in their niche during the twenties and early thirties did not depend so directly on a patina of "respectability." See, though, Ann duCille's ("Blues Notes on Black Sexuality") challenge of the tendency among contemporary scholars like Gloria Hull, Barbara Christian, and Cheryl Wall to essentialize and romanticize the folk culture of the blues. See also Hazel V. Carby, " 'It Jus Be's Dat Way Sometime': The Sexual Politics of Women's Blues," in *Radical America* 20, no. 4 (1986); and Angela Y. Davis, *Blues Legacies and Black Feminism: Gertrude "Ma" Rainey, Bessie Smith, and Billie Holiday* (New York: Pantheon, 1998).

81 The "sexual abandon" of the "Jazz Age" was also a treacherous minefield for many white women, whose "respectability" was now judged by far more subtle gradations of acceptability than had pertained previously. As once-risqué behaviors and costumes were incorporated into "acceptable" society, "self-policing" was required. See Katherine B. Davis, *Factors in the Sex Life of Twenty-Two Hundred Women* (New York: Harper Bros., 1929). Or see the movie *IT*, which models the allegedly crucial, but sometimes invisible difference between "it" girls and "bad" girls when Clara Bow stands in for an unwed mother.

82 See Frank Presbrey (*The History and Development of Advertising*) for a typical expression of faith in advertising's civilizing function.

83 Lillie P. Howard ("A Lack Somewhere") concludes that the problem is just "a lack somewhere in [Helga's] character" (225), and that this "suggests the impotence of the period for many" (232). There's a contradiction here, since she seems to say that Helga's inability to accept her Blackness is only a personality flaw, but then asserts that this flaw or lack—which she has written off as a quirk—says something (what, I'm not sure) about the quality of the entire period. Without citing Howard, Hazel Carby criticizes her approach, remarking that "the representation of alienation as a state of mind reduces history to an act of thought and leads to a political conservatism" (*Reconstructing Womanhood*, 170).

84 Pond's ad, *Harper's Bazaar*, December 1928, 117.

85 In a now-classic essay, Raymond Williams contrasts "alternative" and "oppositional" cultural practices. *Quicksand* suggests that subcultures, too, can be confining, particularly to the extent that they are shaped by the defensive exigencies of their relationship to an unfriendly dominant culture. Sheer opposition implies a

more energetic, analytic response to that relationship than alternativity per se (Raymond Williams, "Base and Superstructure in Marxist Cultural Theory," *New Left Review* 82 [November/December 1973]: 9–11).

86 See Robert E. Fleming, "The Influence of *Main Street* on Nella Larsen's *Quicksand*," *Modern Fiction Studies* 31, no. 3 (fall 1985): 547–54.

87 "Larsen represented the ideologies of consumerism, of capitalism, and of sexuality as being intimately connected" (Carby, *Reconstructing Womanhood*, 174).

88 How different is the work performed by Helga's cataloging of colors from this ad campaign copy for hose in 1929, ostensibly a wired list from a participating society woman: "[To] J. Walter Thompson Co., Chicago. Sun burnt beige *name* corsica golden beige *name* claret greyish beige *name* nuage grege *name* mistral tourterelle *name* ombre *stop* four nude beiges *name* chantilly soiree rosette chablis. [Signed,] Lady Egerton-Caret" (*Newsletter*, 1 July 1929, JWT Archives).

89 Deborah E. McDowell treats the issue of lesbian desire in her introduction to Larsen's *Passing*, which features an extended, but still "flirtatious" handling of the attraction between two women (xxiii–xxxiii).

90 Judith Butler, "Imitation and Gender Subordination," in *The Lesbian and Gay Studies Reader*, ed. Henry Abelove, Michele Aina Barale, and David M. Halperin (New York: Routledge, 1993), 316. See also Butler's treatment of the same theme in her treatment of Joan Riviere's discussion of masquerade (*Gender Trouble*, 50–54); and Diana Fuss, "Fashion and the Homospectatorial Look," in *On Fashion*, ed. Shari Benstock and Suzanne Ferriss (New Brunswick, N.J.: Rutgers University Press, 1994), 211–32.

91 See Laura Mulvey's clear-cut, unproblematized distinction between scopophilic desire and the identificatory gaze in "Visual Pleasure and Narrative Cinema" (1975), in *The Sexual Subject: A "Screen" Reader in Sexuality*, ed. John Caughie, Annette Kuhn, and Mandy Merck (New York: Routledge, 1992), 22–34.

92 Fuss, "Homospectatorial Look," 228.

Chapter 5

1 See Nancy Milford, *Zelda: A Biography* (New York: Harper and Row, 1970), 264, with regard to the first run. See Harry T. Moore, preface to *Save Me the Waltz*, by Zelda Fitzgerald (Carbondale: Southern Illinois University Press, 1966), x, with regard to the 1958 edition.

2 Matthew J. Bruccoli, ed., *Zelda Fitzgerald: The Collected Writings* (New York: Macmillan, 1991), 5.

3 Zelda Fitzgerald, *Save Me the Waltz*, in *Zelda Fitzgerald: The Collected Writings*, ed. Matthew J. Bruccoli (New York: Macmillan, 1991). See also Milford, *Zelda*. Fitzgerald was hospitalized at the Phipp's Clinic in Johns Hopkins Hospital for much of the first half of 1932, where she wrote the first draft of *Waltz* in around a month.

4 Marcel Duchamp, Man Ray, and Hans Bellmer are three of the surrealists whose work revolves around these concerns.

5 On *Najda*, see Susan Rubin Suleiman, *Subversive Intent: Gender, Politics, and the Avant-Garde* (Cambridge, Mass.: Harvard University Press, 1990), esp. 99–103.

6 On women and surrealism, see Whitney Chadwick, ed., *Mirror Images: Women, Surrealism, and Self-Representation* (Cambridge, Mass.: MIT Press, 1998); Whitney Chadwick, *Women Artists and the Surrealist Movement* (Boston: Little, Brown, 1985); Suleiman, *Subversive Intent;* Mary Ann Caws et al., eds., *Surrealism and Women* (Cambridge, Mass.: MIT Press, 1991); and Renée Riese Hubert, *Magnifying Mirrors: Women, Surrealism, and Partnership* (Lincoln: University of Nebraska Press, 1994). On surrealism in general, see André Breton, *Nadja*, trans. Richard Howard (New York: Grove, 1960); Marcel Jean, ed., *The Autobiography of Surrealism* (New York: Viking, 1980); Maurice Nadeau, *The History of Surrealism*, trans. Richard Howard (Cambridge, Mass.: Harvard University Press, 1989); and Hal Foster, *Compulsive Beauty* (Cambridge, Mass.: MIT Press, 1993).

7 See Leonora Carrington, "The Debutante," in *The House of Fear: Notes from Down Below* (New York: E. P. Dutton, 1988), 48.

8 Jean Baudrillard, "Simulacra and Simulations," in *Selected Writings*, ed. Mark Poster (Cambridge, U.K.: Polity Press, 1988), 167.

9 Carl Naether, *Advertising to Women* (New York: Prentice Hall, 1928), 234.

10 *Confessions of a Copywriter, by a Widely-Known New York Advertising Man Who Chooses to Conceal His Identity in Order to Give Unhampered Play to His Pen* (Chicago: Dartnell Corp., 1930). Originally published as a serial in the Dartnell magazine *Printed Salesmanship* (n.d.).

11 Dorothy Dignam, "It's Better When You Get Acquainted," Box 3, 18, Dignam Papers, Schlesinger Library, Radcliffe College; hereafter cited as Schelesinger Library.

12 James R. Mellow, *Invented Lives: F. Scott and Zelda Fitzgerald* (Boston: Houghton Mifflin, 1984), flapcover copy.

13 Christine Frederick, *Selling Mrs. Consumer* (New York: Business Bourse, 1929), 337.

14 Ad for Pond's, *New Yorker,* 29 September 1928, 81. See Stuart Ewen, *Captains of Consciousness: Advertising and the Social Roots of the Consumer Culture* (New York: McGraw-Hill, 1976), 61.

15 *Newsletter,* no. 90, 23 July 1925, 4, J. Walter Thompson Archives, Duke University; hereafter cited as JWT Archives.

16 W. F. Haug, *Critique of Commodity Aesthetics: Appearance, Sexuality, and Advertising in Capitalist Society* (Minneapolis: University of Minnesota Press, 1986), 19.

17 Perhaps exclusion of their rise to fame functions primarily to keep the novel's focus squarely and unblinkingly on Alabama's work, not her husband's. Linda W. Wagner comments that the book structures itself around Alabama's story and that a tracking of "David's ostensible success would have alleviated the sense of tragedy implicit in the story line of his wife" ("*Save Me the Waltz:* An Assessment in Craft," *Journal of Narrative Technique* 12, no. 3 [fall 1982]: 201–9).

18 The phrase is Baudrillard's, "Simulacra and Simulations," 166.

19 Walter B. Neuberg, "Cosmetics: Woman's Heritage through the Ages," n.d.,

A–114, File 25, 2, Dignam Papers, Schlesinger Library. Dorothy Dignam may well have been the ghostwriter for this piece.

20 Zelda Fitzgerald, "What Became of the Flappers?" *McCall's,* October 1925, in Bruccoli, *Collected Writings,* 397–99.

21 Naether (*Advertising to Women*) lists effective slogans for beauty products where changeability is the only constant: "Phrases designed to emphasize self and variety of a person's complexes. . . . To emphasize self: Your radiant self. Her changeable self. Interesting complexities of your nature. To emphasize variety of a person's complexes: Rainbow moods. Rainbow of perfumes. Rainbow personality. Rainbow of thoughts" (204).

22 *Ladies Home Journal,* October 1928, 142. One wonders which odeurs should accompany the less "lovely" "feminine moods"! On perfume as cultural currency, see also Jennifer Craik, *The Face of Fashion: Cultural Studies in Fashion* (New York: Routledge, 1994), 164–72; Marilyn Revell DeLong and Elizabeth Kergeh Bye, "Apparel for the Sense: The Use and Meaning of Fragrances," *Journal of Popular Culture* 24 (winter, 1990): 81–88; and Veleda J. Boyd and Marilyn M. Robitaille, "Scent and Femininity: Strategies of Contemporary Perfume Ads," in *Gender and Utopia in Advertising: A Critical Reader,* ed. Luigi Manca and Alessandra Manca (Lisle, Ill.: Procopian Press, 1994): 49–54.

23 This approach was popular enough to inspire parody in one 1930 treatise on mob mentality. In a chapter revolving around a department store's perfume sale, the author quotes at length from an invented perfume advertisement about women's many moods, and the scent available to match each one, in a color-coded series of flagons (Frank K. Notch, *King Mob: A Study of the Present-Day Mind* [New York: Harcourt, Brace, 1930]).

24 Friedrich Nietzsche, "Our Virtues," *Beyond Good and Evil,* trans. Helen Zimmern (1907; reprint, London: George Allen and Unwin, 1967), 239.

25 Roland Barthes, *The Fashion System,* trans. Matthew Ward and Richard Howard (1967; reprint, New York: Hill and Wang), 255.

26 Even here Naether misfires. In the twenties, advertisers were convinced that anything dubbed Parisian would sell, a belief contradicted by these consumer responses to a J. Walter Thompson marketing survey: "The French process does not interest me," "The French method means nothing to me," "I don't know French soaps," "I am not interested in the French appeal," and so on ("Lux Toilet Soap survey," 1925, Microfilm Reel no. 47, 16 mm. series, JWT Archives).

27 Note that the sisters' names, Dixie and Alabama, cast them in the vehicular role: they represent and augment the appeal of the South.

28 See also the woman-at-her-vanity ads reproduced in Roland Marchand, *Advertising the American Dream: Making Way for Modernity, 1920–1940* (Berkeley: University of California Press, 1985), 176–77.

29 John Berger, *Ways of Seeing* (London: BBC/Penguin, 1972), 46.

30 "Masquerade . . . attributes to the woman the distance, alienation, and divisive-

ness of self (which is constitutive of self in psychoanalysis) rather than the closeness
and excessive presence which are the logical outcome of the psychoanalytic drama
of sexualized linguistic difference" (Mary Ann Doane, "Masquerade Reconsidered:
Further Thoughts on the Female Spectator," *Discourse* 11, no. 1 [fall/winter 1988–
1989]: 47; emphasis added).

31 Elinor Glynn and Clarence Badger (producers), "*IT*" (Los Angeles: Paramount
Pictures, 1927). In an early example of multimedia marketing, the movie *IT* was a
spin-off of a contemporary article by the same name. Elinor Glynn wrote a *Cos-
mopolitan* article identifying Clara Bow as the "IT" girl. In the same year, 1927,
Paramount Pictures presented *IT,* with Elinor Glynn as coproducer and writer and
Clara Bow as star. Characters in the movie pore over and refer to the article, and
Glynn herself makes a cameo appearance to describe "It." Lori Landay reports that
Bow's father ran a restaurant in Beverly Hills for a time that went by the name It,
and that soon after the movie's release, an ad campaign for Murine Eye Drops also
used the term and concept as its structuring theme (*Madcaps, Screwballs, and Con
Women: The Female Trickster in American Culture* [Philadelphia: University of
Pennsylvania Press, 1998], 88).

32 Bow's lack of inhibition does not read merely as a predisposition, a personal
temperament. Although the story of a store clerk marrying her boss ostensibly
should be a celebration of American opportunity, of a democratic milieu that
triumphs over class, in fact, the vigor of Bow's performance is entirely class-
inflected, and its widespread appeal, its "Itness," indicates the audience's desire for
a working-class heroine. This Gracie Axelrod is rewarded for her appetite, not in
spite of its class-specific manifestations, but because of it.

33 Landay, *Madcaps.*

34 Even *Save Me the Waltz* mentions "It":
"What is this 'it' I saw in the papers?" said the eight-year-old voice.
"Don't be silly, it's only sex appeal," answered the voice of ten.
"Only beautiful ladies can have it in the movies," said Bonnie. (170)

35 In 1973, Gloria Steinem remarked, "I don't mind drag—women have been female
impersonators for some time" (quoted in Marjorie B. Garber, *Vested Interests: Cross-
Dressing and Cultural Anxiety* [New York: Harper, 1992], 65).

36 Christine Stansell suggests (in conversation) that the figures Fitzgerald uses to
describe Gabrielle link her to a set of objects that might decorate a thoroughly
nineteenth-century parlor: implying the contempt of the modern for old "things."

37 This phantasmatic terrain of warfare contrasts with F. Scott Fitzgerald's real-life
failure—about which he expressed deep regret—to see actual combat, despite his
lieutenancy (see Mellow, *Invented Lives,* 56).

38 In a 1931 letter characteristic of many Zelda sent Scott from the hospital, she
referred to similar love notes: "[There] are kisses splatterring [*sic*] you[r] balcony
to-night from a lady who was once, in three separate letters, a princess in a high
white tower and who has never forgotten her elevated station in life and who is

waiting once more for her royal darling" (quoted in Milford, *Zelda*, 189). The eager submission to metaphoric confinement is replaced by resistance the following year, when Zelda uses the letters to a different end in *Waltz*.

39 See Kate Chopin, *The Awakening* (1899; reprint, New York: Penguin Classics, 1986); Henry James, *The Portrait of a Lady* (1881; reprint, New York: Dell, 1969); Charlotte Perkins Gilman, *The Yellow Wallpaper* (1889; reprint, New York: Feminist Press, 1973); and Edith Wharton, *The House of Mirth* (1905; reprint, New York: Collier, 1987).

40 Fitzgerald, "Flappers?" 397–99. Interestingly, both of Zelda's "flapper" pieces, this and "Eulogy on the Flapper" (1922), describe the flapper as extinct, an already pinned butterfly.

41 In a way, this parallels Fitzgerald's handling of David's rise to fame, which also goes undiscussed, yet here the physical "reward" for popular success is not a luxurious bed but bleeding feet—and more work (see Mellow, *Invented Lives*).

42 The pursuit of authenticity was an obsession propounded at least as much by commercial culture as by "high" culture. According to Jackson Lears, there is a profound link between the commodified world Alabama ostensibly leaves behind and the search for authenticity as an organizing motivation (see "The Pursuit of the Real," in *Fables of Abundance: A Cultural History of Advertising in America* [New York: Basic Books, 1994], 345–78).

43 James Joyce, *A Portrait of the Artist as a Young Man* (1916; reprint, New York: Penguin, 1986), 171.

44 This ad helpfully reminds us: "Every woman dreads—and rightly dreads—the day when she must leave the twenties and be definitely classified among the thirties" ("The Long Twenty-Nine," Pond's Cold Cream ad, in *Punch, or the London Charivari*, 13 June 1928, xvii, Account Files: Chesebrough-Pond's, JWT Archives).

45 In *Shopping with Freud*, Rachel Bowlby depicts the elitist reliance on an artificial contrast between high art's purity and a supposedly crass, superficial commercial culture. She reveals the borders between the two as being fantastically tenuous (New York: Routledge, 1993). See also Lawrence Levine, *Highbrow/Lowbrow: The Emergence of Cultural Hierarchy in America* (Cambridge, Mass.: Harvard University Press, 1988).

46 See my discussion of Frances Maule's 1935 manual *She Strives to Conquer: Business Behavior, Opportunities and Job Requirements for Women*, in " 'Complex Little Femmes': Adwomen and Theories of the Female Consumer." See also Marchand, *Advertising the American Dream*, 16–20, 208–17.

47 Although Mary Gordon does indeed call *Waltz* "a kind of jazz *Bildungsroman*," she rushes to stipulate that it avoids the genre's "usual inwardness and speculation" (introduction in Bruccoli, *Collected Writings*, xxi).

48 The term is Jann Matlock's, quoted in Emily Apter, *Feminizing the Fetish: Psychoanalysis and Narrative Obsession in Turn-of-the-Century France* (Ithaca, N.Y.: Cornell University Press, 1991), 66.

49 "Scott Fitzgerald felt that Zelda using the same material (their lives) in *Save Me the*

Waltz that he was planning to use in *Tender Is the Night* was a personal betrayal," explains Mary Gordon (introduction in Bruccoli, *Zelda Fitzgerald: The Collected Writings*, xvii). In *Night*, though, he felt free to quote Zelda's letters at length. See also F. Scott Fitzgerald, *Tender Is the Night* (1933; reprint, New York: Macmillan, 1982). Scott viewed Nicole Diver as a composite portrait of Zelda and Sara Murphy (see Milford, *Zelda*, 285).

50 Frederick, *Selling Mrs. Consumer*, 334.

51 On the dominatrix as employee or assistant, see the Barbet Schroeder film *Maitresse*, 1976, Warner Brothers; and Gilles Deleuze, "Coldness and Cruelty," in *Masochism* (New York: Zone Books, 1989), 20, 41. On the relations between fellow "slaves," see Leopold von Sacher-Masoch, "Venus in Furs," in *Masochism* (New York: Zone Books, 1989), 234–46.

52 Deleuze, "Coldness and Cruelty," 21–22. For an applied version of masochism-as-mysticism, see *Bodyplay and Modern Primitives Quarterly* 7 (fall 1993). (Thanks to Erika Reynolds, roving gender representations reporter in the field.) See also Gaylyn Studlar, "Masochism, Masquerade, and the Erotic Metamorphoses of Marlene Dietrich," in *Fabrications: Costume and the Female Body*, ed. Jane Gaines and Charlotte Herzog (New York: Routledge, 1990), 229–49.

53 Kathy Acker, "Against Ordinary Language: The Language of the Body," in *The Last Sex: Feminism and Outlaw Bodies*, ed. Arthur Kroker and Marilouise Kroker (New York: St. Martin's Press, 1993), 24. See also Hal Foster, *Compulsive Beauty* (Cambridge, Mass.: October Books, 1993), which traces surrealism's obsession with repetition and the death wish.

54 Foster, *Compulsive Beauty*, 113.

55 Trinh T. Minh-ha, quoted in Whitney Chadwick, "An Infinite Play of Empty Mirrors: Women, Surrealism, and Self-Presentation," in Chadwick, *Mirror Images*, 3.

56 André Breton, *Manifeste du Surréalisme* (1924), in *The Autobiography of Surrealism*, ed. Marcel Jean (New York: Viking, 1980), 117–26.

57 Philippe Soupault, *La Révolution surréaliste*, in *The Autobiography of Surrealism*, ed. Marcel Jean (New York: Viking, 1980), 136–37.

58 See Eleanor Lanahan, ed., *Zelda, an Illustrated Life: The Private World of Zelda Fitzgerald* (New York: Harry Abrams, 1996), 86–103.

59 Held at the Galerie Beaux-Arts, Paris. See Richard Martin, *Fashion and Surrealism* (New York: Rizzoli, 1987), 56–59, 193.

60 On *Najda*, see Suleiman, *Subversive Intent*, 99–103.

61 For a discussion on self-portraits in the work of Leonora Fini, Leonora Carrington, Frida Kahlo, and Kay Sage, see Chadwick, *Women Artists*, 66–102.

62 The term *femme enfant* is André Breton's. Chadwick (*Women Artists*) and Suleiman (*Subversive Intent*) both discuss the attitude of male surrealists toward the women in their midst. In Breton's work, the avant-garde woman figures predominantly as a muse and gender performer. For example, see *Soluble Fish*, no. 13. It describes the "charming stratagem" of a young girl's toilette; she uses "chalk, a live coal, and an extremely rare green diamond" for her makeup, then makes her way across town in

a "calaber-fur coat" and "two mouse-skins," to plant herself beneath the stairs of the stock exchange, where she functions not as an artist herself, but "as a subterranean Fame blowing . . . the trumpet of ruin" (Jean, *Autobiography of Surrealism*, 126).

63 In one series, Man Ray posed a nude Meret Oppenheim with a printing press, she inked like a blank page on the verge of inscription (*Man Ray: Photographs* [New York: Thames and Hudson, 1991], 69). See also biographic appendices in Chadwick, *Women Artists;* and Caws, *Surrealism and Women.*

64 See Chadwick, *Women Artists,* 66–102.

65 See ibid., 106; and Martin, *Fashion and Surrealism,* 155. Some might complain that the surrealists were struggling against the notion of fashion or trend setting. Yet Meret Oppenheim, Lee Miller, Jacqueline Lamba, and Valentine Hugo were among the women in surrealism who worked for the fashion industry as models, photographers, designers, and writers. Richard Martin's *Fashion and Surrealism* documents the cross-pollination between the two worlds.

66 The canonization of dance remains uneasy. "Ballet has always been regarded as a less important art" (Angela McRobbie, "Dance Narratives and Fantasies of Achievement," in *Meaning in Motion: New Cultural Studies in Dance,* ed. Jane C. Desmond [Durham, N.C.: Duke University Press, 1997], 208).

67 Regarding Ernst and Carrington, see Susan Rubin Suleiman, "The Bird Superior Meets the Bride of the Wind: Leonora Carrington and Max Ernst," in *Significant Others: Creativity and Intimate Partnership,* ed. Whitney Chadwick and Isabelle de Courtivron (London: Thames and Hudson, 1993), 97–118.

68 Susan Rubin Suleiman, *Risking Who One Is: Encounters with Contemporary Art and Literature* (Cambridge, Mass.: Harvard University Press, 1994), 111.

69 Consider, for example, Meret Oppenheim, who would not allow her work to be reproduced in a book that covered only the women of surrealism, modeled extensively for Man Ray, and in 1936, created the ultimate surrealist object: the fur-covered teacup and saucer. With the addition of luxurious fur, the cup's functionality is decoupled completely from its exchange value; fur doubles as a symbol of affluence and fetishized stand-in for pubic hair—feminine pubic hair, since a teacup is womblike. The furry cup is a comment, if ever there was one, on the fetishization and feminization of the commodity, though Oppenheim claims she was only interested in the juxtaposition of textures and that it was Breton (rather than her) who named the piece *Déjeuner en fourrure,* thereby invoking Sacher-Masoch's "Venus in Furs." For Oppenheim's comments, see Robert J. Belton, "Androgyny: Interview with Meret Oppenheim," in *Surrealism and Women,* eds. Mary Ann Caws et al. (Cambridge, Mass.: MIT Press, 1991), 63–75.

70 As presented by Nancy Milford, Scott's letters reflect initial efforts to downplay the intensity of what was happening to Zelda, followed by repeated attempts to deny his own alcoholism through condemnation of Zelda's mental state (see "Breaking Down," in Milford, *Zelda,* 147–338).

71 Nancy Milford details Zelda's futile, ill-planned efforts to escape hospitalization and return to dancing (ibid.; see 166, for instance).

72 Ibid., 210–16. As Marina Warner explains, *Down Below* was originally "written in English (text now lost), dictated in French to Jeanne Megnen in 1943, [and then] published in *VVV*, No. 4, February 1944, in a translation from the French by Victor Llona" (introduction to *The House of Fear: Notes from Down Below*, by Leonora Carrington [New York: Dutton, 1988], 216).

73 William McFee, quoted in Milford, *Zelda*, 263.

74 See Lanahan, *Zelda, an Illustrated Life*, 14.

75 See Chadwick, *Women Artists*, 130–40.

76 Suleiman, *Subversive Intent*, esp. 179–80.

77 See Lanahan, *Zelda, an Illustrated Life*, 42. See also reproductions in Kaye McDonough, *Zelda: Frontier Life in America* (San Francisco: City Lights Books, 1978), 48, 84.

78 Georges Bataille, *Erotism: Death and Sensuality*, trans. Mary Dalwood (San Francisco: City Lights Books, 1986), 11.

79 Ibid., cover, plates 2 and 13. Mitchell Breitwieser remarks, in conversation, that this repeated motif of the exposed throat in Fitzgerald's work has an unsettling and surely significant resemblance to an erect phallus.

80 Leonora Carrington, *La Dame Ovale* (Paris: G. L. M. Editions, 1939).

81 Carrington, *The House of Fear*, 44–48.

82 Reproduced in Whitney Chadwick, *Leonora Carrington: La Realidad de la Imaginacion* (Calzada Mexico–Coyoacan: Ediciones Era Galeria, 1994), plate 1.

83 Jane Livingston comments on this androgyny in "On the Art of Zelda Fitzgerald," in Lanahan, *Zelda, an Illustrated Life*, 83.

84 See Lanahan, *Zelda, an Illustrated Life*, 104–8, for Fitzgerald's series of paper doll design gouaches for *Little Red Riding Hood*.

Epilogue

1 See Lawrence Levine, *Highbrow/Lowbrow: The Emergence of Cultural Hierarchy in America* (Cambridge, Mass.: Harvard University Press, 1988).

2 Karl Marx, *The Eighteenth Brumaire of Louis Napoleon*, in *On Revolution*, ed. and trans. Saul K. Padover (1852; reprint, New York: McGraw-Hill, 1971), 243–328.

3 See Stephen Fox, *The Mirror-Makers: A History of American Advertising and Its Creators* (New York: William Morrow and Co., 1984).

4 See Jackson Lears, *Fables of Abundance: A Cultural History of Advertising in America* (New York: Basic Books, 1994), 204–5.

5 See Sacvan Bercovitch, *The American Jeremiad* (Madison: University of Wisconsin Press, 1978). In *The Gold Standard and the Logic of Naturalism: American Literature at the Turn of the Century*, Walter Benn Michaels further complicates the notion of resistance literature by showing how market-based ideology molds even critiques of our culture (Berkeley: University of California Press, 1987).

6 Thomas Frank, "Babbitt Rex: Boob and Boho in the Businessman's Republic," *Baffler* 10: 9.

7 Chantal Mouffe, "Hegemony and Ideology in Gramsci," in *Gramsci and Marxist Theory*, ed. Chantal Mouffe (New York: Routledge, 1979), 168–204.

8 See Mikhail M. Bakhtin, *The Dialogic Imagination: Four Essays by M. M. Bakhtin*, ed. Michael Holquist, trans. Caryl Emerson and Michael Holquist (Austin: University of Texas Press, 1981).

9 Edith Lewis, "A New Kind of Beauty Contest," *Newsletter*, 31 March 1929, J. Walter Thompson Archives, Duke University.

Bibliography

Primary Materials

Adams, Henry Foster. *Advertising and Its Mental Laws.* New York: Macmillan, 1916.

——. "The Dynamo and the Virgin." In *The Harper American Literature,* edited by Donald McQuade et al. New York: Harper and Row, 1987.

Alden, James. *Careers in Advertising.* New York: Macmillan, 1932.

Alger, Horatio. *Ragged Dick: Or, Street Life in New York* (1868). In *"Ragged Dick" and "Struggling Upward,"* edited by Carl Bode. New York: Penguin, 1985.

Barnum, P. T. *The Humbugs of the World.* New York: Carleton, 1866.

——. *Struggles and Triumphs, or Forty Years' Recollections of P. T. Barnum.* Buffalo: Courier Co., 1875.

Barton, Bruce. *The Man Nobody Knows.* 1922. Reprint, Indianapolis, Ind.: Bobbs-Merrill, 1980.

Beaton, Cecil. *Cecil Beaton's Scrapbook.* London: B. T. Batsford, 1937.

——. *The Glass of Fashion.* Garden City, N.Y.: Doubleday, 1954.

Beecher, Catherine, with Harriet Beecher Stowe. *American Women's Home.* New York: J. B. Ford and Co., 1869.

Bishop, W. H. "Story-Paper Literature." *Atlantic Monthly* 44 (September 1879).

Bok, Edward. *The Americanization of Edward Bok: The Autobiography of a Dutch Boy Fifty Years After.* New York: Scribner's, 1921.

Bourne, Randolph. *History of a Literary Radical: And Other Essays.* Edited by Van Wyck Brooks. New York: B. W. Huebsch, 1920.

Breton, André. *Nadja.* Translated by Richard Howard. New York: Grove, 1960.

——. *Manifeste du Surréalisme.* 1924. In *The Autobiography of Surrealism,* edited by Marcel Jean. New York: Viking, 1980.

Calkins, Earnest Elmo. *Business the Civilizer.* Boston: Little, Brown and Co., 1928.

Carnegie, Dale. *How to Win Friends and Influence People.* New York: Simon and Schuster, 1937.

Carrington, Leonora. "The Debutante." In *The House of Fear: Notes from Down Below.* New York: E. P. Dutton, 1988.

Chase, Stuart, with the Labor Bureau. *The Tragedy of Waste.* New York: Macmillan, 1925.

Confessions of a Copywriter, by a Widely-Known New York Advertising Man Who Chooses to Conceal His Identity in Order to Give Unhampered Play to His Pen. Chicago: Dartnell Corp., 1930. Originally published as a serial in the Dartnell magazine *Printed Salesmanship* (n.d.).

Davis, Katherine B. *Factors in the Sex Life of Twenty-two Hundred Women.* New York: Harper Bros., 1929.

Dos Passos, John. *U.S.A.* New York: Modern Library, 1937.

Dreiser, Theodore. *Sister Carrie.* Edited by Lee Clark Mitchell. 1900. Reprint, New York: Oxford University Press, 1991.

Durstine, Roy. *Making Advertisements and Making Them Pay.* New York: Scribner's, 1920.

——. *This Advertising Business.* New York: Scribner's, 1928.

Emerson, Ralph Waldo. "The Over-Soul." In *Selected Essays,* edited by Larzer Ziff. New York: Penguin, 1982.

Fitzgerald, F. Scott. *Tender is the Night.* 1933. Reprint, New York: Collier, 1986.

——. *The Stories of F. Scott Fitzgerald.* 1920. Reprint, New York: Macmillan, 1987.

——. *The Short Stories of F. Scott Fitzgerald.* Edited by Matthew J. Bruccoli. New York: Scribner's, 1989.

——. *The Great Gatsby.* 1925. Reprint, New York: Macmillan, 1993.

Fitzgerald, Zelda. *Zelda Fitzgerald: The Collected Writings.* Edited by Matthew J. Bruccoli. Introduction by Mary Gordon. New York: Macmillan, 1991.

Fleischman, Doris E. (a.k.a. Mrs. Edward Bernays), ed. *An Outline of Careers for Women: A Practical Guide to Achievement.* Garden City, N.Y.: Doubleday, Doran, 1931.

Fletcher, Frank Irving. *Lucid Interval: Confessions of a Custodian of the Convictions of Others.* New York: Harper and Bros., 1938.

Franklin, Benjamin. *Autobiography and Other Writings.* Edited by Ormond Seavery. 1788. Reprint, New York: Oxford University Press, 1993.

Frederick, Christine. *Selling Mrs. Consumer.* New York: Business Bourse, 1929.

——. "Advertising and the So-Called 'Average Woman.'" Chapter 14 of an undisclosed book, Christine Isobel MacGaffey Frederick Papers, Schlesinger Library, Radcliffe College.

Furniss, Edgar, with Lawrence R. Guild. *Labor Problems: A Book of Materials for Their Study.* Boston: Houghton Mifflin, 1925.

Gilman, Charlotte Perkins. *Women and Economics: A Study of the Economic Relation between Men and Women as a Factor in Social Evolution,* 1898. Reprint, New York: Harper and Row, 1966.

Goode, Kenneth M. and Harford Powell Jr. *What About Advertising?* In *The Plastic Age, 1917–1930,* edited by Robert Sklar. New York: George Braziller, 1970.

Hamburger, Estelle. *It's a Woman's Business.* New York: Vanguard Press, 1939.

Harrison, Reverend Jonathan Baxter. *Certain Dangerous Tendencies in American Life, and Other Papers.* Boston: Houghton, Osgood, and Co., 1880.

Higley, Merle. *Women in Advertising in New York Agencies.* New York: Young Women's Christian Association, 1924.

Hopkins, Claude. *My Life in Advertising.* New York: Harper, 1927.

Hotchkiss, G. B. *Advertising Copy.* New York: Harper and Bros., 1924.

Howells, William Dean. *A Hazard of New Fortunes.* 1890. Reprint, New York: Penguin, 1980.

——. *The Rise of Silas Lapham.* 1885. Reprint, New York: Penguin, 1983.

Hoyt, Elizabeth. *The Consumption of Wealth*. New York: Macmillan, 1928.

Hurlock, Elizabeth B. *Motivation in Fashion*. New York, 1929.

———. *The Psychology of Dress*. New York: Ronald Press Co., 1929.

James, Henry. *The Ambassadors*. New York: Oxford University Press, 1985.

———. *The Bostonians*. 1886. Reprint, New York: Penguin, 1986.

James, William. *Essays in Pragmatism*. New York: Hafner, 1948.

———. *The Varieties of Religious Experience: A Study in Human Nature*. 1902. Reprint, New York: Viking Penguin, 1982.

Joyce, James. *A Portrait of the Artist as a Young Man*. 1916. Reprint, New York: Penguin, 1986.

Kyrk, Hazel. *A Theory of Consumption*. Houghton Mifflin, 1923.

Larsen, Nella. *"Quicksand" and "Passing."* 1928. Reprint, New Brunswick, N.J.: Rutgers University Press, 1989.

Lewis, Sinclair. *Babbitt*. 1922. Reprint, New York: Penguin, 1980.

———. *Selected Short Stories of Sinclair Lewis*. Edited by James Tuttleton. Chicago: Elephant Press, 1990.

Lombroso, Caesar. *The Female Offender*. New York: D. Appleton and Co., 1909.

Lombroso, Gina. *The Soul of Woman: Reflections on Life*. New York: Dutton, 1923.

Lorimer, George Horace. *Letters from a Self-Made Merchant to His Son*. Chicago: Gregg Publishing, 1903.

Marden, Orison Swett. *Every Man a King, or Might in Mind-Mastery*. New York: T. Y. Crowell, 1906.

Maule, Frances. *She Strives to Conquer: Business Behavior, Opportunities, and Job Requirements for Women*. New York: Funk and Wagnall's, 1934.

Melville, Herman. *The Confidence Man: His Masquerade*. Edited by Tony Tanner. 1857. Reprint, New York: Oxford University Press, 1989.

Mencken, H. L., and George Jean Nathan. *The American Credo*. New York: Knopf, 1920.

Montross, Lynn. "Bass Drums." In *Town and Gown*, edited by Lynn Montross. 1923. Reprint, Freeport, N.Y.: Books for Libraries Press/Doubleday, 1970.

Munsterberg, Hugo. *Psychology and Industrial Efficiency*. Boston: Houghton Mifflin, 1913.

———. *Business Psychology*. Chicago: La Salle Extension University, 1921.

Naether, Carl. *Advertising to Women*. New York: Prentice Hall, 1928.

Nietzsche, Friedrich. "Our Virtues." *Beyond Good and Evil*. 1907. Translated by Helen Zimmern. Reprint, London: George Allen and Unwin, 1967.

Notch, Frank K. *King Mob: A Study of the Present-Day Mind*. New York: Harcourt, Brace, 1930.

Nystrom, Paul. *The Economics of Fashion*. New York: Ronald Press, 1928.

Patten, Simon. *The Theory of Prosperity*. New York: Macmillan, 1902.

Poiret, Paul. *The King of Fashion: The Autobiography of Paul Poiret*. Translated by Stephen Haden Guest. Philadelphia: J. B. Lippincott, 1931.

Powell, Harford, Jr. *The Virgin Queene*. Boston: Little, Brown and Co., 1928.

Presbrey, Frank. *The History and Development of Advertising.* Garden City, N.Y.: Doubleday and Doran, 1929.

Reisner, Christian. *Church Publicity: The Modern Way to Compel Them to Come In.* New York: Methodist Book Concern, 1913.

Rowell, George H. *Forty Years an Advertising Agent, 1865–1905.* New York: Printers Ink, 1906.

Sacher-Masoch, Leopold von. "Venus in Furs" (1870). In *Masochism.* New York: Zone Books, 1989.

Scott, Walter Dill. *The Psychology of Advertising.* Boston: Small, Maynard, 1903.

Sigourney, Lydia Hunt. *Letters to Young Ladies.* New York: Harper and Bros., 1836.

Sinclair, Upton. *The Jungle.* 1906. Reprint, Urbana: University of Illinois Press, 1988.

Soupault, Philippe. *La Révolution Surréaliste.* In *The Autobiography of Surrealism,* edited by Marcel Jean. New York, Viking, 1980.

Southard, Earnest Elmo. "The Mental Hygiene of Industry: A Movement that Particularly Concerns Employment Managers." *Industrial Management* 59 (1920): 100–106.

Strong, Edward K. *The Psychology of Selling and Advertising.* New York: McGraw-Hill, 1925.

Taylor, Frederick Winslow. *The Principles of Scientific Management.* 1911. Reprint, New York: W. W. Norton, 1967.

Trine, Ralph Waldo. *The Power that Wins: Henry Ford and Ralph Waldo Trine in an Intimate Talk on Life—the Inner Thing—the Things of the Mind and Spirit—and the Inner Powers and Forces that Make for Achievement.* Indianapolis, Ind.: Bobbs-Merrill, 1929.

Twain, Mark. *A Connecticut Yankee in King Arthur's Court.* 1889. Reprint, Berkeley: University of California Press, 1983.

Veblen, Thorstein. *The Theory of Business Enterprise.* New York: Scribner's, 1904.

——. *Theory of the Leisure Class: An Economic Study of Institutions.* 1899. Reprint, New York: Modern Library, 1934.

Waldo, Ruth. "Advertising." In *An Outline of Careers for Women: A Practical Guide to Achievement,* edited by Doris E. Fleischman. Garden City, N.Y.: Doubleday, Doran, 1931.

Washington, Booker T. *Up from Slavery.* 1901. Reprint, Garden City, N.Y.: Doubleday, 1963.

Wells, H. G. *Tono-Bungay.* 1908. Reprint, Duffield and Co., 1927.

West, Nathanael. *"Miss Lonelyhearts" and "The Day of the Locust."* 1933. Reprint, New York: New Directions, 1969.

Wharton, Edith. *The House of Mirth.* 1905. Reprint, New York: Macmillan, 1987.

Whittaker, Captain Fred. *Larry Locke, Man of Iron* (1883). In *The Knights in Fiction: Two Labor Novels of the 1880s,* edited by Mary C. Grimes. Urbana: University of Illinois Press, 1986.

Woodward, Helen. *Through Many Windows.* New York: Harper and Bros., 1926.

Woodward, William E. *The Gift of Life: An Autobiography.* New York: E. P. Dutton and Co., 1947.

History and Theory

Acker, Kathy. "Against Ordinary Language: The Language of the Body." In *The Last Sex: Feminism and Outlaw Bodies,* edited by Arthur Kroker and Marilouise Kroker. New York: St. Martin's Press, 1993.

Adorno, Theodor W., and Max Horkheimer. *The Dialectic of Enlightenment.* 1944. Reprint, New York: Herder and Herder, 1972.

Allen, Jeanne. "The Film Viewer as Consumer." *Quarterly Review of Film Studies* 5, no. 4 (fall 1980): 481–99.

Althusser, Louis. "Ideological State Apparatuses." In *Lenin and Philosophy and Other Essays,* translated by Ben Brewster. London: New Left Books, 1971.

Apter, Emily. *Feminizing the Fetish: Psychoanalysis and Narrative Obsession in Turn-of-the-Century France.* Ithaca, N.Y.: Cornell University Press, 1991.

Armstrong, Nancy. *Desire and Domestic Fiction: A Political History of the Novel.* New York: Oxford University Press, 1987.

Bakhtin, Mikhail M. *The Dialogic Imagination: Four Essays by M. M. Bakhtin.* Edited by Michael Holquist. Translated by Caryl Emerson and Michael Holquist. Austin: University of Texas Press, 1981.

Barthes, Roland. *The Fashion System.* Translated by Matthew Ward and Richard Howard. 1967. Reprint, New York: Hill and Wang, 1983.

——. "Myth Today." In *Mythologies.* 1957. Reprint, Hill and Wang, 1986.

Bataille, Georges. *Erotism: Death and Sensuality.* Translated by Mary Dalwood. 1957. Reprint, San Francisco: City Lights, 1986.

——. *Story of the Eye.* Translated by Joachim Neugroschel. 1928. Reprint, San Francisco: City Lights, 1987.

Baudrillard, Jean. *A l'Ombre des Majorités Silencieuses, ou La Fin du Social.* Fontenay-sous-Bois: Imprimerie Quotidienne, 1978.

——. *Jean Baudrillard: Selected Writings.* Edited by Mark Poster. Cambridge, U.K.: Polity Press, 1988.

——. *The System of Objects.* Translated by James Benedict. New York: Verso, 1996.

Beale, Marjorie. "Metaphors of Management in French Advertising and Film in the 1920s." Paper presented at the Managing the Visuals of Desire conference, Doreen B. Townsend Center for the Humanities, University of California at Berkeley, September 1993.

Bederman, Gail. *Manliness and Civilization: A Cultural History of Gender and Race in the United States, 1880–1917.* Chicago: University of Chicago Press, 1995.

Benjamin, Walter. "The Work of Art in the Age of Mechanical Reproduction." In *Illuminations,* translated by Harry Zohn. New York: Schocken Books, 1968.

——. "Paris: Capital of the Nineteenth Century." In *Reflections: Essays, Aphorisms, and*

Autobiographical Writings, translated by Edmund Jephcott. New York: Schocken Books, 1978.

Bennett, Tony, Colin Mercer, and Janet Woollacott. *Popular Culture and Social Relations.* Philadelphia: Open University Press, 1986.

Benson, Susan Porter. *Counter Cultures: Saleswomen, Managers, and Customers in American Department Stores, 1890–1940.* Urbana: University of Illinois Press, 1986.

Bercovitch, Sacvan. *The American Jeremiad.* Madison: University of Wisconsin Press, 1978.

Berger, John. *Ways of Seeing.* London: BBC/Penguin, 1972.

Berlant, Lauren. "National Brands/National Body: *Imitation of Life.*" In *Comparative American Identities: Race, Sex, and Nationality in the Modern Text,* edited by Hortense Spillers. New York: Routledge, 1991.

Bhabha, Homi. "Difference, Discrimination, and the Discourse of Colonialism." In *The Politics of Theory,* edited by Frances Parker et al. Colchester, U.K.: University of Essex Press, 1983.

Boddewyn, J. J. *Advertising Self-Regulation and Outside Participation: A Multinational Companion.* New York: Quorum Books, 1988.

Boisvert, Bill. "Apostles of the New Entrepreneur: Business Theory and the Management Crisis." *Baffler,* no. 6: 69–81.

Boorstin, Daniel J. *The Image: A Guide to Pseudo-Events in America.* New York: Harper, 1961.

Bordwell, David, and Kristin Thompson. *Film Art.* Reading, Mass.: Addison-Wesley, 1980.

Bowlby, Rachel. *Just Looking: Consumer Culture in Dreiser, Gissing, and Zola.* New York: Methuen, 1985.

——. *Shopping with Freud.* New York: Routledge, 1993.

Boyd, Veleda J. and Marilyn M. Robitaille. "Scent and Femininity: Strategies of Contemporary Perfume Ads." In *Gender and Utopia in Advertising: A Critical Reader,* edited by Luigi Manca. Lisle, Ill.: Procopian Press, 1994.

Brennan, Teresa. *History after Lacan.* New York: Routledge, 1993.

Brewer, John, and Roy Porter, eds. *Consumption and the World of Goods.* New York: Routledge, 1993.

Briner, Bob. *The Management Methods of Jesus.* Nashville, Tenn.: Thomas Nelson Inc., 1996.

Bristow, Edward J. *Prostitution and Prejudice: The Jewish Fight against White Slavery, 1870–1939.* New York: Schocken, 1983.

Bronner, Simon J. *Consuming Visions: Accumulation and Display of Goods in America, 1880–1920.* New York: W. W. Norton, 1989.

Brown, Gillian. *Domestic Individualism: Imagining Self in Nineteenth-Century America.* Berkeley: University of California Press, 1990.

Burke, Timothy. *Lifebuoy Men, Lux Women: Commodification, Consumption, and Cleanliness in Modern Zimbabwe.* Durham, N.C.: Duke University Press, 1996.

Burnam, John C. *Psychoanalysis and American Medicine, 1894–1918.* New York: International Universities Press, 1967.

Butler, Judith. *Gender Trouble: Feminism and the Subversion of Identity.* New York: Routledge, 1990.

——. *Bodies That Matter: On the Discursive Limits of "Sex."* New York: Routledge, 1993.

——. "Imitation and Gender Subordination." In *The Lesbian and Gay Studies Reader,* edited by Henry Abelove, Michele Aina Barale, and David M. Halperin. New York: Routledge, 1993.

——. *Excitable Speech: A Politics of the Performative.* New York: Routledge, 1997.

Carby, Hazel V. "On the Threshold of the Women's Era': Lynching, Empire, and Sexuality in Black Feminist Theory." In *"Race," Writing, and Difference,* edited by Henry Louis Gates Jr. Chicago: University of Chicago Press, 1986.

——. *Reconstructing Womanhood: The Emergence of the Afro-American Woman Novelist.* New York: Oxford University Press, 1987.

Caughie, John, Annette Kuhn, and Mandy Merck, eds. *The Sexual Subject: A* Screen *Reader in Sexuality.* New York: Routledge, 1992.

Caws, Mary Ann, et al., eds. *Surrealism and Women.* Cambridge, Mass.: MIT Press, 1991.

Chadwick, Whitney. *Women Artists and the Surrealist Movement.* Boston: Little, Brown, 1985.

——. *Leonora Carrington: La Realidad de la Imaginacion.* Calzada Mexico–Coyoacan: Ediciones Era Galeria, 1994.

——, ed. *Mirror Images: Women, Surrealism, and Self-Representation.* Cambridge, Mass.: MIT Press, 1998.

Collins, Patricia Hill. *Black Feminist Thought: Knowledge, Consciousness, and the Politics of Empowerment.* New York: Routledge, 1991.

Craik, Jennifer. *The Face of Fashion: Cultural Studies in Fashion.* New York: Routledge, 1994.

Cross, Gary. *Time and Money: The Making of a Consumer Culture.* New York: Routledge, 1993.

Crouthamel, James. *Bennett's "New York Herald" and the Rise of the Popular Press.* Syracuse, N.Y.: Syracuse University Press, 1989.

Culver, Stuart. "What Manikins Want: *The Wonderful Wizard of Oz* and *The Art of Decorating Dry Goods Windows." Representations* 21 (winter 1988): 97–116.

Curtis, Susan. *A Consuming Faith: The Social Gospel and Modern American Culture.* Baltimore, Md.: Johns Hopkins University Press, 1991.

Davidson, Martin. *The Consumerist Manifesto: Advertising in Postmodern Times.* New York: Routledge, 1992.

Davis, Angela Y. *Women, Race, and Class.* New York: Vintage/Random House, 1983.

——. *Blues Legacies and Black Feminism: Gertrude "Ma" Rainey, Bessie Smith, and Billie Holiday.* New York: Pantheon, 1998.

Debord, Guy. *Society of the Spectacle.* 1967. Reprint, Detroit: Black and Red, 1983.

de Certeau, Michel. *The Practice of Everyday Life.* Berkeley: University of California Press, 1984.

Deleuze, Gilles. "Coldness and Cruelty." In *Masochism*. New York: Zone Books, 1989.

Delong, Marilyn Revell, and Elizabeth Kergeh Bye. "Apparel for the Sense: The Use and Meaning of Fragrances." *Journal of Popular Culture* 24 (winter 1990): 81–88.

D'Emilio, John, and Estelle B. Freedman. *Intimate Matters: A History of Sexuality in America*. New York: Harper and Row, 1988.

Doane, Mary Ann. *The Desire to Desire: The Woman's Film of the 1940s*. Bloomington: Indiana University Press, 1987.

———. "Masquerade Reconsidered: Further Thoughts on the Female Spectator." *Discourse* 11, no. 1 (fall/winter 1988–1989): 42–53.

Douglas, Ann. *The Feminization of American Culture*. New York: Doubleday, 1988.

———. *Terrible Honesty: Mongrel Manhattan in the 1920s*. New York: Farrar, Straus and Giroux, 1995.

Douglas, Mary. *Purity and Danger: An Analysis of the Concepts of Pollution and Taboo*. London: Ark, 1984.

Doyle, Laura. *Bordering on the Body: The Racial Matrix of Modern Fiction and Culture*. New York: Oxford University Press, 1994.

duCille, Ann. "Blues Notes on Black Sexuality: Sex and the Texts of Jessie Fauset and Nella Larsen." In *American Sexual Politics: Sex, Gender, and Race since the Civil War*, edited by John C. Fout and Maura Shaw Tantillo. Chicago: University of Chicago Press, 1993.

Duffy, Margaret. "Body of Evidence: Studying Women and Advertising." In *Gender and Utopia in Advertising: A Critical Reader*, edited by Luigi Manca and Alessandra Manca. Lisle, Ill.: Procopian Press, 1994.

Eckert, Charles. "The Carole Lombard in Macy's Window." In *Fabrications: Costume and the Female Body*, edited by Jane Gaines and Charlotte Herzog. New York: Routledge, 1990.

Edwards, Paul K. *The Southern Urban Negro as a Consumer*. New York: Prentice Hall, 1932.

Enloe, Cynthia H. *Bananas, Beaches, and Bases: Making Feminist Sense of International Politics*. Berkeley: University of California, 1990.

Enrico, Roger, and Jesse Kornbluth. *The Other Guy Blinked: How Pepsi Won the Cola Wars*. New York: Bantam, 1986.

Erenberg, Lewis A. *Steppin' Out: New York Nightlife and the Transformation of American Culture, 1890–1930*. Westport, Conn.: Greenwood Press, 1981.

Ewen, Stuart. *Captains of Consciousness: Advertising and the Social Roots of the Consumer Culture*. New York: McGraw-Hill, 1976.

———. *All Consuming Images: The Politics of Style in Contemporary Culture*. New York: Basic Books, 1988.

Ewen, Stuart, and Elizabeth Ewen. *Channels of Desire: Mass Images and the Shaping of American Consciousness*. New York: McGraw-Hill, 1982.

Fass, Paula. *The Damned and the Beautiful: American Youth in the 1920s*. New York: Oxford University Press, 1977.

——. "Making and Remaking an Event: The Leopold and Loeb Case in American Culture." *Journal of American History* 80, no. 3 (December 1993): 919–51.

Fisher, Philip. "Acting, Reading, Fortune's Wheel: *Sister Carrie* and the Life History of Objects." In *Hard Facts: Setting and Form in the American Novel*. New York: Oxford University Press, 1985.

——. "Appearing and Disappearing in Public: Social Space in Late-Nineteenth-Century Literature and Culture." In a special issue, "Reconstructing American Literary History," ed. Sacvan Bercovitch, *Harvard English Studies* 13 (1986).

Fleming, Robert E. "The Influence of *Main Street* on Nella Larsen's *Quicksand.*" *Modern Fiction Studies* 31, no. 3 (fall 1985): 547–54.

Forseth, Roger. " 'Alcoholite at the Altar': Sinclair Lewis, Drink, and the Literary Imagination." *Modern Fiction Studies* 31, no. 3 (fall 1985): 581–608.

Foster, Hal. *Compulsive Beauty*. Cambridge, Mass.: MIT Press, 1993.

Foucault, Michel. *The History of Sexuality, Volume I: An Introduction*. Translated by Robert Hurley. New York: Random House, 1990.

——. "The Spectacle and the Scaffold." In *Discipline and Punish: The Birth of the Prison*, translated by Alan Sheridan. New York: Vintage, 1979.

——. *Power/Knowledge: Selected Interviews and Other Writings, 1972–1977*. Edited by Colin Gordon. Brighton, Sussex: Harvester Press, 1980.

Fox, Richard Wightman, and T. J. Jackson Lears, eds. *The Culture of Consumption: Critical Essays in American History, 1880–1980*. New York: Pantheon, 1983.

Fox, Stephen. *The Mirror-Makers: A History of American Advertising and Its Creators*. New York: William Morrow and Co., 1984.

Frank, Thomas. "Babbitt Rex: Boob and Boho in the Businessman's Republic." *Baffler* 10: 3–16.

Frye, Northrop. *The Modern Century*. Toronto: Oxford University Press, 1967.

Fung, Richard. "Burdens of Representation, Burdens of Responsibility." In *Constructing Masculinity*, edited by Brian Wallis and Simon Watson. New York: Routledge, 1995.

Fuss, Diana. "Fashion and the Homospectatorial Look." In *On Fashion*, edited by Shari Benstock and Suzanne Ferriss. New Brunswick, N.J.: Rutgers University Press, 1994.

Gaines, Jane, and Charlotte Herzog, eds. *Fabrications: Costume and the Female Body*. New York: Routledge, 1990.

Garber, Marjorie B. *Vested Interests: Cross-Dressing and Cultural Anxiety*. New York: Harper, 1992.

Garvey, Ellen Gruber. *The Adman in the Parlor: Magazines and the Gendering of Consumer Culture, 1880s to 1910s*. New York: Oxford University Press, 1996.

Giddens, Anthony. *The Transformation of Intimacy: Sexuality, Love, and Eroticism in Modern Societies*. Stanford: Stanford University Press, 1992.

Gilfoyle, Timothy. *City of Eros: New York City, Prostitution, and the Commercialization of Sex, 1790–1920*. New York: W. W. Norton, 1992.

Gilman, Sander. *Smart Jews: The Construction of the Image of Superior Jewish Intelligence.* Lincoln: University of Nebraska Press, 1996.

Grebstein, Sheldon Norman. *"Babbitt:* Synonym for a State of Mind." In *The Merrill Studies in "Babbitt,"* edited by Martin Light. Columbus, Ohio: Merrill, 1971.

Green, Nancy L. *Ready-to-Wear, Ready-to-Work: A Century of Industry and Immigrants in Paris and New York.* Durham, N.C.: Duke University Press, 1997.

Grossberg, Lawrence, Cary Nelson, and Paula Treichler, eds. *Cultural Studies.* New York: Routledge, 1992.

Habermas, Jürgens. *The Structural Transformation of the Public Sphere: An Inquiry into a Category of Bourgeois Society.* Translated by Thomas Burger and Frederick Lawrence. Cambridge, Mass.: Harvard University Press, 1991.

Haineault, Doris-Louise, and Jean-Yves Roy. *Unconscious for Sale: Advertising, Psychoanalysis, and the Public.* Translated by Kimball Lockhart with Barbara Kerslake. Vol. 86 of *Theory and History of Literature.* Minneapolis: University of Minnesota Press, 1993.

Hale, Nathan G., Jr. *Freud and the Americans: The Beginnings of Psychoanalysis in the United States, 1876–1917.* New York: Oxford University Press, 1971.

———. *The Rise and Crisis of Psychoanalysis in America: Freud and the Americans, 1917–1985.* New York: Oxford University Press, 1995.

Halttunen, Karen. *Confidence Men and Painted Women: A Study of Middle-Class Culture in America, 1830–1870.* New Haven, Conn.: Yale University Press, 1982.

Harris, Neil. *Humbug: The Art of P. T. Barnum.* Boston: Little, Brown, 1973.

Haug, W. F. *Critique of Commodity Aesthetics: Appearance, Sexuality, and Advertising in Capitalist Society.* Minneapolis: University of Minnesota Press, 1986.

Hayden, Dolores. *The Grand Domestic Revolution: A History of Feminist Designs for American Homes, Neighborhoods, and Cities.* Cambridge, Mass.: MIT Press, 1981.

Heilbroner, Robert J. *The Nature and Logic of Capitalism.* New York: Norton, 1985.

Herzog, Charlotte. " 'Powder Puff' Promotion: The Fashion Show-in-the-Film." In *Fabrications: Costume and the Female Body,* edited by Jane Gaines and Charlotte Herzog. New York: Routledge, 1990.

Higashi, Sumiko. *Virgins, Vamps, and Flappers: The American Silent Movie Heroine.* Montreal: Eden Press Women's Publications, 1978.

Hollander, Anne. *Seeing through Clothes.* New York: Viking, 1978.

Holtz, William, and Speer Morgan, eds. "Fragments from a Marriage: Letters from Sinclair Lewis to Grace Hegger Lewis." *Missouri Review* 11, no. 1 (1988): 71–98.

hooks, bell. "Selling Hot Pussy: Representation of Black Female Sexuality in the Cultural Marketplace." In *Writing on the Body: Female Embodiment and Feminist Theory,* edited by Katie Conboy, Nadia Medina, and Sarah Stanbury (New York: Columbia University Press, 1997).

Horowitz, Daniel. *The Morality of Spending: Attitudes toward the Consumer Society in America, 1875–1940.* Baltimore, Md.: Johns Hopkins University Press, 1985.

Howard, Lillie P. " 'A Lack Somewhere': Nella Larsen's *Quicksand* and the Harlem

Renaissance." In *The Harlem Renaissance Re-examined,* edited by Victor A. Kramer. New York: AMS Press, 1987.

Hubert, Renée Riese. *Magnifying Mirrors: Women, Surrealism, and Partnership.* Lincoln: University of Nebraska Press, 1994.

Hutchisson, James M. *The Rise of Sinclair Lewis, 1920–1930.* University Park: Pennsylvania State University Press, 1996.

Illouz, Eva. *Consuming the Romantic Utopia: Love and the Cultural Contradictions of Capitalism.* Berkeley: University of California Press, 1997.

Irigaray, Luce. "This Sex Which Is Not One." Translated by Claudia Reeder. In *New French Feminisms.* Edited by Elaine Marks and Isabelle de Courtivron. Brighton, U.K.: Harvester, 1980.

Jean, Marcel, ed. *The Autobiography of Surrealism.* New York: Viking, 1980.

Jenkins, Henry. *Textual Poachers: Television Fan and Participatory Culture.* New York: Routledge, 1992.

Jewell, Sue K. *From Mammy to Miss America and Beyond: Cultural Images and the Shaping of U.S. Social Policy.* New York: Routledge, 1992.

Kaplan, Amy. *The Social Constructions of American Realism.* Chicago: University of Chicago Press, 1988.

Kipnis, Laura. "Adultery." *Intimacy,* a special issue of *Critical Inquiry* 24, no. 2 (winter 1998): 289–327.

Kirby, Lynne. "Gender and Advertising in American Silent Film: From Early Cinema to *The Crowd.*" *Discourse* 13, no. 2 (spring/summer 1991): 3–20.

Lacan, Jacques, and the École Freudienne. *Feminine Sexuality.* Edited by Juliet Mitchell and Jacqueline Rose. Translated by Jacqueline Rose. New York: Pantheon, 1982.

Laipson, Peter. "I Have No Genius for Marriage: Bachelorhood in Urban America, 1870–1930." Ph.D. diss., University of Michigan, 1996.

Lanahan, Eleanor, ed. *Zelda, an Illustrated Life: The Private World of Zelda Fitzgerald.* New York: Harry Abrams, 1996.

Landay, Lori. "Getting 'It': Elinor Glynn, Clara Bow, and the Common Ground of Female Sexuality." Paper presented at the American Studies Association Conference, Pittsburgh, Pa., 10 November 1995.

——. *Madcaps, Screwballs, and Con Women: The Female Trickster in American Culture.* Philadelphia: University of Pennsylvania Press, 1998.

Langbauer, Laurie. "The City, the Everyday, and Boredom: The Case of Sherlock Holmes." *Differences* 5, no. 3 (fall 1993): 80–120.

Larson, Erik. *The Naked Consumer: How Our Private Lives Become Public Commodities.* New York: Henry Holt, 1992.

Leach, William. "Herbert Hoover's Emerald City and Managerial Government." In *Land of Desire: Merchants, Power, and the Rise of a New American Culture.* New York: Pantheon, 1993.

Lears, T. J. Jackson. *No Place of Grace: Anti-Modernism and the Transformation of American Culture, 1880–1920.* New York: Pantheon, 1981.

——. "From Salvation to Self-Realization: Advertising and the Therapeutic Roots of the Consumer Culture, 1880–1930." In *The Culture of Consumption: Critical Essays in American History, 1880–1980,* edited by Richard Wightman Fox and T. J. Jackson Lears. New York: Pantheon, 1983.

———. "The Courtship of Art and Advertising." Paper presented at the Conference on Popular Culture East and West, Indiana University, 1986.

———. "The Ad Man and the Grand Inquisitor: Intimacy, Publicity, and the Administrative State in America, 1880–1940. Paper presented at the Davis Center Seminar, Princeton University, 30 March 1990.

———. *Fables of Abundance: A Cultural History of Advertising in America.* New York: Basic Books, 1994.

Leverenz, David. *Manhood and the American Renaissance.* Ithaca, N.Y.: Cornell University Press, 1989.

Levine, Lawrence. *Highbrow/Lowbrow: The Emergence of Cultural Hierarchy in America.* Cambridge, Mass.: Harvard University Press, 1988.

———. "The Folklore of Industrial Society: Popular Culture and Its Audiences." *American Historical Review* 97, no. 5 (December 1992): 1369–1430.

———. *The Unpredictable Past: Explorations in American Cultural History.* New York: Oxford University Press, 1993.

Lewis, Grace Hegger. *With Love from Gracie: Sinclair Lewis, 1912–1925.* New York: Harcourt Brace and Co., 1955.

Light, Martin. "Editor's Preface," to a special issue on Sinclair Lewis, *Modern Fiction Studies* 31, no. 3 (fall 1985): 479–94.

Lindberg, Gary. *The Confidence Man in American Literature.* New York: Oxford University Press, 1982.

Lott, Eric. "White Like Me: Racial Cross-Dressing and the Construction of American Whiteness." In *Cultures of United States Imperialism,* edited by Amy Kaplan and Donald E. Pease. Durham, N.C.: Duke University Press, 1993.

Love, Glen A. *"Babbitt": An American Life.* New York: Twayne, 1993.

Lunbeck, Elizabeth. *The Psychiatric Persuasion: Knowledge, Gender, and Power in Modern America.* Princeton, N.J.: Princeton University Press, 1994.

Lutz, Thomas. *American Nervousness, 1903: An Anecdotal History.* Ithaca, N.Y.: Cornell University Press, 1991.

Manca, Luigi, and Alessandra Manca, eds. *Gender and Utopia in Advertising: A Critical Reader.* Lisle, Ill.: Procopian Press, 1994.

Marchand, Roland. *Advertising the American Dream: Making Way for Modernity, 1920–1940.* Berkeley: University of California Press, 1985.

Martin, Richard. *Fashion and Surrealism.* New York: Rizzoli, 1987.

Martin, Robert A. "Fitzgerald in Hollywood: After Paradise." In *The Short Stories of F. Scott Fitzgerald: New Approaches in Criticism,* edited by Jackson R. Bryer. Madison: University of Wisconsin Press, 1982.

Marx, Karl. *The Eighteenth Brumaire of Louis Napoleon,* 1852. In *On Revolution.* Edited and translated by Saul K. Padover. New York: McGraw Hill, 1971.

———. *Capital: A Critique of Political Economy.* Vol. 1. Edited by Friedrich Engels.

Translated by Samuel Moore and Edward Aveling. New York: International Publishers, 1977.

Massé, Michelle A., and Karen Rosenblum. "Male and Female Created They Them: The Depiction of Gender in the Advertising of Traditional Men's and Women's Magazines." *Women's Studies International Forum* 11, no. 2 (1988): 127–44.

Matthews, Glenna. *"Just a Housewife": The Rise and Fall of Domesticity in America*. New York: Oxford University Press, 1987.

May, Lary. *Screening out the Past: The Birth of Mass Culture and the Motion Picture Industry*. New York: Oxford University Press, 1980.

McClintock, Anne. *Imperial Leather: Race, Gender, and Sexuality in the Colonial Contest*. New York: Routledge, 1995.

McDonough, Kaye. *Zelda: Frontier Life in America*. San Francisco: City Lights Books, 1978.

McQuade, Donald A., and Elizabeth Williamson. "Advertising." In *Handbook of American Popular Culture*, edited by M. Thomas Inge. 2d ed. New York: Greenwood Press, 1989.

McRobbie, Angela. "Dance Narratives and Fantasies of Achievement." In *Meaning in Motion: New Cultural Studies in Dance*, edited by Jane C. Desmond. Durham, N.C.: Duke University Press, 1997.

Mellow, James R. *Invented Lives: F. Scott and Zelda Fitzgerald*. Boston: Houghton Mifflin, 1984.

Menten, Theodore. *Advertising Art in the Art Deco Style*. New York: Dover, 1975.

Merish, Lori. " 'The Hand of Refined Taste' in the Frontier Landscape: Caroline Kirkland's *A New Home, Who'll Follow?* and the Feminization of American Consumerism." *American Quarterly* 45, no. 4 (December 1993): 485–523.

Michaels, Walter Benn. *The Gold Standard and the Logic of Naturalism: American Literature at the Turn of the Century*. Berkeley: University of California Press, 1987.

———. *Our America: Nativism, Modernism, and Pluralism*. Durham, N.C.: Duke University Press, 1995.

Milford, Nancy. *Zelda: A Biography*. New York: Harper and Row, 1970.

Modleski, Tania, ed. *Studies in Entertainment: Critical Approaches to Mass Culture*. Bloomington: Indiana University Press, 1986.

Moore, Harry T. Preface to *Save Me the Waltz*, by Zelda Fitzgerald. Carbondale: Southern Illinois University Press, 1967.

Motts, Frank Luther. *History of American Magazines*. Vol. 2. Cambridge, Mass.: Harvard University Press, 1938.

Mouffe, Chantal. "Hegemony and Ideology in Gramsci." In *Gramsci and Marxist Theory*, edited by Chantal Mouffe. New York: Routledge, 1979.

Mulvey, Laura. "Visual Pleasure and Narrative Cinema." In *The Sexual Subject: A Screen Reader in Sexuality*, edited by John Caughie, Annette Kuhn, and Mandy Merck. New York: Routledge, 1992.

Murphy, Jacqueline Shea. "Unrest and Uncle Tom: Bill T. Jones/Arnie Zane Dance Company's *Last Supper at Uncle Tom's Cabin/The Promised Land*." In *Bodies of the*

Text: Dance as Theory, Literature as Dance, edited by Jacqueline Shea Murphy and Ellen W. Goellner. New Brunswick, N.J.: Rutgers University Press, 1995.

Nadeau, Maurice. *The History of Surrealism.* Translated by Richard Howard. Cambridge, Mass.: Harvard University Press.

Ohmann, Richard. *Selling Culture: Magazines, Markets, and Class at the Turn of the Century.* New York: Verso, 1996.

Pacteau, Francette. *The Symptom of Beauty.* Cambridge, Mass.: Harvard University Press, 1994.

Partington, Angela. "Popular Fashion and Working-Class Affluence." In *Chic Thrills: A Fashion Reader,* edited by Juliet Ash and Elizabeth Wilson. Berkeley: University of California Press, 1992.

Peiss, Kathy. *Cheap Amusements: Working-Women and Leisure in Turn-of-the-Century New York.* Philadelphia: Temple University Press, 1986.

———. "Making up, Making Over: Cosmetics, Consumer Culture, and Women's Identity." In *The Sex of Things: Gender and Consumption in Historical Perspective,* edited by Victoria de Grazia and Ellen Furlough. Berkeley: University of California Press, 1996.

———. *Hope in a Jar: The Making of America's Beauty Culture.* New York: Henry Holt, 1998.

Penley, Constance. "Feminism, Psychoanalysis, and the Study of Popular Culture." In *Cultural Studies,* edited by Lawrence Grossberg, Cary Nelson, and Paula Treichler. New York: Routledge, 1992.

Pinkus, Karen. *Bodily Regimes: Italian Advertising under Fascism.* Minneapolis: University of Minnesota Press, 1995.

Pope, Daniel. *The Making of Modern Advertising.* New York: Basic Books, 1983.

Radner, Hilary. *Shopping Around: Feminine Culture and the Pursuit of Pleasure.* New York: Routledge, 1993.

Radway, Janice. *Reading the Romance: Women, Patriarchy, and Popular Literature.* Chapel Hill: University of North Carolina Press, 1984.

Rakow, Lana. " 'Don't Hate Me Because I'm Beautiful': Feminist Resistance to Advertising's Irresistible Meanings." *Southern Journal of Communication* 57, no. 2 (1992): 132–42.

Reynolds, David. *Beneath the American Renaissance: The Subversive Imagination in the Age of Emerson and Melville.* New York: Knopf, 1988.

Richards, I. A. *The Philosophy of Rhetoric.* New York: Oxford University Press, 1936.

Richards, Thomas. *The Commodity Culture of Victorian England: Advertising and Spectacle, 1851–1914.* Stanford, Calif.: Stanford University Press, 1990.

Ridless, Robin. *Ideology and Art: Theories of Mass Culture from Walter Benjamin to Umberto Eco.* New York: P. Lang, 1984.

Riesman, David. *The Lonely Crowd: A Study of the Changing American Character.* New Haven, Conn.: Yale University Press, 1950.

Riviere, Joan. "Womanliness as a Masquerade." In *Formations of Fantasy,* edited by Victor Burgin, James Donald, and Cora Kaplan. New York: Methuen, 1986.

Roche, Thomas P., Jr. "The Children of the Legend: A Reading of *Scottie: The Daughter of. . . .*" *Princeton University Library Chronicle* 58, no. 2 (winter 1996): 267–86.

Ross, Andrew, ed. *No Sweat: Fashion, Free Trade, and the Rights of Garment Workers.* New York: Verso, 1997.

Runciman, W. G., ed. *Max Weber: Selections in Translation.* Translated by Eric Matthews. Cambridge: Cambridge University Press, 1978.

Scanlon, Jennifer. *Inarticulate Longings: "The Ladies Home Journal," Gender, and the Promises of Consumer Culture.* New York: Routledge, 1995.

Scarry, Elaine. *Resisting Representation.* New York: Oxford University Press, 1994.

Schneider, Sara K. *Vital Mummies: Performance Design for the Show-Window Mannequin.* New Haven, Conn.: Yale University Press, 1995.

Schudson, Michael. *Advertising, the Uneasy Persuasion: Its Dubious Impact on American Society.* New York: Basic Books, 1986.

Sedgwick, Eve Kosofsky. *Epistemology of the Closet.* Berkeley: University of California Press, 1990.

Sicherman, Barbara. *The Quest for Mental Health in America, 1890–1917.* 1967. Reprint, New York: Arno Press, 1980.

Snyder, Katherine. *Bachelor Narrative: Gender and Representation in Anglo-American Fiction, 1850–1914.* Cambridge, Mass.: Yale University Press, 1991.

Sloterdijk, Peter. *Critique of Cynical Reason.* Translated by Michael Eldred. London: Verso, 1988.

Spears, Timothy B. " 'All Things to All Men': The Commercial Traveler and the Rise of Modern Salesmanship." *American Quarterly* 45, no. 4 (December 1993): 524–55.

Sombart, Werner. *The Jews and Modern Capitalism.* Translated by M. Epstein. New Brunswick, N.J.: Transaction Books, 1981.

Spitzer, Leo. "American Advertising Explained as Popular Art." In *Leo Spitzer: Representative Essays,* edited by Alban K. Forcione et al. Stanford, Calif.: Stanford University Press, 1988.

Stecopoulus, Harry, and Michael Uebel, eds. *Race and the Subject of Masculinities.* Durham, N.C.: Duke University Press, 1997.

Strasser, Susan. *Satisfaction Guaranteed: The Making of the American Mass Market.* New York: Pantheon, 1989.

——. " 'The Smile that Pays': The Culture of Travelling Salesmen, 1880–1920." In *The Mythmaking Frame of Mind: Social Imagination and American Culture,* edited by James Gilbert et al. Belmont, Calif.: Wadsworth Publishing, 1993.

Suleiman, Susan Rubin. *Subversive Intent: Gender, Politics, and the Avant-Garde.* Cambridge, Mass.: Harvard University Press, 1990.

——. "The Bird Superior Meets the Bride of the Wind: Leonora Carrington and Max Ernst." In *Significant Others: Creativity and Intimate Partnership,* edited by Whitney Chadwick and Isabelle de Courtivron. London: Thames and Hudson, 1993.

——. *Risking Who One Is: Encounters with Contemporary Art and Literature.* Cambridge, Mass.: Harvard University Press, 1994.

Susman, Warren I. *Culture as History: The Transformation of American Society in the Twentieth Century.* New York: Pantheon, 1984.

Torgovnick, Marianna. *Gone Primitive: Savage Intellects, Modern Lives.* Chicago: University of Chicago Press.

Tompkins, Jane. *Sensational Designs: The Cultural Works of American Fiction, 1790–1860.* New York: Oxford University Press, 1985.

Turner, Victor. *The Ritual Process: Structure and Anti-Structure.* Chicago: Aldine Pub. Co., 1969.

Twitchell, James B. *AdCult USA: The Triumph of Advertising in American Culture.* New York: Columbia University Press, 1996.

Vaughn, Steven. *Holding Fast the Inner Lines: Democracy, Nationalism, and the Committee on Public Information.* Chapel Hill, N.C.: University of North Carolina Press, 1980.

Vinikas, Vincent. *Soft Soap, Hard Sell: American Hygiene in an Age of Advertisement.* Ames: Iowa State University Press, 1992.

Walker, Nancy, ed. *Women's Magazines, 1940–1960: Gender Roles and the Popular Press.* Boston: Bedford Books, 1998.

Weber, Max. *The Protestant Ethic and the Spirit of Capitalism.* Translated by Talcott Parsons. 1958. Reprint, New York: Scribner's, 1976.

Wernick, Andrew. "From Voyeur to Narcissist: Imaging Men in Contemporary Advertising." In *Beyond Patriarchy: Essays by Men on Pleasure, Power, and Change,* edited by Michael Kaufman. New York: Oxford University Press, 1987.

Wicke, Jennifer. *Advertising Fictions: Literature, Advertisement, and Social Reading.* New York: Columbia University Press, 1988.

——. "Lingerie and (Literary) History: Joyce's *Ulysses* and Fashionability." *Critical Quarterly* 36, no. 2 (summer 1994): 25–41.

——. " 'Who Is She When She's at Home?' Molly Bloom and the Work of Consumption." In *Molly Blooms: A Polylogue on "Penelope" and Cultural Studies,* edited by Richard Pearce. Madison: University of Wisconsin Press, 1994.

Williams, Raymond. "Base and Superstructure in Marxist Cultural Theory." *New Left Review* 82 (November/December 1973): 9–11.

Williamson, Judith. *Consuming Passions: The Dynamics of Popular Culture.* New York: Marion Boyers, 1986.

Wilson, Christopher P. "Sinclair Lewis and the Passing of Capitalism." *American Studies* 34, no. 2 (fall 1983): 95–108.

Žižek, Slavoj. *Looking Awry: An Introduction to Jacques Lacan through Popular Culture.* Cambridge, Mass.: MIT Press, 1991.

Zuckerman, Mary Ellen, with John Tebbel. *The Magazine in America, 1771–1990.* New York: Oxford University Press, 1991.

Zunz, Oliver. *Making America Corporate, 1870–1920.* Chicago: University of Chicago Press, 1990.

Index

Simone Weil Davis is Assistant Professor of English at Long Island University's
C.W. Post campus.

Library of Congress Cataloging-in-Publication Data
Davis, Simone Weil
Living up to the Ads : gender fictions of the 1920s / Simone Weil Davis.
    p.   cm.
Includes bibliographical references and index.
ISBN 0-8223-2411-3 (cloth : alk. paper).
— ISBN 0-8223-2446-6 (pbk. : alk. paper)
1. Sex role in advertising—United States—History—20th century.   2. Sex role in
literature—History—20th century.
HF5827.85.D38   2000
659.1'042—dc21   99-37024